T0305427

The Ecological Economics of Consumption

CURRENT ISSUES IN ECOLOGICAL ECONOMICS

Series Editors: Sylvie Faucheux, *Professor of Economic Science* and Martin O'Connor, *Associate Professor of Economic Science, C3ED, Université de Versailles Saint Quentin en Yvelines, France,* John Proops, *Professor of Ecological Economics, School of Politics, International Relations and the Environment, Keele University,* UK and Jan van der Straaten, *Retired Senior Lecturer, Department of Leisure Studies, Tilburg University, the Netherlands*

The field of ecological economics has emerged as a result of the need for all social sciences to be brought together in new ways, to respond to global environmental problems. This major new series aims to present and define the state-of-the-art in this young and yet fast-developing discipline.

This series cuts through the vast literature on the subject to present the key tenets and principal problems, techniques and solutions in ecological economics. It is the essential starting point for any practical or theoretical analysis of economy–environment interactions and will provide the basis for future developments within the discipline.

Titles in the series include:

Greening the Accounts
Edited by Sandrine Simon and John Proops

Nature and Agriculture in the European Union
New Perspectives on Policies that Shape the European Countryside
Edited by Floor Brouwer and Jan van der Straaten

Waste in Ecological Economics
Edited by Katy Bisson and John Proops

Environmental Thought
Edited by Edward A. Page and John Proops

The Ecological Economics of Consumption
Edited by Lucia A. Reisch and Inge Røpke

Modelling in Ecological Economics
Edited by John Proops and Paul Safanov

The Ecological Economics of Consumption

Edited by

Lucia A. Reisch

Lecturer at the University of Hohenheim, Germany

Inge Røpke

Associate Professor at the Technical University of Denmark, Denmark

CURRENT ISSUES IN ECOLOGICAL ECONOMICS

Edward Elgar

Cheltenham, UK • Northampton, MA, USA

Published by
Edward Elgar Publishing Limited
The Lypiatts
15 Lansdown Road
Cheltenham
Glos GL50 2JA
UK

Edward Elgar Publishing, Inc.
William Pratt House
9 Dewey Court
Northampton
Massachusetts 01060
USA

A catalogue record for this book
is available from the British Library

ISBN 978 1 84376 512 7

Contents

Figures

Tables

Contributors

Claudia Empacher is an independent researcher and consultant and works as a freelancer at the Institute for Social-Ecological Research (ISOE), Frankfurt am Main. She studied socio-economy with emphasis on environmental economics and economic psychology. Her main research interests are sustainable consumption, consumption behaviour, lifestyles, sustainable nutrition, social sustainability and corporate social responsibility (empacher. kofler@t-online.de).

Konrad Götz, sociologist, is senior researcher in the research area 'mobility and lifestyle analysis' of the Institute for Social-Ecological Research (ISOE), Frankfurt am Main (goetz@isoe.de). He was instrumental in developing ISOE's social-ecological lifestyle approach and has carried out numerous qualitative and quantitative empirical studies with target group orientation in the fields of mobility, nutrition, textiles, tourism and leisure. Before his job at ISOE, he was working in the field of industrial sociology and as a market researcher at the SINUS-Institute in Heidelberg.

Kirsten Gram-Hanssen is a senior researcher at the governmental research institute Danish Building and Urban Research, Department of Housing and Urban Renewal (kgh@by-og-byg.dk). She is educated as a socio-engineer with a Masters and a PhD from the Technical University of Denmark. Her main research interest concerns differences in consumption practices related to housing and urban life. She has conducted numerous empirical studies on energy consumption, lifestyle and everyday life using different combinations of quantitative and qualitative methods.

Tim Jackson is Professor of Sustainable Development at the Centre for Environmental Strategy in the University of Surrey (T.Jackson@surrey. ac.uk). He has lectured and carried out research in the social, economic and technical dimensions of sustainable development for 18 years. His current research interests include consumer behaviour and the environment, sustainable energy systems, ecological economics and environmental philosophy. Since January 2003, he has been employed at CES on a research fellowship, funded under the Economic and Social Research Council's Sustainable Technologies Programme, on the 'social psychology of sustainable consumption'.

Wander Jager is a social psychologist at the University of Groningen (NL), Faculty of Management and Organisation (w.jager@bdk.rug.nl). His main interests are consumer behaviour, common resource management, behavioural dynamics, market dynamics, societal transition dynamics and multi-agent computer simulation of behaviour. He is involved in the European Social Simulation Association.

Mikko Jalas is a researcher and a PhD student at the Helsinki School of Economics, Department for Management (jalas@hkkk.fi) and holds a degree in Industrial Management. His major research interests are the producer–consumer–relationships in the eco-modernistic debate as well as the history of time-use surveys and other indices of well-being. His PhD thesis works towards a collective account of consumption and eco-efficiency.

Jesper Jespersen has been Professor of Economics at the Faculty of Social Sciences, Roskilde University since 1996 (jesperj@ruc.dk). He received his PhD from The European University in Firenze, September 1979. In 1998 and 2001/02 he was awarded a Carlsberg overseas fellowship at Churchill College, Cambridge doing research in Post Keynesian Macroeconomics. His main research interests are related to macroeconomic theory and methodology, and environmental macroeconomics. He is a member of the Post Keynesian Economic Study Group, the Nordic Network of Keynesian Inspired Economics, and the Danish Network of Environmental Economics Research.

Laurie Michaelis is an associate fellow of the Environmental Change Institute at Oxford University (laurie.michaelis@eci.ox.ac.uk). His main interests are in collective choice, cultural change and their roles in shaping consumption patterns within communities. He was director of research for the Oxford Commission on Sustainable Consumption from 1999 to 2002, and is currently working mainly with Quaker meetings in Britain.

Lucia A. Reisch is Lecturer at the University of Hohenheim in Stuttgart, Department of Consumption Theory and Consumer Policy (lureisch@uni-hohenheim.de). She holds a PhD in economics and received MBA training at UCLA (US). Her major research interest is empirical consumer behaviour research in the field of ecologically and socially responsible consumer behaviour. As a member of the Scientific Advisory Board for Consumer, Food and Nutrition Policies to the German Federal Ministry of Consumer Protection, Food and Agriculture, she was in charge of a Strategy Paper that represented the groundwork for the Ministry's new consumer policy strategy.

Inge Røpke is a socio-economist and Associate Professor at the Technical University of Denmark, Department of Manufacturing Engineering and Management (ir@ipl.dtu.dk). Her main research interests are the development and present state of ecological economics, the relations between consumption and the environment and the interplay between technological change and long-term changes of everyday life. She has been actively involved in the International Society for Ecological Economics since the early 1990s.

Elizabeth Shove is a Reader in Sociology at Lancaster University, England (e.shove@lancaster.ac.uk). She has worked on questions of energy consumption and environmental change for a number of years and recently coordinated a European Science Foundation funded programme of summer schools, workshops and exchanges on 'consumption, everyday life and sustainability'. She is interested in ordinary technologies and the transformation of routines and practices and has written *Comfort, Cleanliness and Convenience: The Social Organization of Normality* (2003). She is currently working on kitchens, bathrooms and future concepts of comfort.

Joachim H. Spangenberg is a biologist, ecologist and economist, invited professor at the University of Versailles Saint Quentin-en-Yvelines invited expert at UNCSD, UNDP, OECD and national ministries, and vice-president of SERI, the Sustainable Europe Research Institute in Vienna (Joachim.Spangenberg@seri.de). His main interests are integrated sustainability scenarios and indicators for policy and household use, bridging the gap between social, institutional, economic and environmental aspects of sustainable development and consumption. He is a member of ESEE and ISEE, and executive committee member of the International Network of Engineers and Scientists for Global Responsibility.

Sigrid Stagl is Lecturer at the University of Leeds, School of the Environment (sts@env.leeds.ac.uk). She was awarded the first PhD in Ecological Economics worldwide (Rensselaer Polytechnic Institute, Troy, NY). Her main research interests are human behaviour and social institutions, sustainable consumption, participatory multi-criteria evaluation and sustainable rural development. She is currently vice-president of the European Society of Ecological Economics.

Richard Wilk was trained as an archaeologist and cultural anthropologist, and is now professor of anthropology and gender studies at Indiana University (wilkr@indiana.edu). His recent research has been concerned with consumer culture in poor countries with a focus on food and gender, and in rich countries on energy and the moral economy. He is past president of the Society for Economic Anthropology.

1. The place of consumption in ecological economics

Inge Røpke and Lucia A. Reisch

Research concerning consumption in an environmental perspective has become very dynamic in recent years. Throughout the 1990s contributions have emerged from several different disciplines and approaches, and the research now covers a wide variety of topics. As ecological economics is open for considering all aspects of the interactions between humans and the environment, and simultaneously has the ambition of promoting transdisciplinary work, it is not surprising to see an increasing number of contributions on consumption and environment emerge at ecological economics conferences and in journals related to the field. This anthology can be seen as part of this wave of interest. As a background for presenting the contributions of this volume, this introduction outlines the history behind the present wave of interest in consumption and environment. Without aiming at completeness, the intention of the following is to give an idea of the disciplinary and methodological breadth and variety of research concerning consumption and environment, and to place ecological economic contributions in perspective.

1.1 THE DEVELOPMENT OF A RESEARCH AREA

Studies on consumption date back to the turn of the 20th century, a first milestone being Thorstein Veblen's (1899) splendid sociological analysis of the 'leisure class'. Another landmark was economist Harvey Leibenstein's (1950) article on bandwagon, snob and Veblen effects, which inspired a whole strain of research on demonstration and status effects and, later, positional goods, and was about the first to explicitly thematize social external effects of private consumption. Until the early 1970s, consumption studies tended to look at the consumer society in a critical perspective, for instance the seminal works of John Kenneth Galbraith, Erich Fromm, Roy F. Harrod, Herbert Marcuse, Roland Barthes and Jean Baudrillard.

While the number of contributions was sparse compared to analysis of the production side, outstanding examples have been very influential. Critical writings drew attention to issues such as: the endogeneity of wants, the creation and manipulation of needs, the symbolic, compensatory and pseudotherapeutical nature of consumption, the dubious achievements of consumer society with regard to quality of life, the alienation, emptiness and conformism related to mass consumption, the egoism, hedonism and limitlessness of consumption, and the priority of private goods over collective goods.

In this early critique of consumer society, environmental impacts of consumption were usually not part of the discourse. Environmentally motivated critique of consumption began to emerge soon after the environmental discourse took off in the 1960s. Environmentalists questioned the dominant societal aims of maximum economic growth and increasing consumption because of the related environmental costs. In terms of economic theory it was argued that environmental externalities are pervasive and the norm rather than the exception (Daly 1968; Ayres and Kneese 1969). In these and other contributions, which were formative for the later emergence of ecological economics, consumption was viewed mainly as an abstract aggregate and not an object for more detailed study. In the more popular environmentalist discourse, which also influenced ecological economics, consumption was often dealt with in moralistic terms ('we ought to reduce consumption'). From the beginning, there was the promise of a 'double dividend' idea that curbing consumption would simultaneously make us better off (Spargaaren 1997). In this sense, the environmentalist critique became an add-on to the established critique of consumption. Fred Hirsch (1976) was one of the first economists to combine both discourses analytically. He argued that, beyond ecological limits, there are social limits to growth that arise due to inbuilt consumption externalities and defensive costs.

While the starting environmental discourse motivated research efforts on consumption in an environmental perspective, the contributions were relatively few and isolated. The 1970s brought about research that dealt more specifically and practically with consumption and the environment, focusing on individual consumer behaviour patterns, and heavily focused on energy use and waste disposal behaviour. Motivated by the energy crises, there was an increasing research interest in energy use and saving behaviour, encouraging engineers to take up social aspects such as 'lifestyles' and gradually attracting social scientists to energy studies. Several publications emerged combining energy and lifestyle, from papers in *Science* (for example, Mazur and Rosa 1974) to very good popular literature (including Nørgård and Christensen 1982, based on research results from the 1970s).

In the 1980s, consumer behaviour and policy research began to place consumption in an environmental perspective, something that had been called for by the field's leading thinkers before (for example, Katona et al. 1971; Strümpel 1977; van Raaij 1979). As an academic discipline, consumer behaviour research has a rather long tradition. Developed within the marketing departments of US business schools in the 1950s, it gradually separated from marketing, and new, more macro-oriented subfields such as consumer policy began to emerge (Belk 1995). Liisa Uusitalo, a Finnish economist, did some of the early empirical studies on consumer behaviour in an environmental perspective, and some of the first anthologies on 'consumption and environment' (for example, Joerges 1982; Uusitalo 1983) have their roots in this field.

And yet another strain of research, dealing more generally – and less 'moralistically' – with consumption issues, began to emerge across several social science and humanistic disciplines. When Douglas and Isherwood published their anthropological work *The World of Goods* in 1978 and Bourdieu published *La Distinction: Critique Sociale du Jugement* in 1979, these were isolated contributions, but they heralded a new era of interest in understanding consumption in a more comprehensive way. From the mid-1980s on, the number of contributions exploded, and seminal works appeared such as Miller (1987) and Campbell (1987). Looking back, British consumption sociologist Colin Campbell (1991) observed in a paper about the new wave of consumption research in the humanities and the social sciences: 'Occasionally a special combination of events causes a topic or field of study to spring into prominence in several disciplines at approximately the same time. This is indeed what has happened over the past decade with respect to "consumption".' In 1995, another British consumption sociologist, Daniel Miller (1995), documented the first decade of the 'new consumption studies' in the multi-disciplinary volume *Acknowledging Consumption*. The collection illustrates the widespread interest in consumption with reviews of the developments in the fields of consumer behaviour, sociology, political economy, history, geography, psychology, anthropology and media studies. With that, the consumption concept became applied to a bewildering range of goods and services, everything from art to shopping, receiving welfare and visiting a zoo (Edgell et al. 1996). These 'new studies' showed an only limited interest in environmental issues.

In spite of the broad variety of studies constituting this new wave, some common characteristics can be identified. Compared to the earlier contributions the new studies are less normative and try to provide both a much broader and a deeper understanding of consumption imperatives and of the role of consumption in social, cultural and economic change. According to Miller (1995), the new studies challenged the key myths of consumption that have been widespread both in academia and in public. For instance, the idea that mass consumption causes global homogenization, that consumption is opposed to sociality and authenticity, and that consumption creates particular kinds of social being. Consumption as such, Miller contends, is neither good nor bad; it is integrated in our social practices, embedded in our cultures, and can be related to anything from egoistic to altruistic intentions. Yet, since First World consumption can have disastrous consequences in the Third World – via international demonstration effects, via specific demand structures, via unfair pricing of resources etc – he calls for politicizing consumption in its North–South dimension. Indeed, a philosophical and psychological debate on the ethics of consumption, the good life, justice and global stewardship (Crocker and Linden 1998) has been developing simultaneously.

As mentioned above, environmental issues had a very low priority in these new consumer studies (Miller 1995; Jacoby et al. 1998). The same appears to be true in *The Consumer Society*, where Goodwin and colleagues (1997) summarize a wide array of literature on consumption, and only a few contributions, all from the 1990s, deal with the environment. These studies emerged from an increasing interest in consumption issues in relation to environmental studies. The Brundtland Report, the Rio Conference and the formulation of Agenda 21 in 1992 signalled a change in the focus of environmental policies. The almost exclusively production-oriented perspective was widened to also include consumption and the local activities of citizens. Although the level of consumption in the rich countries was not directly thematized in the beginning, it was difficult to avoid the issue in a situation with increasing interest in problems such as global warming. Furthermore, the trend towards ecological modernization, combined with the trend towards economic liberalization in the 1990s, implied the inclusion of more actors in relation to environmental regulation and global governance. Environmental improvements were expected to occur to a larger extent through voluntary measures, backed by political consumers and labelling of green products. The political situation thus encouraged increased research interest in consumption issues in relation to the fields working with the environment.

1.2   THE CONCEPT OF CONSUMPTION IN ECOLOGICAL ECONOMICS

In ecological economics, the interest in consumption appeared slowly. Ecological economics was institutionalized as a field by the end of the 1980s (for an outline of the early history of ecological economics see Røpke, forthcoming). An interest in consumption issues follows naturally from the foundational ideas in ecological economics. Stated very briefly, the basic idea is that the human economy is embedded in nature and that it can take up more or less 'space' in the geo-biosphere. The scale of the human economy in relation to natural systems is now so large that basic life support systems for humans are threatened. As the continuous growth of the economy's scale ought to be curbed, it is not possible to rely on economic growth to solve the global problems of poverty, so the issue of equity and distribution comes to the fore. In other words, to improve the environmental space for increasing living standards for the poor, the rich have, at least, to stop the increase in their appropriation of natural resources and pollution absorption capacity. Technological change can be relied on to do some of the job, but such an 'efficiency revolution' has to be accompanied by a 'sufficiency revolution' among the richest fifth of the world population, if the ethical challenge is to be taken seriously.

Against this background, consumption issues had to appear on the agenda with questions such as: How can consumption be conceptualized? What are the environmental impacts of consumption? What are the driving forces behind growing consumption? How are resources appropriated for the achievement of high consumption levels? How does consumption relate to quality of life? How can consumption patterns be changed?

At first, the contributions were sparse. Indirectly, research in trade, unequal exchange and so on, can contribute to the knowledge about the appropriation mechanisms behind high consumption levels, but it seldom brings consumption directly onto the agenda. Slowly, a more specific discussion on consumption in relation to ecological economics took off, which was based on and inspired by four early starting points. Firstly, Herman Daly's steady state economics (1991), where he dealt with basic conceptual issues related to consumption, whether consumption should be considered a means or an aim, and how to conceptualize the relationship between welfare and the throughput of materials and energy. Secondly, the discussion of needs and wants and the concept of satisfiers in the work of Manfred Max-Neef (1992). Thirdly, the mechanisms behind consumption growth, in particular Juliet Schor's work (1991) on the work-and-spend cycle that set the stage for more work on lock-in effects. And fourthly, the gradual application of different measures of environmental impacts such as energy accounting, materials flow accounting, and ecological footprints in assessments of environmental impacts of consumption.

By the middle of the 1990s, consumption studies gained momentum in ecological economics. At the inaugural conference of the European Society of Ecological Economics in 1996, many papers dealt with consumption, including the plenary speech by Faye Duchin. Some of the papers later appeared in *Ecological Economics*, including a Special Section in 1999. The field of energy studies, which had a long tradition for dealing with lifestyle and consumer behaviour, grew rapidly and overlapped with ecological economics.

Simultaneously with the breakthrough of consumption issues in ecological economics, several of the fields mentioned above as 'new studies of consumption' began to deal with environmental issues. As mentioned, the field of research in consumer behaviour and consumer policy had provided some of the early studies on consumption and environment, but in the 1990s, the number of contributions rose tremendously, also in the related field of economic psychology. In the cross-field between the relatively new-born sociology of consumption and environmental sociology (dating back to the beginning of the 1970s), studies of environment and consumption began to emerge. These studies built on some of the sociologists and anthropologists with experience from energy studies, including Elizabeth Shove, who initiated a European network for studies on consumption and environment (see www. comp.lancs.ac.uk/sociology/esf/papers.htm). Similar activities encouraging research and networking in the field took place in the United States (Westra and Werhane 1998; Cohen and Murphy 2001; Princen et al. 2002) and in different European countries, for example, Germany (Scherhorn et al. 1997), the Netherlands (Noorman and Schoot Uiterkamp 1998), Switzerland (Häberli et al. 2002), and the Nordic countries (Stø 1995).

During the past decade, we have thus witnessed a wide variety of contributions on environment and consumption from many different perspectives and from different academic fields. However, it is difficult to perceive the establishment of one coherent research field, as the contributions typically refer to different academic fields. Contributions related to ecological economics are often characterized by the application of a problem-oriented approach that implies transdisciplinarity. They take their point of departure in a problem and then search for answers from many different adjacent fields. So, ecological economists happily tap into the knowledge provided by other fields dealing with consumption. This makes it difficult to say what are and what are not ecological economic studies of consumption. Yet, in our opinion, this is not crucial – the important point is that ecological economics has included the consumption issue and is open to a variety of perspectives (as demonstrated, for example, in Reisch 2003). Furthermore, it is worth noting that different perspectives coexist in ecological economics. Some contributors keep the line back to the old classics and adhere to the 'double dividend' idea that cutting back consumption will both improve the environment and the quality of life for the richest fifth of the global population, whereas others adhere more to the new sociological and anthropological studies of consumption and argue that we face a real dilemma, as the ethical challenge to reduce consumption will interfere with well-established and highly appreciated patterns of life and consumption as a central field of meaning, relation and identity. However, there is a basic agreement that the growing appropriation of resources by the richest fifth has to be curbed. The question is how.

1.3 ABOUT THIS BOOK

In accordance with the transdisciplinary basis of ecological economics, this volume encompasses contributions from different perspectives, often cutting across disciplines. It is divided into three parts that group contributions on:

- *problematizing consumption* both as a concept and as an economic and social force with high environmental impact (Part I);
- *explaining consumption* as an attempt of individuals to satisfy different types of needs while being embedded in certain lifestyles and constrained by time and daily routines (Part II), and;
- *changing consumption* towards less environmentally damaging consumption patterns, brought about through national sustainability and consumer policy measures as well as through community building and individual action (Part III).

The contributions compiled in Part I all problematize both the concept and the impact of consumption. American anthropologist Richard Wilk questions some common assumptions about consumption that have been part of the discussion of sustainable consumption. First, he queries the term 'consumption' itself, arguing that the term has been used with such imprecision that it obscures essential issues relating to the differences between goods and services, stocks and flows. Second, he addresses the idea that the historical development of consumer culture can be 'reversed', suggesting that the past can never be a good model for a sustainable future. Instead, we need to better understand the social and psychological adjustments of people in the present who are voluntarily and involuntarily lowering their standards of living. Finally, the chapter addresses units and levels of analysis, questioning work that is based on a world of individual consumers faced with abstract social and economic forces.

The chapter by Joachim H. Spangenberg, a German biologist, ecologist and economist, deals mainly with the environmental impacts of household consumption, describing their historical emergence, the role of products in a consumer society, and some of the social and psychological forces driving household and individual consumption. To assess the environmental impact of consumption, input-based material flow analysis and environmental space estimates are suggested as a proxy for a variety of environmental pressures. As the resource intensity of different consumption patterns can be measured, he argues that it is possible to compare consumption options and to identify environmentally more benign alternatives. According to the author, environmental responsibility of consumers exists when consumption is environmentally relevant and if consumers have a significant influence. This applies to only three consumption clusters, constituting priority fields of action: construction/housing, nutrition/food chain and mobility/ transport. For these, an actor matrix of stakeholders involved is presented as an ordinal measurement of households' potential to ease the burden on the environment.

The third chapter in Part I, by Danish ecological economist Inge Røpke, deals with 'work-related consumption drivers and consumption at work'. The main message in her chapter is that the discussion on sustainable consumption should also incorporate the consumption that occurs in relation to work and, more generally, the relationship between consumption at work and consumption at home. She starts by considering how domestic consumption is encouraged by work-related factors and then considers how consumption activities occur in the workplace, so illustrating that production and consumption are intertwined. The main part of the chapter deals with the conceptual distinction between production and consumption. Inspiration is drawn from both ecology and economics with focus on some important predecessors for ecological economics. She concludes with reflections on how to proceed with consumption studies to provide the basis for promoting more sustainable life patterns.

The contributions of Part II aim at explaining consumption from different perspectives. The first chapter is co-authored by an international, interdisciplinary team: Tim Jackson, a British professor of Sustainable Development, Wander Jager, a Dutch social psychologist and consumer behaviour specialist, and Austrian ecological economist Sigrid Stagl. The authors argue that the conceptual framework of human needs provides a potentially useful but often contentious vantage point from which to view contemporary debates about consumption and sustainability. In their chapter, they review a variety of different perspectives on needs, set out the relevance of modern needs theories for sustainable development and discuss some of the principal arguments for and against a needs-theoretical view of human well-being. They conclude by drawing out some lessons for sustainability from the continuing debate on needs, drawing attention in particular to key questions about the material requirements associated with social and psychological functioning.

British sociologist Elizabeth Shove reviews in her chapter three distinctive ways of conceptualizing behaviour, lifestyle and sustainable consumption. These approaches – which variously represent consumers as decision-makers and shoppers, as citizens influencing the provision of more or less sustainable options, and as practitioners implicated in the reproduction of taken-for-granted conventions – revolve around fundamentally incompatible theories of social change. These divisions have important consequences for policy and practice. She uses the example of escalating expectations of indoor comfort to suggest that popular and pervasive ways of thinking about consumption and the environment are fundamentally limited. In particular, dominant understandings of consumer choice have the unfortunate effect of obscuring processes and dynamics that are vital for sustainability but which fall outside the frame of environmental policy as it is conventionally configured.

Studies have shown that domestic electricity consumption depends on the socio-economic status of the household. However, households from similar socio-economic groups can also have big differences in consumption patterns. Kirsten Gram-Hanssen, a Danish socio-engineer, shows that these differences relate to the number and use of technologies, and not to the energy efficiency of the technologies in everyday life. This is the reason why she takes a closer look at the relation between user and appliances. The work is based on both quantitative and qualitative studies. It is shown that there are substantial differences between how residents relate to different types of technology, both in questions of acquisition and in use. Thoughts from anthropological and sociological consumer theories are presented in connection with the interpretation of the empirical material. It is argued that the main reason why some families use twice or three times as much electricity as other families with a similar socio-economic background is due to different attitudes towards consumption – whether the family finds pleasure primarily in saving or in consuming.

Mikko Jalas from Helsinki School of Economics, is investigating whether sustainability in everyday life is (also) a matter of time, exploring the potential of time-use survey data in tracking environmentally relevant changes in everyday life. The author claims that the data on the non-market activities of the households contribute to a more comprehensive view of the flows of energy and materials in the society. The chapter also expounds on the argument that such data help to elucidate the conditions for changes in the volume and the structure of the economy. Previous attempts to link time use and consumption expenditure data at the macro-level constitute a sporadic line of inquiry, and furthermore, the empirical studies show that the time-use changes have impacted the structure of the economy only modestly. Despite these results the chapter suggests that time-use data are central in the debate on sustainable consumption, and the current efforts to harmonize time-use survey methods and the accumulating body of empirical data facilitate more coherent work on time-use statistics.

Part III comprises chapters that discuss different ways to change consumption towards more sustainable patterns. German economist and consumer policy specialist Lucia Reisch focuses on the new development of a 'sustainable consumer policy' in Germany. She explains that for the first time since consumer policy had emerged as a distinctive policy field in post-war Europe, a normative notion that goes far beyond the classical direct individual consumer benefits has been put at the core of a consumer policy strategy: sustainable consumption and production. Her chapter discusses how far sustainable consumption has been (the empirical question) and can be (the normative question) defined as a consumer policy issue. She starts out by sketching the scope and goals of contemporary consumer policy in Europe in general and Germany specifically. It is argued that a broadened policy field calls for a correspondingly broadened view of its actors and subjects – the consumers. The chapter proposes an integrated view of the consumer filling three different but interrelated roles: consumers as market actors, as consumer-citizens and as participants in the informal sector. The implications of such a broad approach for consumer policy and the chances and pitfalls of emphasizing a normative concept as new *Leitbild* are discussed.

The concept of a sustainable consumption policy is also the focus of Claudia Empacher and Konrad Götz, both from the Frankfurt-based Institute for Social-Ecological Research. They represent lifestyle research as an important means to promote sustainable consumption patterns. The lifestyle concept has been developed in both social sciences as a concept of social structure analysis and market research for targeting specific consumer groups. However, the authors argue, aims and needs in the field of sustainable consumption differ from both approaches, therefore a social-ecological lifestyle concept is needed. The text presents the results of a German empirical study on sustainable consumption patterns that was based on a social-ecological lifestyle concept. The potentials of such an approach for the promotion of sustainable consumption are pointed out: by differentiating groups of people according to their attitudes, social situation and actual behaviour, a holistic picture of the respective groups can be drawn, their specific rationality becomes comprehensible, potentials for changing behaviour can be identified and thus, innovative approaches to different target groups can become visible.

In his contribution 'Community, reflexivity and sustainable consumption', Laurie Michaelis from the Environmental Change Institute at Oxford University provides a community-based approach to change consumption. Governments, he contends, recognize the need for sustainable consumption, but are reluctant to impose measures to change lifestyles. They view consumption patterns as central to meeting human needs. But most of the means chosen to satisfy our needs are collectively determined. Our choices are shaped by markets, infrastructure, technology, social structures and cultural norms. Our social environment supports unsustainable consumption trends, yet some subcultures buck the trend. Growing reflexivity in society offers the possibility that more sustainable cultures may emerge. Reflexive processes are being used to develop more sustainable lifestyle ethics by organizations including: Global Action Plan, which works through neighbourhood 'EcoTeams'; a network of British Quakers, who are exploring their collective approach to sustainable living; and the Permaculture Association, which adopts an 'action learning' approach to search for solutions to sustainable communities. Each has its strengths, and could learn from the others' experiences.

Last, but certainly not least, Danish economist Jesper Jespersen focuses on the macroeconomic implications of sustainable development. Is it possible, he asks, within a market economy with private property rights to diminish the ecological pressure through a reduced material production without causing unemployment? He argues that the obvious solution to the question is a zero-growth policy combined with a labour sharing mechanism that could be organized through a system of tradable work permits. In a market economy the growth rate is determined by effective demand. Hence, macroeconomic policies play a crucial role. If the growth rate is fixed below the trend in labour productivity the number of unemployed people will increase. Such a development can be prevented through a proportional reduction of the average working hours per person employed. That would require an institutional change that simultaneously reduces the total numbers of hours worked within the macroeconomy. Each member of the labour force could be given work permits matching a proportional share of the total number of working hours. Trade in these work permits could be organized as a regular market.

As the presentation above illustrates, the authors have different disciplinary backgrounds, different nationalities, and in some cases, their approaches are basically different. We find that such variety best reflects the openness of ecological economics and the willingness to be informed by the insights of others. We are well aware that, in spite of the broad variety of contributions, many other perspectives could have been included. The field has grown so tremendously during the last few years that it is impossible to provide a comprehensive overview. As a part of the preparations for this volume we arranged a session on consumption at the Sixth Nordic Environmental Social Sciences Conference in Turku, Finland in June 2003, and the response to our call for papers was overwhelming and illustrative of the present interest in the field. However, the limitations of this volume have only allowed us to include a small part of the issues we would have liked to deal with. Among the important omissions are: the mechanisms in the global political economy that make possible the high level of consumption in the industrialized countries, consumption issues related to developing countries, ethical questions, risk and consumption, and gender issues. It will not be difficult to find materials for more volumes.

All of the contributions are original contributions for this reader. We do thank the authors for their creative and valuable contributions. As editors and authors, we hope that the anthology can contribute to consumption studies gaining a stronger foothold inside ecological economics.

REFERENCES

Ayres, R.U. and A. V. Kneese (1969), 'Production, consumption, and externalities', *The American Economic Review*, **59**, 282–97.
Belk, Russell (1995), 'Studies in the new consumer behaviour', in Daniel Miller (ed.), *Acknowledging Consumption. A Review of New Studies*, London: Routledge, pp. 58–95.
Campbell, Colin (1987), *The Romantic Ethic and the Spirit of Modern Consumerism*, Oxford: Basil Blackwell.
Campbell, C. (1991), 'Consumption: The new wave of research in the humanities and social sciences', *Journal of Social Behavior and Personality*, **6**, 57–74.
Cohen, Maurie J. and Joseph Murphy (eds) (2001), *Exploring Sustainable Consumption. Environmental Policy and the Social Sciences*, Amsterdam: Pergamon Press.
Crocker, David A. and Toby Linden (eds) (1998), *Ethics of Consumption. The Good Life, Justice, and Global Stewardship*, Lanham: Rowman and Littlefield.
Daly, H.E. (1968), 'On economics as a life science', *Journal of Political Economy*, **76**, 392–406.
Daly, Herman E. (1991), *Steady-State Economics*, Second Edition with New Essays, Washington DC: Island Press.
Edgell, Stephen, Kevin Hetherington and Alan Warde (eds) (1996), *Consumption Matters. The Production and Experience of Consumption*, Oxford/Cambridge: Blackwell.
Goodwin, Neva R., Frank Ackerman and David Kiron (eds) (1997), *The Consumer Society*, Washington DC/Covelo, CA: Island Press.
Häberli, Rudolf, Rahel Gessler, Walter Grossenbacher-Mansuy and Daniel Lehmann Pollheimer (2002), *Vision Lebensqualität*, Zurich: vdf Hochschulverlag.
Hirsch, Fred (1976), *The Social Limits to Growth*, Cambridge, MA: Harvard University Press.
Jacoby, J., G. V. Johar and M. Morrin (1998), 'Consumer behaviour: A quadrennium', *Annual Review of Psychology*, **49**, 319–44.
Joerges, Bernward (ed.) (1982), *Verbraucherverhalten und Umweltbelastung. Materialien zu einer verbraucherorientierten Umweltpolitik*, Frankfurt/New York: Campus.

Katona, George, Burkhard Strümpel and Ernest Zahn (eds) (1971), *Zwei Wege zur Prosperität. Konsumverhalten, Leistungsmentalität und Bildungsbereitschaft in Amerika und Europa*, Düsseldorf/Vienna: Econ.

Leibenstein, H. (1950), 'Bandwagon, snob and Veblen effects in the theory of consumers' demand', *The Quarterly Journal of Economics*, **44**, 183–207.

Max-Neef, Manfred (1992), 'Development and human needs', in Paul Ekins and Manfred Max-Neef (eds), *Real-life Economics. Understanding Wealth Creation*, London: Routledge, pp. 197–214.

Mazur, A. and E. Rosa (1974), 'Energy and lifestyle: Cross-national comparison of energy consumption and quality of life indicators', *Science*, **186**, 607–10.

Miller, Daniel (1987), *Material Culture and Mass Consumption*, Oxford: Basil Blackwell.

Miller, Daniel (ed.) (1995), *Acknowledging Consumption. A Review of New Studies*, London: Routledge.

Noorman, Klass Jan and Ton Schoot Uiterkamp (eds) (1998), *Green Households? Domestic Consumers, Environment, and Sustainability*, London: Earthscan.

Nørgård, Jørgen S. and Bente L. Christensen (1982), *Energihusholdning*, Copenhagen: Fællesforeningen for Danmarks Brugsforeninger.

Princen, Thomas, Michael Maniates and Ken Conca (eds) (2002), *Confronting Consumption*, Cambridge, MA and London: MIT Press.

Reisch, Lucia A. (2003), 'Consumption', in Edward A. Page and John Proops (eds), *Environmental Thought*, Current Issues in Ecological Economics Series, Cheltenham, UK and Northampton, MA, US: Edward Elgar, pp. 217–42.

Røpke, Inge (forthcoming), 'The early history of modern ecological economics', Accepted for publication in *Ecological Economics*.

Scherhorn, Gerhard, Lucia A. Reisch and Sabine Schrödl (1997), *Wege zu nachhaltigen Konsummustern*, Marburg: Metropolis.

Schor, Juliet B. (1991), *The Overworked American. The Unexpected Decline of Leisure*, New York: BasicBooks.

Shove, Elizabeth (1997), 'Revealing the Invisible: Sociology, Energy and the Environment', in Michael Redclift and Graham Woodgate (eds) (1997), *The International Handbook of Environmental Sociology*, Cheltenham, UK and Lyme, MA, US: Edward Elgar, pp. 261–73.

Spaargaren, Gert (1997), *The Ecological Modernisation of Production and Consumption: Essays in Environmental Sociology*, Wageningen: Landbouw University.

Stø, Eivind (ed.) (1995), *Sustainable Consumption*, Report from the International Conference on Sustainable Consumption at Lillehammer, February 1995, Lysager, Norway: National Institute for Consumer Research.

Strümpel, Burkhard (1977), *Die Krise des Wohlstands: Das Modell einer humanen Wirtschaft*, Stuttgart: Kohlhammer.

Uusitalo, Liisa (ed.) (1983), *Consumer Behaviour and Environmental Quality*, Aldershot: Gower.

van Raaij, Fred (1979), 'Das Interesse für ökologische Probleme und Konsumentenverhalten', in Heribert Meffert, Hartwig Steffenhagen and Hermann Freter (eds), *Konsumentenverhalten und Information*, Wiesbaden: Gabler, pp. 355–74.

Veblen, Thorstein B. (1899), *The Theory of the Leisure Class: An Economic Study in the Evolution of Institutions*, New York: Augustus M. Kelley.

Westra, Laura and Patricia H. Werhane (eds) (1998), *The Business of Consumption. Environmental Ethics and the Global Economy*, Lanham: Rowman and Littlefield.

PART I

Problematizing consumption

2. Questionable assumptions about sustainable consumption

Richard Wilk

2.1 INTRODUCTION

To date there has been a considerable amount of thought and writing on the topic of sustainable consumption, some of it contentious, but most of it well intentioned and intended to be constructive (for example, Brown and Cameron 2000; Burgess 2003; Jackson and Michaelis 2003; Reisch 2003). The notion of a whole world of people consuming at the rate of the average North American is enough to make anyone who thinks seriously about the future want to cringe. This sword of Damocles hanging over all of our heads, the palpably unsustainable nature of present forms of consumption and production in the affluent parts of the world, gives a sense of urgency to scholarship on the topic. The obvious moral correctness of those who recognize the seriousness of the consumption problem – a position I completely agree with – has both positive and negative consequences.

On the plus side, it has led to a lot of interdisciplinary cooperation and intellectual boundary-crossing that does not occur in other research areas. Scholarship on consumption has been remarkably open to many intellectual approaches and methodologies. There is nothing like a crisis looming on the horizon to put disciplinary boundaries and disputes over methodology into proper perspective. There has also been a commendable amount of cooperation on consumption issues between scholars and political and environmental activists, and in Europe at least, with some government agencies. In Germany, for instance, the Federal Ministry of Consumer Protection, Food and Agriculture has built its General Strategy on the concept of sustainable consumption (see Reisch in this book).

On the negative side, the common agreement on goals has created a situation where nobody really wants to 'rock the boat' by asking difficult questions. As a recent exchange between Daniel Miller (2001) and Wilk (2001) illustrates, the convergence between scientists and activists is maintained only by a willingness to leave some fundamental issues out of discussion. Miller argues that scientists need to expose the ethnocentric and class-based moral agendas that lie behind a lot of activist rhetoric, while Wilk questions the need to undercut an important alliance. In this exchange Miller points out that utopian fantasies about how much happier everyone would be if they gave up their cars and became vegetarians are not a substitute for sound public policy that will move the majority – not just a committed fringe – towards a less environmentally destructive society.

That is not to say that there is nothing but rosy agreement about consumption in the research and activist communities. Some, for example, see consumerism as largely a behavioral problem that requires a transformation in attitudes and values (Brown and Cameron 2000; De Geus 2003). Others point out that consumption practices are deeply embedded in physical infrastructure and social institutions, which severely limits the possibility of effective change in individual behavior (Sanne 2002). Or we can take the level of analysis to the global structures of inequality that channel the environmental impacts of the consumption of the rich onto the poor and helpless (Fischer-Kowalski and Amann 2001). As Reisch (2003) and others show, even very fundamental ideas about what makes people consume the way they do are diverse, poorly articulated and sometimes mutually incompatible (also Wilk 2002).

Rather than being symptoms of disarray or incoherence, I think the fact that we are coming to grips with the complexity of consumption is a good sign that the scholarship on consumption and sustainability is becoming mature enough for us to face more difficult and fundamental problems that presently lie beneath a surface of common agreement. Therefore, I think it is time to ask some 'subversive' questions and make some points that might lead to lateral and creative thinking about consumption and sustainability. The *sustainability* side of the phrase has been debated and discussed innumerable times, so here I will focus on the concept of consumption.

2.2   IS CONSUMPTION THE PROBLEM?

While the term consumption appears to have an obvious physical meaning, it actually includes a complex mix of metaphor and connotation that complicate its use. Cognitive and historical linguistic analysis shows that in English at least, the word's earliest meaning is 'destruction by fire', a process that takes something useful, and turns it into waste. Since then, the word has acquired most of its meaning through close association with the metaphor of eating, so that shopping is metaphorical hunting, buying is like catching, using is like eating, and throwing things away is like defecating (Wilk 2004). The metaphorical connection is so strong that we tend to ignore the many ways that what we call consumption is not at all like eating. For instance, one can consume a film on DVD over and over again without ever producing waste; many objects are never thrown away, but are curated and stored and may be rebuilt or modified, and even end up in public museums. Shopping itself can be no more than entertainment – it does not have to lead to the purchase or use of objects. In fact, there would be much less waste in the world if people did more shopping and less actual buying, if they were more obsessed with finding the right goods, and less willing to take what was easily available. A society of exacting and demanding shoppers might be considerably more sustainable.

When we liken consumption to eating we emphasize its active nature (hunting, catching, using) when in fact many consuming activities are passive and involve little choice. They may be habitual, predetermined by regulations or markets, and otherwise channeled by infrastructure.

The metaphorical content of the term consumption explains why it is so difficult to define in a straightforward way that captures all activities that seem to belong to the category. Despite the attempts by various physical scientists, economists and ecologists to find a scientific definition of consumption (for example as entropy, or actions that diminish the value of substances) all efforts founder on a host of exceptions, things that we intuitively consider to be consumption, but which elude concise definition (Narotzky 1997; Stern 1997; Nordman 1998). Where is the boundary between simply using something and consuming it, especially when consumption is itself a form of work (Cowan 1987)? Am I consuming a car the whole time I am using it, or only when I abandon it on the street? And then there are so many things that are ambiguously consumption-like: buying stocks and bonds (is investment a form of consumption?), borrowing and lending (am I consuming the hammer I borrowed from you?), and even recycling, which requires energy and work in order to transform waste back into goods. And if consumption is impossible to define concisely, then terms like 'overconsumption' and 'waste' should also be treated gingerly.

Once we break the metaphorical tie between *consumption* (which can be cyclic, non-linear, prolonged, shared, divisible) and *eating*, which is linear, discrete and indivisible, we can see that environmental problems caused by extraction, burning fossil fuels and waste disposal are far different from the moral problems of overeating or starvation that so often inform attitudes about consumption. The issue of sustainability is not about simply consuming *less* (metaphorically putting ourselves on a diet), but of rates of flow, transport costs, length of curation, types of cycling, recycling, and reuse, alternative sources and trade-offs, all problems that are complex and cannot be reduced to the idea that 'consuming less is better for the planet'.

One can think of many counter-examples. It may be better to consume a large amount of used clothing from a thrift store than small amounts of new clothes; but there might be a great difference in that balance if we compare polyester made from oil by-products with cotton grown with an overdose of pesticides, or garments made by union workers in Europe and those sewn in a sweatshop in Honduras. And what about the 'consumption' of services, like insurance, live music in bars, museum exhibits, or legal advice? For many kinds of services, once infrastructure costs are paid, the costs of use are negligible. When I listen to the radio, what is consumed, besides a smidgen of electricity? Some of the things we call consumption have no inputs, and no outputs, and therefore almost no direct environmental impact. The more money I spend on the brand value of branded goods, the less I have available for other material purchases. 'Wasting' money on useless gadgets and idle entertainments may be much better than 'saving' and investing my money in a bank that finances commercial development or suburban sprawl.

The flow of materials in consumer-industrial society is completely unlike eating in two other fundamental ways. First, the produce–consume–waste cycle of food is continuous, and little more than energy and waste is left behind. But in society, a huge proportion of what is produced ends up sunk into goods and infrastructure that are not just used up and discarded – instead they have very long lives, and may become permanent infrastructure. Building a dam may 'consume' huge amounts of concrete, but it could be hundreds of years before the dam gradually becomes useless and is abandoned or destroyed. Consumption is not always a moral balance between too little and too much. When people are accused of being 'wasteful', it is usually because they have *accumulated* large amounts of clothes, or goods, or summer houses, or cars, not because they have actually *consumed* them.

Owning, collecting and appreciating objects may actually increase their value – it could be seen as environmentally benign, or even productive and positive. And, as Lilienfeld and Rathje (1998) show, recycling itself is often wasteful of both materials and energy – no more than a symbolic form of virtue. The answer then is more than 'use less stuff', it must combine a concern with quantity and qualities like origins, use life, embodied energy, transportation and permanence. The use of the term 'consumption' easily leads to simple metrics like overconsumption or underconsumption, rather than to a complementary focus on the qualities of objects and services. In terms of environmental impact, it can make much more sense to 'consume' more instead of less, depending entirely on the qualities of goods consumed, and *substitution effects* that are very poorly understood. If lowering the consumption of one item merely frees up money and time that can be spent on something else (which was the case with rising fuel efficiency standards in the USA), then there is no net benefit. Similarly, if an 'organic' or 'green' label makes us comfortable with higher levels of overall consumption, there may be a net increase in environmental impact. Rather than seeing a problem of overindulgence, as people simply spending too much, we might think in terms like 'over-earning' or 'poor curation skills'.

The second major problem that makes consumption a term of dubious utility is that we try to use it for both the flow of goods, and the flows of money that we use to buy goods. But when I 'consume' my savings on a spending spree, that money does not become waste or disappear – it goes to the vendor who keeps some and sends the rest to a supplier, who pays workers with some, and uses some to pay for materials, and so on. My spending moves money that enables other spending on and on: it is circulation, *not* consumption. Is it therefore better that I save my money? Then it just goes to a bank that puts it back into circulation in the form of loans, enabling more spending and buying. Investing it in a 'green' industry may just lead to more circulation and more consumption. From this perspective, anything that *wastes money* is a good thing if it leads to a reduction in consumption. Gambling, frivolous expenditure on music, wildly expensive art and other intangibles should all be encouraged, because they divert surplus money away from direct purchase of energy and materials-intensive goods. The solution is not making people *spend less*, but actually *promoting* the purchase of goods that have less impact – this is a subtle but important difference.

De Vries (1993) argues for the importance of taking 'consumption' apart to think more systematically about stocks and flows, durables and consumables, and the impacts of each on the economy. Obviously consumer capitalism has historically progressed by turning durables into consumables, through cultivating fashion (that is, planned obsolescence) and producing cheap 'throwaway' items that replace more expensive, reparable, and longer-lasting goods. This creates a stratified system, where the rich can afford durables and the poor buy cheap 'junk' that is broken and replaced on a faster cycle. In the long run the poor can end up paying much more for the same services (think about the contrast between prefabricated 'mobile' homes and permanent houses in the USA). Buying in smaller packages also means a higher ratio of packaging to contents, so the poor produce more waste per unit consumed (Rathje and Murphy 1992). Reducing flow therefore might require providing cheap credit or leasing arrangements that would allow poorer people access to more durable goods. As Moltoch (2003, pp. 244–6) says, reducing overall throughput of energy and materials may require *promoting* consumption of durable and less material-intensive options.

Perhaps the most pernicious influence of using the term 'consumption' in uncritical ways is that it focuses attention on an abstract individual called 'the consumer'. As industrial ecologists remind us, for many problems of 'consumption', individual consumer choices have little effect, since the vast majority of energy and materials are used by industry, which also produces well over 90 percent of the waste stream in the US (Lilienfeld and Rathje 1998). Industrial designers, rather than consumers, therefore make choices with huge environmental consequences, often with only a tenuous idea of, or concern for what consumers want or need (Moltoch 2003). The cultures that we most need to understand, in order to promote sustainability, might be those of industrial design, advertising agencies, accountants and marketing departments. For some goods, 'consumers' may be the least important people in the product lifecycle, from raw materials to waste.

Clearly, the term *consumption* creates as many problems as it solves, leading many of the more quantitatively inclined to substitute terms like 'cost', 'throughput' and 'use', each of which have their own definition problems. I know that most of us will continue to use it, but we need to be much more specific about what we mean when we do.

2.3   CAN CONSUMERISM BE REVERSED?

When most activists talk about a society with dramatically reduced ecological footprint, they call up images of an earlier era, a simpler time when people had more appreciation for local products, were more self-sufficient, and were happier with less. By implication, the more sustainable future is going to mean, in some ways, a return to the past, albeit a past with better tools and higher technology. All the calls for a 'simpler' lifestyle, for 'simple living', and a 'return' to self-restraint and moderation are calling on this notion of reversibility (De Geus 2003). But everything we know about human history tells us that there is no possibility of a return to the past; in history, most movements that claim to be conservative or revivalist are actually agents of change, creating new forms in the name of the old. They make reference to the past only as justification for a radical program. In any case, historians and archaeologists lend little weight to the idea that life was somehow easier or simpler in the past. The assumption of some form of primordial self-sufficiency and sustainability also flies in the face of archaeological and anthropological evidence (see, for example, Edgerton 1992). Archaeologists tell us that even when great civilizations collapsed, people did not simply return to the preceding agrarian village lifestyles.

What if all changes in consumption are directional and irreversible? One of the most fundamental directionalities is what sociologists call the 'level of consumer aspiration', or what economists call the 'standard of living'. It seems to be a basic characteristic of consumer capitalism that people think both historically and socially about their own level of comfort (Illich 1977). They compare their present state with the way they used to live, and with the way other people live. One provides a reference point below which people do not want to 'fall', and the other provides both cautionary tales about what could happen if one did fall, and an image of how a higher level of consumption would be better. This is not simply scorn for the poor and envy of the rich, but a much more complex calculus of both 'fitting in' and 'standing out'. This combination produces what Shove (2003) calls a *ratchet effect*: individually and socially people interpret any decline in material abundance and comfort as a problem that requires alleviation. Even if they do not expect a constant rise, they will not accept a fall. Studies of countries, like Brazil, where middle-class real incomes fell dramatically during hyper-inflation show that people are willing to work harder and make other sacrifices in order to maintain what they considered a necessary level of consumption (O'Dougherty 2002).

The flow of technological change and fashion also ensures that there is no reversibility; the contents of the 'market basket' of consumables used to calculate the Consumer Price Index have to be changed periodically to reflect the passing of some items (cake laundry soap, lamp oil, salt fish) out of common use. Directionality also means that you cannot reason from the present uses of objects to their past uses. The way we use telephones today cannot explain why people first started to use them (this is a familiar problem in biological evolution). Going forward cannot be done by reversing the past; we cannot reason from the present state of consumer culture back to some underlying 'primitive' condition and original causes. Instead of holding out any kind of past state as a model, or creating impossible utopias, we would do better to look at examples of the ways that people reduce their needs in the present, at the people who are exceptions to the rule that living standards can only rise.

It might be useful, for instance, to look at the consuming lives of middle-class students, who usually experience a dramatic decline in their levels of consumption (of most things) when they enter university. Are they just delaying their return to formerly high standards, or does this experience of relative poverty lead to lasting change in their goals, and their experience of comfort and abundance? Newman's (1989) study of 'downwardly mobile' middle-aged upper middle-class Americans during the 1980s found high levels of depression, social dysfunction and divorce, as many people were unable to reconcile themselves to permanently lower income. In the USA many women who become single mothers through divorce experience a similar fall from the consumption levels of the middle class. Some do manage the transition, and even report being happier without the stress of higher level positions. How do they experience the dramatic lowering of income, the loss of the use of a car, moving from a house to an apartment, selling their furniture and dispersing their jewelry and other highly personal objects?

Another common form of lowered material standards is that experienced by the elderly. In many countries, part of the lifecycle transition to old age is a process of dispersing possessions and moving into smaller (and usually more efficient) housing. While some dread and delay this transition, many others report pleasure in escaping the burden of possessions, and others enjoy the process of giving their valuables away, for a variety of reasons. Price et al. (2000) and Millman (1991) both report that these gifts can be manipulative and even vindictive. Another more extreme sort of renunciation takes place during entry into religious orders or sects that demand that devotees give up their personal possessions entirely. While not very common in Europe or North America, religious renunciation is still an important element of Buddhist and Hindu traditions. What can we learn about living with less from the experiences of these diverse people? I would argue that we are much more likely to find valuable insights from them, than from any conjuring of an imaginary past or a notion of simplicity that exists only in the imagination.

2.4   WHAT'S LOVE GOT TO DO WITH IT?

When most ecological economists think about consumption and sustainability, they are working at an abstract level that includes whole societies, sectors and countries as units of analysis. Arguments about sustainability call on moral issues of north and south, of global inequalities and long-term stewardship. But while it is certainly important to understand the implications of modern consumer society at the macro-level, 'society' is only an abstraction, far from the everyday experiences of most people. While some members of sustainable-living groups ground their actions in a global social morality (for example, how can I consume so much when so many have nothing?), the vast majority of people look no further than their own families in their daily and longer-term decisions about work, housing, transportation and child-bearing.

Though shaped by large-scale global phenomena and forces, actual daily behavior is still overwhelmingly local and highly contextual. The global and national-scale patterns of consumption that we see are no more than the aggregate of these millions of extremely local, familial and personal actions. Therefore, while it may make sense to speak abstractly about how changes in 'policy' affect 'consumer behavior', such statements have no explanatory power; they explain one abstraction by reference to another. We must remember that terms like 'social competition', or 'household budgets' are post-hoc analytical terms, part of our own attempt to make sense out of patterns of behavior. One of the most basic lessons of ethnography is that we should not confuse *analytical models* and *folk models* – the latter are the ones that actually exist in people's minds, informing and shaping their goals, social interactions and behavior. Effective policy interventions meant to change consuming behavior has to address the folk model, not the analytical abstraction (see in particular the work of Kempton 1986, 1991, 1997).

One approach to changing daily behavior is to think of ways that people could be inspired to think more about the long-term and global implications of their daily habits and choices (Ryan and Durning 1997; McKibben 2001). This could mean connecting commodity chains so people could learn more about where things come from, and the social and environmental impacts of producing their everyday commodities (Robbins 2000; Barndt 2002). Given the chance, so this logic goes, people will make more moral decisions; all they need is more information and some encouragement. But will they?

One problem with this approach is high transaction and information costs. It is extremely difficult and time-consuming for *experts* to calculate the environmental costs of goods. Faced with thousands of goods and many alternatives for each (some branded, some not), the amount of information that consumers would have to process is daunting. Even green branding may raise new questions and complications for consumers that increase their transaction costs, in an environment where time is often very precious.

The information-flow solution also focuses on buying as the key decision point in the overall environmental impact of behavior. But as I point out above, flow is equally important; the durability and reparability of goods may be more important than their embodied energy and materials. And the most common form of information provided on product labels allows buyers to compare one brand of item against another – a hybrid instead of a diesel, or fair trade coffee instead of plantation-grown – rather than between one *kind* of good and another – a motorcycle instead of a car, or tea instead of coffee.

More to the point is whether the moral appeal alone will change people's behavior. The comparative evidence is that appeals to the common good, or to long-term benefits, can draw interest and provide an initial burst of added value to products and services, but there have to be other social or economic benefits if most people are going to sustain a change in their lifestyles in the long run (see Wilk 1996; Etzioni 1998). In other words, many people will try a product that promises green benefits, but they will only make it a routine part of their lives if it saves them money or time, increases their comfort, or confers some kind of valued social status or recognition.

On a more fundamental level, people's everyday moral concerns are much more about other people in their immediate social sphere than they are about the well-being of the planet or people in the distant future. As Daniel Miller (1998) convincingly shows in his *A Theory of Shopping*, everyday buying is an act of love and sacrifice, bounded by the needs and perceptions of close kin. Social aspirations have more to do with the expectations of parents, in-laws and spouses than with some abstract social class or 'reference group'. Instead of selfish individualists, empirical studies of both Western and non-Western consumers find people who are expressing love and concern for their families by providing goods for them. They give gifts and treats, spoil their children and compete with their siblings; even when they indulge themselves they often see this as what Miller calls 'self-gifting', rewards for good behavior and accomplishments.

The household and family are especially important units for understanding both restraint and expansiveness in buying, using, accumulating and wasting goods and services. My own research finds large variations in the way households pool and manage their funds, their division of authority over property and purchasing, and in the way they provide money and goods to children (Wilk 1994). Couples may polarize each other so that one becomes the 'saver' and the other the 'spender', leading to conflicts and arguments (Zelizer 1994). Middle-class families can develop 'virtuous cycles' of restraint, saving and substitution of social time for money and goods, or they can create a downward spiral into debt and bankruptcy. Most of these phenomena have direct implications for the problem of sustainability, yet they are still largely unexplored by social scientists of any persuasion (Commuri and Gentry 2000). Abstract aggregates like 'standards of living' and 'consumer aspirations' are driven by these mundane and everyday interactions and behaviors, not by abstract forces like 'materialism' or 'pressures of advertising'.

This explains why religious appeals to moderation and charity have a very limited effect on people's actual ambitions and behavior. Compared to a motive like proving to one's parents that you are a worthy and successful son or daughter, fulfilling one's role as a good provider, or making sure your children have more than you did and are not ashamed to have their friends visit home, ultimate moral precepts remain no more than nagging background noise. In almost every society studied by anthropologists, we find the same thing; people's everyday social relationships are created, maintained, symbolized and actualized using material culture. And as example after example shows, making people give up significant parts of that material culture inevitably causes major social disruption and even cultural dissolution (Salisbury 1962; Bodley 1982). This poses a clear set of obstacles to any wholesale attempt to transform consumer culture quickly from one based on material abundance and high throughput to one that is more frugal (Brown and Cameron 2000). Instead, changes will have to be incremental. A moral appeal may work well for a few, but for the majority, less energy using and material-intensive goods will have to offer other values, ones that are familiar to anyone immersed in mass advertising. They will have to be fashionable or sexy or capable of expressing love and affection. And they do not even have to be material; the most effective new products from the point of view of sustainability, dematerialize services and values. For example, one might think of giving broadband Internet access and an mp3 music player to a teenager instead of an old car.

2.5   CONCLUSIONS

In this chapter I have not shied away from asking difficult questions for which I have few answers. In my self-appointed role as annoying gadfly, I hope to encourage people to look at problems of sustainability in a new way. In particular, we cannot become intellectual prisoners of our own analytical terms. While using the word 'consumption' can often be convenient, in practice it channels thought and conceals key issues.

My conclusions are that a movement towards sustainable consumer culture cannot be based on a repudiation of all contemporary customs, values and institutions. *Anti-consumption* or *overconsumption* may be good moral rhetoric, and they may provoke feelings of righteousness and guilt, but they are analytically useless and make for poor policy. They have use as political rhetoric aimed at building mass public support for changes in the tax and policy structure to favor more sustainable options. But as a political platform the concepts must be used carefully and judiciously; in the USA they may be having the opposite of the intended effect. They feed the widespread assumption that sustainability means a lower standard of living, and less of everything at higher cost. Instead, as I argue above, more 'sustainable consumption' actually means *increasing* certain kinds of 'consumption'. The whole issue is about *what kinds* of goods and services people buy, use and throw away – this is a fundamentally different issue from 'reducing consumption'. Only a specialist in industrial ecology and global commodity chains can possibly tell what kinds of consumption are actually reducing the total material and energy throughput of a complex economic system. And the whole question of how the flow of money relates to the flow of energy and materials is still largely unanswered (Hornborg 2001; Bunker and Ciccantell n.d.).

Giving consumers more information and trusting them to make good choices is another wishful strategy with limited practical utility. The sheer volume of goods on the market, the constant turnover of new brands and models, and outsourcing mean that the same product could come from many different sources, some sustainable, some not. And what is the consumer to do when faced with an alternative between a product that is 'green' and one that is 'fairly traded' or 'no sweatshop'? Even the most conscientious people do not want *more* ethical and moral dilemmas when they shop; they already have to balance cost, quality and a host of emotional and social weights.

In thinking about how more sustainable products could successfully enter the marketplace, we could take some guidance from the experience of the advertising profession, which is after all the only business fully devoted to changing consumer culture. Through much of the first half of the 20th century, advertisements were seen as a form of education. They imparted information about products, listing their superior qualities and values (Marchand 1986). After a few decades, though, consumers were saturated with information and dubious of its veracity. By mid-century, advertisers turned to using appeals and images that targeted the most powerful sources of emotion: family roles, social status and sexuality. Whatever moral qualms one might have about these methods, they have created the cultural and economic context of consumer culture. Like the Media Foundation that publishes *Adbusters* magazine, one can identify the whole system as the enemy, but is it practical to wait for the overthrow of consumer capitalism before moving towards sustainability?

Ultimately, this last question is a facet of the fundamental moral and ethical issues faced by anyone bent on social change. To what extent are you willing to compromise and work with a system that is ultimately destructive? How far can the ends justify the means?

My concern is that so far the community working for this thing called sustainable consumption has been almost puritanical in its public voice on issues of the common good and ecological balance. In the contemporary culture of consumption, the vast majority of people (especially the ones who are consuming at the most prodigious rate) are totally oblivious to this kind of schoolmaster's nagging; if anything they resent it. They react badly to what they perceive as a tone of smug superiority and moral certainty.

This is the response I get from about 70 percent of the students in my classes on globalization and consumer culture. They feel like I am just trying to spoil their fun. On the other side, I can always count on a small group of students who experience something like a religious conversion, becoming vegetarians and green activists, joining our local Center for Sustainable Living and working in our green campus initiative. I worry about them as much as the oblivious majority, for as much as I admire the glow of their idealism, they are probably doomed to disillusionment. Idealism alone does not give them the knowledge and skills they need to be effective agents of change. We have to find a path towards sustainability that reaches and motivates all these different kinds of people, which speaks an appropriate language and addresses the issues of everyday life, as well as the ultimate fate of the planet.

REFERENCES

Barndt, Deborah (2002), *Tangled Routes: Women, Work, and Globalization on the Tomato Trail*, Boulder, CO: Westview Press.

Bodley, John (1982), *Victims of Progress*, San Francisco: Benjamin Cummings.

Brown, P. and L. Cameron (2000), 'What can be done to reduce overconsumption?', *Ecological Economics*, **32**, 27–41.

Bunker, Stephen and John Ciccantell (n.d.), 'Space, matter, and technology in globalization past and future', in C. Chase-Dunn and E. N. Anderson (eds), *The Historical Evolution of World-Systems*, New York: Palgrave (in press).

Burgess, J. (2003), 'Sustainable consumption: is it really achievable?', *Consumer Policy Review*, **11** (3), 78–84.

Commuri, Suraj and James Gentry (2000), 'Opportunities for family research in marketing', *Academy of Marketing Science Review*, http://www.amsreview.org/articles/commuri08-2000.pdf

Cowan, Susan (1987), 'The consumption junction: a proposal for research strategies in the sociology of technology', in Wiebe E. Bijker, Thomas P. Hughes and Trevor Pinch (eds), *The Social Construction of Technological Systems: New Directions in the Sociology and History of Technology*, Cambridge, MA: MIT Press, pp. 261–80.

De Geus, Marius (2003), *The End of Overconsumption: Towards a Lifestyle of Moderation and Self-Restraint*, Utrecht: International Books.

De Vries, Jan (1993), 'Between purchasing power and the world of goods: understanding the household economy in early modern Europe', in John Brewer and Roy Porter (eds), *Consumption and the World of Goods*, London and New York: Routledge, pp. 85–132.

Edgerton, Robert B. (1992), *Sick Societies*, New York: Free Press.

Etzioni, A. (1998), 'Voluntary simplicity: Characterization, select psychological implications, and societal consequences', *Journal of Economic Psychology*, **19**, 619–43.

Fischer-Kowalski, Marina and Christof Amann (2001), 'Beyond IPAT and the Kuznets curves: Globalization as a vital factor in analyzing the environmental impact of socio-economic metabolism', *Population and Environment*, **23** (1), 7–47.

Hornborg, Alf (2001), *The Power of the Machine: Global Inequalities of Economy, Technology, and Environment*, Walnut Creek, CA: AltaMira Press.

Illich, Ivan (1977), *Toward a History of Needs*, Pantheon: New York.

Jackson, Tim and Laurie Michaelis (2003), *Policies for Sustainable Consumption*, London: UK Sustainable Development Commission.

Kempton, W. (1986), 'Two theories of home heat control', *Cognitive Science*, **10**, 75–90.

Kempton, W. (1991), 'Public understanding of global warming', *Society and Natural Resources*, **4** (4), 331–45.

Kempton, W. (1997), 'How the public views climate change', *Environment*, **39** (9), 12–21.

Lilienfeld, Robert and William Rathje (1998), *Use Less Stuff: Environmental Solutions For Who We Really Are*, New York: Ballantine.

Marchand, Roland (1986), *Advertising the American Dream: Making Way for Modernity, 1920–1940*, Berkeley: University of California Press.

McKibben, Bill (2001), *What Would Jesus Drive?*, Grist online, http://www.gristmagazine.com/grist/maindish/mckibben060501.stm.

Miller, Daniel (1998), *A Theory of Shopping*, London: Polity Press.

Miller, Daniel (2001), 'The poverty of morality', *Journal of Consumer Culture*, **1** (2), 225–44.

Millman, Marcia (1991), *Warm Hearts and Cold Cash: The Intimate Dynamics of Families and Money*, New York: Free Press.

Moltoch, Harvey (2003), *Where Stuff Comes From*, New York and London: Routledge.

Narotzky, Susana (1997), *New Directions in Economic Anthropology*, London: Pluto Press.

Newman, Katherine (1989), *Falling from Grace: The Experience of Downward Mobility in the American Middle Class*, New York: Vintage Books.

Nordman, Bruce (1998), *Celebrating Consumption*, Lawrence Berkeley National Laboratory, http://eetd.lbl.gov/EA/Buildings/BNordman/C/cons3.html.

O'Dougherty, Maureen (2002), *Consumption Intensified: The Politics of Middle-Class Daily Life in Brazil*, Durham, NC: Duke University Press.

Price, L., E. Arnould and C. Curasi (2000), 'Older consumers' disposition of special possessions', *Journal of Consumer Research*, **27** (3), 179–201.

Rathje, William and Cullen Murphy (1992), *Rubbish!: The Archaeology of Garbage*, New York: HarperCollins.

Reisch, Lucia (2003), 'Consumption', in Edward A. Page and John Proops (eds), *Environmental Thought*, Current Issues in Ecological Economics Series, Cheltenham, UK and Northampton, MA, US: Edward Elgar, pp. 217–42.

Robbins, Richard (2000), *The Political Economy of Twinkies*, http://www.plattsburgh.edu/legacy.

Ryan, John C. and Alan Thein Durning (1997), *Stuff: The Secret Lives of Everyday Things*, Seattle: Northwest Environment Watch.

Salisbury, Richard (1962), *From Stone to Steel*, Cambridge, MA: Cambridge University Press.

Sanne, Christer (2002), 'Willing consumers – or locked-in? Policies for sustainable consumption', *Ecological Economics*, **42** (1–2), 273–87.

Shove, Elizabeth (2003), *Comfort, Cleanliness and Convenience: The Social Organizaton of Normality*, London: Berg.

Stern, Paul (1997), 'Toward a working definition of consumption for environmental research and policy', in P. Stern, T. Dietz, V. Ruttan, R. Socolow, and J. Sweeney (eds), *Environmentally Significant Consumption*, Washington DC: National Academy Press, pp. 12–25.

Wilk, Richard (1994), 'Inside the economic institution: Modeling household budget structures', in James Acheson (ed.), *Anthropology and Institutional Economics*, Lanham, MD: University Press of America, pp. 365–90.

Wilk, Richard (1996), *Economies and Cultures: Foundations of Economic Anthropology*, Boulder, CO: Westview Press.

Wilk, Richard (2001), 'Consuming morality', *Journal of Consumer Culture*, **1** (2), 245–60.

Wilk, Richard (2002), 'Consumption, human needs, and global environmental change', *Global Environmental Change*, **12** (1), 5–13.

Wilk, Richard (2004), 'Morals and metaphors: Why consumption is an illusion', in press Karin Ekström (ed.), *Elusive Consumption*, London: Berg Publishers.

Zelizer, Viviana (1994), *The Social Meaning of Money*, New York: BasicBooks.

3. The society, its products and the environmental role of consumption

Joachim H. Spangenberg

3.1 INTRODUCTION

Sustainable development does not provide an ideological blueprint for a future society: nobody knows what the future will look like, although we are all involved in creating it. For this creation process we need an orientation, a compass indicating the direction of what is probably desirable, offering a sustained quality of life in particular in the long run, and for all the Earth's citizens. For implementing these insights, for making them operational and relevant in day-to-day decision-making we need a democratic, highly participative political process to translate the general orientation, based on the values of the society, into concrete strategies and politics. However, while this participatory approach calls upon responsible citizens (or selfish ones with an enlightened self-interest), the same individuals are consumers as well. How can and should they contribute to sustainable development in this role, and which motives would orient their preferences towards sustainable development and environmentally benign consumption (Røpke 2001)?

For mainstream neoclassical economists it is simple: preferences are exogenously given, and they do not change endogenously. Every consumer is a homo oeconomicus with full information, taking decisions exclusively based on selfish utility maximisation: social or ethical values, emotions and affection are not relevant for this 'ideal' person's 'rational' behaviour (unless interpreted as basically selfish motivations). In a truly Orwellian use of language, consumers are all taken to behave like the kind of guy you would not invite for dinner (Bossel 2000), and this is called 'rational'. Furthermore, all these 'homini' are identical in their behaviour (so they are rather 'homunculi'), permitting to aggregate their un-individual behaviour into household demand curves and match them with supply.

Reality is more complex, however, and thus ecological economics has to deal with the challenge of a more realistic perception of human beings (*Ecological Economics* 2000). Fashion, taste and thus preferences change over time, are individually differentiated and influenced by social groups and public discourses. Humans are *social individuals*: neither can societal processes be predicted by just aggregating independent individuals, nor can individual behaviour be explained without taking the social context duly into account. Whereas basic needs like food, shelter, and so on are relatively easy to define, the means to satisfy these needs vary considerably between cultures, income groups and according to gender (Max-Neef 1991) and evolve over time. The history of production and consumption indicates how the environmental problems emerged, and how deeply they are rooted in our model of civilisation (Section 2).

Furthermore, the preferences expressed at the shopping counter result from a blend of interwoven intrinsic and extrinsic motivations, deep values and spontaneous emotions, influencing each other and co-evolving over time and income, but with different sensitivities, time scales and levels of resilience. Nonetheless they are not irrational: the way our society and economy functions provides perfectly rational reasons for ongoing consumption without any sign of saturation – not necessarily so, but definitely for the time being (Røpke 1999).

Products and services are not only economic goods (measured in monetary terms) with a social meaning, but physical objects as well, tangible or – like many services – otherwise physically enjoyed. No economic good exists without a physical footprint, and the resulting matter–money dichotomy can be considered as important for modern, that is, ecological economics, as the wave–particle dichotomy for modern physics. Consequently, any definition of sustainable consumption must reflect on the physical, social and economic processes behind production and consumption (Reisch and Scherhorn 1999), and institutional regulation, formal or informal, must take all of them into account to be effective. As a result, the challenges of measuring and reducing the environmental impact of consumption are manifold, despite the 50 years of debate on consumption since Vance Packard (1960) and the obvious needs to change *'the unsustainable pattern of consumption and production, particularly in industrialized countries'* as a *'major cause of the continued degradation of the global environment'* (United Nations 1993, Section 4). Open questions to deal with include:

- Who are the consumers to be analysed; do they include business, the state or only the households? As an immediate answer, we focus on households and their role as actors for sustainable consumption.
- What is the environmental relevance of household consumption? An answer to this question is only possible by deriving integrative indicators for environmental pressures and to relate them to

consumption options. Some such universal yardsticks are introduced in Section 2.
• What is the impact consumers have on consumption decisions? Answering this question necessitates a brief look into consumption motivations and what influences them (Section 3), plus describing the interaction of a plethora of actors shaping the final decision, when wishes and realities have to be accommodated at the same time (Section 4).

3.2   THE ARTEFACTS OF SOCIETIES

The history of humankind can be read as a history of its products – and vice versa. Our knowledge of earlier societies is not based on understanding their tradition and culture, but on analysing their artefacts, or, more precisely, the waste they left behind. Without arrow tips, bones or potsherds we would know little about their lives. Our way of interpreting human history is to a large degree an anthropology of products and their waste.

Products as such had been with human development since its first day (for a long time, using instruments has even been considered a key criterion distinguishing between humans and animals). With industrialisation, however, a new mode of production took over. Products were no longer manufactured by handicraft workers in the neighbourhood and exchanged against farmers' goods. Instead, major facilities produced a high volume of more and more specialised products on their assembly belts, based on the disintegration of production processes into small repetitive steps to increase productivity (Taylorism). The products were traded on an increasingly globalised market – at the end of the 19th century, trade volumes (relative to production size) and economic integration were higher than in the early 21st (*The Economist* 2000). Traditional goods were produced in high quantities at low prices, new products were invented, and increasingly the satisfaction of all kinds of human needs was commodified. Like the production of material goods, capitalism is trying to turn knowledge, caring for people, entertainment and nature into commodities, thus making access to them wealth dependent – a surprisingly still valid extension of Marx's comment that capitalism reduces everything to the 'cash nexus' (Giddings et al. 2002).

Mass production, however, faced one serious challenge: who should buy the products? It was Henry Ford who decided to pay a decent wage to his workers so that they could afford the products they were producing. Fordism is the basis of mass consumption, and the traditional cornerstone of our social models: when mass income declined, the result was almost inevitably a decline in consumption, production, employment and tax revenue. With mass production and increasing purchasing power of consumers, consumption soared, and with it resource depletion, emissions and waste generation.

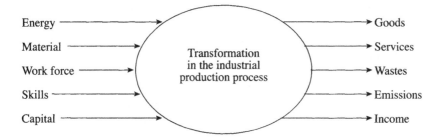

Figure 3.1　The industrial transformation system

Waste is the Janus face of products and production, its undesired but unavoidable backside. Its sheer volume developed into a key determinant of urban planning already in Ancient Rome, was the breeding ground for the plague killing a third of the European population in the 14th to 17th century and accelerated its growth with the emerging Industrial Revolution. Industrialisation was only possible based on new infrastructure, production facilities, roads and railways, their construction and maintenance. The growth of waste heaps and brownfields would have been the most telling symbol of the new era, even more so than the smoking chimneys (Spangenberg 1994). The pattern of production and consumption that emerged and in its basic traits remained unchanged right into the 21st century is a waste-intensive one (see Figure 3.1): the vast majority of all materials activated never enters the production chain. Vance Packard (1960) was right to call our societies 'wasteful societies' – products become waste after use, and with decreasing product life and recycling rates of less than 2 per cent of all materials activated, the production process is essentially a 'wastisation' process of labour and resources (Spangenberg 1996). So, long before any consumer is involved, every production process begins with waste generation; in terms of physical volumes, the goods and services we consume are just a mere by-product, albeit a desired one, and the main product of our productive processes is waste.

For instance, while as of today the total volume of resources needed to provide a vacuum cleaner for households is several hundred kilograms, its total time of service delivery (that is, the use time accumulated over the life time) is about two weeks, and for an electric drill it is less than two days (Striewski 2003). An average German car is produced by turning about

10 tons of resources into 1 ton of a technical artefact used to transport on average 100 kilograms of humans. Its service, enhanced mobility, is used mainly in cities where the average car transport velocity is about 15 kilometres per hour, well below the 17–20 kilometres per hour of the horse carriage, and for distances of less than 1 kilometre, where it would have been faster to go on foot. Its use is enjoyed for an aggregate time of about three months (average use in Germany 200 hours per year or 33 minutes per day over 12 years, making the car an 'auto*stabile*' rather than an 'auto*mobile*'), and then the car is thrown away; recycling of spare parts plays no significant role so far. Adding a much praised environmental device, the catalytic converter, consumes resources at least equivalent to the mass of the whole car. The relation of resource consumption and environmental impact to the volume of services generated is rather absurd, let alone the social and economic cost incurred.

3.3 PRODUCTION, CONSUMPTION AND POLLUTION

Sustainable consumption integrates social, economic and institutional as well as environmental aspects. However, the current international discourse is most advanced as far as environmental sustainability is concerned. Social sustainability criteria are just about to be formulated, but economic and institutional ones (except inoperational objectives like maintaining the respective capital stocks) are still rare and preliminary. So focusing on the environmental aspects, what are the criteria of progress towards environmentally sustainable consumption? Mainstream economists and environmental scientists have different world views, which ecological economics tries to integrate: whereas the cyclic flows of money are the basis of the economic analysis, the physical analysis is confronted with mainly linear flows through the economy and their transformation in the course of this process.

Every production process begins with an intellectual act: recognising the use potential embodied in a part of nature and landscape, be it land for grazing, wood for construction or ores for mining. In the next step, a value is attributed to what is now no longer perceived as a part of nature but a resource (although physically probably nothing has changed so far: the perception counts). This attribution of a value refers to the potential market value of the resource, that is, the demand people other than the owners have, not to any kind of intrinsic value. The resource is exploited if this market value is higher than the cost of exploring and exploiting the resource (plus the profit margin defined by the owner), which in reality is the cost of waste production. Overburden, drainage water, or waste heaps are all parts of nature that have been in the way of commercial exploitation of a resource – had the resource been defined otherwise, what is now the waste might have been part of valuable product, and vice versa.

In a Western European economy, 50–60 distinct abiotic materials including energy carriers and water but not air have been defined as such resources, are extracted from nature and crossing the border into the economic sphere at about 20 000 points of entry[1] (Spangenberg et al. 1999). There they undergo mechanical, thermal and (bio-)chemical treatment to be transformed into products, production waste and liquid and gaseous effluents. The production process increases the number of substances dramatically: on the output side about 100 000 substances – about 33 000 thereof in significant quantities – and 2 million products leave the human sphere and are returned to the environment (Sturm 2001), at countless exit gates (smokestacks, drainpipes, waste dumps, exhaust pipes...). Thirty thousand or 90 per cent of the mass-produced substances are so-called 'old substances', which have not undergone a state-of-the-art environmental assessment as they were marketed before appropriate chemicals regulations came into force on the EU level in 1981 (Wille 2003).

Obviously, the sheer numbers of substances and their emission points are beyond the scope of effective control, and the massive resistance of economic interest groups makes effective environmental protection even harder to achieve. For instance, the latest initiative of the European Commission, suggesting the registration of all old substances (that is, collecting meaningful data for them) by 2012 and assessing their impacts based on these data by 2020, has been denounced as 'overly ambitious' by the business lobby and consequently watered down by the governments, for example, of Germany and the UK. As a result, even the approximately 1350 cancerogenous and mutagenous (that is, cancer causing and genome damaging) substances and about 150 bio-accumulative ones will be on the market at least for another half generation (Wille 2003).

Given the figures presented on inputs and outputs, input accounting must be considered as an alternative to emission measurement, providing the opportunity for a comprehensive assessment. Although this admittedly neglects the substance-specific environmental impacts, this is not as much of a problem as it might seem at first glance: if a substantial reduction of resource extraction is set as the target, say a factor 4 for energy consumption (von Weizsäcker et al. 1997) or a factor 10 for material flows (Schmidt-Bleek 1994) by the midst of the century, in the course of time most production processes will have to be redesigned, and with them the goods and services consumed. This requires a significant number of innovations, social, economic, but in particular technical ones. Such innovation processes, speeding up the market-based search mechanisms and giving a clear direction to the permanent structural change usual in capitalist economies have to take into account the state of the art regarding environmental impact assessment. The 'old substances' would rather soon disappear from the market, replaced by newly developed ones based on the best of current knowledge, and – due to dematerialisation – used in smaller quantities. In this way, dematerialisation does not ignore detoxification, but rather provides the opportunity to overcome existing inertia also regarding the qualitative aspects of products and processes.

This is why enforcing specific environmental standards, substance legislation and the forthcoming EU framework are not superfluous efforts, but are complementary to any input reduction scheme and need to be implemented as a matter of urgency, and why substituting at least substances with proven harmless characteristics for the suspicious ones in product design would be a significant step forward. However, as long as we do not manage to design our products so as to minimise the consumption of resources from the very beginning, only limited progress towards environmentally benign production and consumption will be possible.

3.3.1 Quantity and Quality

Input accounting is more than a second best option made necessary by the unmanageable complexity of comprehensive output-based accounting. Not only does the quality of certain substances cause environmental concerns, the sheer volume of resource consumption is a reason to worry, as most current environmental problems are closely linked to energy consumption, material flows and land use intensity (UNDESA 1998). As a matter of fact, except for the impacts of small amounts of highly bio-active substances, and of spatial effects (ecosystem fragmentation by infrastructure construction) the most relevant environmental problems in Europe can be traced back to the overconsumption of these basic resources (Spangenberg and Lorek 2002). The consumption of primary energy, total material flows and land use intensity can thus be considered a reliable proxy measure for total environmental stresses. Some authors have tried to enhance the communicative value of input assessment by aggregating all kinds of input into one figure, based either on accounting for (and converting all other impacts into) appropriated energy, emergy or exergy, land use, or material flows. All these measures are useful to illustrate the current 'consumption overshoot', providing complementary rather than competing views (Robert et al. 2002). The broadest of these physical input measures is material flow accounting, since it includes by definition energy carriers (in tons, not in energy units) and erosion as an indicator of land use intensity. For this reason, and since it is less well-known than energy accounting, it is described here in some detail.

The volume of resources activated for maintaining service flows from stocks as well as from consumer goods, that is, the total physical throughput of the economy (Daly 1991) can be assessed in different ways. Like any other meaningful assessment of human-made environmental distortions, diverse as they are in their nature, their causes and their origins, it must be based on a lifecycle-wide approach, from resource mining to final disposal. However, depending on the kind of problem to be dealt with, and on the data available, different kinds of flows and different system boundaries are selected (OECD 2001; see Figure 3.2).

DPO (Domestic Processed Output) covers the traditional way of describing the interaction of effluents from the production and consumption system with the biosphere. It includes all those substance flows from domestic activities that regularly show up in environmental statistics. The steps to be taken into account include along the chain of production, consumption and disposal:

- the use of substances that are deliberately dissipated in the environment for a specific purpose, for example, pesticides or fertilisers in agriculture or salt on icy roads in winter time,
- emissions and deposition of solid, fluid and gaseous wastes, released into the environment as a result or side-effect of human activities like CO_2 from the energy consumption during manufacturing and use of a product.

Domestic output accounting is the basis for some more recent policy instruments like waste taxes and levies.

TDO (Total Domestic Output) adds the domestic hidden flows to the DPO. They comprise all the hidden physical flows like overburden or strip water from mining, and other materials that have not at all entered the production process. These materials are usually characterised by a negative economic value, that is, the cost of waste disposal, and are most frequently not taken into account in the waste statistics (Striewski 2003). Environmentally they represent open bills, irrespective of their economic valuation, causing environmental impacts like acid rain, groundwater contamination and a variety of not yet known damages, which we will have to deal with in future. Some of these effects are more or less stationary like heavy metal pollution in the ground or in sediments, while others spread ubiquitously. In one respect, the resulting pollution pattern from effluents and waste mimics the consumption patterns: the global consumer society

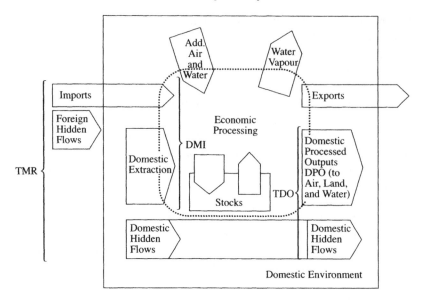

Source: Eurostat 2001.

Figure 3.2   Economy-wide material flows

leaves its footsteps in every corner of the world, from DDT in penguin eggs
to dioxins for breast-fed babies.

DMI (Domestic Material Input) accounts for those physical inputs
into the economy that have been extracted domestically, plus the volume
of imported goods (both without the hidden flows associated with them,
and imports without the production waste generated). As the number of
entry gates and the diversity of substances is much lower on the input side,
accounting for inputs covers the immediate outputs as well as those realised
later due to a period of staying in the stocks. Therefore, input accounting
provides a more comprehensive assessment of the environmental damages
caused by today's activities, and offers itself to innovative instruments for
reducing the total throughput, such as the Swedish tax on gravel (Palm
2002). This tax basis is quite broad: for instance, in Denmark as a highly
trade-dependent country, the DMI in 1997 has been about 185 million tons
or 35 tons per capita. Allocated to final demand, resources have been used
as shown in Table 3.1.

However, these figures do not provide a full picture of the Danish footprint
on the global environment: as the DMI does not take the flows associated
to imports into account, the goods and services purchased by the revenues

from the exports do not show up satisfactorily in the statistics. Nonetheless the table very clearly indicates the importance of the physical dimension of international trade, in addition to the monetary one (Döppe et al. 2003; Giljum and Hubacek 2003), that is, the matter–money dichotomy.

Table 3.1   Danish DMI by final demand 1997

Final demand	Volume (million tons)	Share in national DMI (%)
Capital formation	38	20
Export of goods and services	94	51
Government consumption	10	6
Private consumption	42	23

Source: Pedersen 2002.

TMR (Total Material Requirement) is the all-encompassing measure including the domestic material input plus the hidden flows, both domestically and in the country of origin. As compared to the DMI it covers not only the domestic impacts of economic activities, but their global environmental consequences.

Naturally, the figures for different measurement methodologies diverge. So, for instance, for Sweden, domestic used extraction (DMI minus imports) in 2001 was 20 tons per capita, with DMI 25 tons per capita and TMR 45 tons per capita (Palm 2002).

The figures vary considerably between different countries, due to their level of consumption and to the structure of their domestic industry (for instance, Germany has a high contribution from lignite mining, and the Netherlands a similarly high one from meat production (Adriaanse et al. 1997). Both countries have a TMR of about 70 tons of material use per capita per year, with the German TMR gradually returning to its pre-unification level. Regarding TMR, Denmark also falls quite in line with its neighbour. The lowest annual level is found for Japan and the UK at about 40 tons per capita, while Finland has outgrown the USA (see Figure 3.3): despite its focus on IT industries, Finland's TMR grew from around 60 tons per capita to nearly 100 tons per capita, a rapid increase usually typical for newly industrialising economies. This illustrates that even a modern high-tech business structure cannot exist without underlying traditional and material-intensive production, and provides a warning to all those who hope that the ongoing structural change towards a knowledge-based economy would in itself guarantee a significant dematerialisation of the industrialised economies. Overall, Figure 3.3 illustrates the trend to a relative, but not

Tons per capita

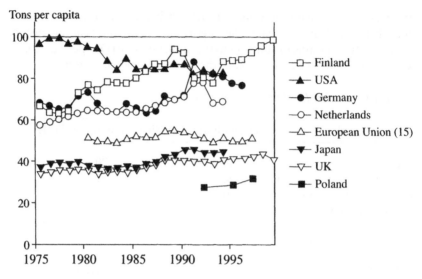

-□- Finland
-▲- USA
-●- Germany
-○- Netherlands
-△- European Union (15)
-▼- Japan
-▽- UK
-■- Poland

Source: Eurostat 2001.

*Figure 3.3   Total material flows between 1975 and 2000 in seven countries
                and the EU 15*

absolute delinkage of economic growth and resource consumption (except
for the USA): despite a growth of at least 50 per cent of the GDP since
the mid-1970s, the TMR did not follow suit but remained rather constant
(Japan, EU 15, UK) or grew less than the GDP.

3.3.2   Take Three: The Environmental Space Concept

Material flow accounting, although the best single unit measurement
available, still suffers from the problem all physical aggregates are confronted
with: essentially, all conversions of resource consumption are rather
arbitrary, as matter, energy and land – the three basic physical categories
– have no common denominator. In the environmental space concept they
are held separate for this reason, providing clear indications for prioritising
changing land use intensity, energy saving and/or dematerialisation, and
making trade-offs and synergies visible. The price to be paid is that there
is not one figure but three and thus no unambiguously best or optimal
result. The concept was developed by Hans Opschoor (Opschoor and
Reijnders 1991) and applied to household consumption by the Dutch NGO
Vereniging Milieudefensie (Buitenkamp et al. 1992). In its current form,
the concept accounts for material flows, primary energy consumption and

land use intensity, defining limits to inputs and measures to halt the loss of biodiversity (Spangenberg 2002). Besides the maximum, it also defines a minimum resource provision necessary to live a dignified life, free of poverty and exclusion. The issue of underconsumption, however, is not the focus of this chapter.

Although environmentally relevant only when they are disseminated, the resources accumulated in the stocks of society deserve a closer look, too. Stocks are public goods like roads or buildings, private goods like refrigerators, cars and houses, or industrial goods like machinery, railway lines and telecommunication infrastructure; they contain a vast amount of embodied material, energy and land. Goods and services can be distinguished according to their lifetime expectancy (short or long) and according to the type of market in which they are sold (fluctuating markets where products are only fashionable for a short time, or saturated markets where products are replacements) (see Table 3.2). Unlike the impression given in much of the consumption debate, not only are short-lived goods a reason for concern, but the accumulation of durables is problematic as well. On the one hand, the mere maintenance of long-lived goods and infrastructures requires an increasing volume of monetary expenditures as well as environmental space use, without providing *additional* welfare: they need to be cleaned, upgraded, repaired or renovated to continue providing the *same* service. This creates a positive feedback cycle: as a rule of thumb, the more materials we have fixed in the stocks, the more flows we need to maintain them. On the other hand, the stocks are bound to become waste as everything else, although after a longer time span. In the meantime, they are a restriction to behavioural options other than those foreseen at the time of their construction.

Table 3.2   Market types and life expectancy

Economic lifetime expectancy	Short	Long
Type of market		
Fluctuating	Tamagotchis	Personal computers
	Plateau soles	Transformers
	DDT	PUR foam
	Rubik's cube	PlayStation
Saturated	Blue jeans	Washing machines
	Newspapers	Water pipes
	Phosphorus	Bricks

Source: van der Voet et al. 2002, modified.

Regarding substance qualities, experts warn that around the middle of the century, when decreasing populations in a number of regions (for example, EU, China) will reduce the demand for housing and transport infrastructure, with the decommissioning of settlements that have exceeded their lifetime, CFC emissions from construction foams will result, their volume about as much as the total releases during the last century. Similarly, the decreasing trend of emissions of heavy metals is expected to be reversed soon, due to releases not from production, but from the stocks of products (van der Voet et al. 2002).

3.4   SUSTAINABILITY, CONSUMPTION AND THE PURSUIT OF HAPPINESS

The World Commission on Environment and Development (WCED or Brundtland Commission) has coined the most frequently quoted description of sustainable development by characterising it as 'development that meets the needs of the present without compromising the ability of future generations to meet their own needs' (WCED 1987, p. 43). Human needs include basic needs like food, clothing and shelter, but also additional material and non-material demands, which if satisfied are supposed to make life more pleasant and entertaining, and a part of these are consumption demands (Max-Neef 1991). Others are the challenge of raising children, gaining reputation from voluntary work in the community or the satisfaction from learning or pursuing a personal hobby. Which demands are articulated depends on a variety of factors, including the idea of what makes the quality of life, what is accepted/admired by the social reference groups, or which options are available and affordable. Time availability plays a central role as well, as time becomes a more and more scarce resource (Cogoy 1995). The resulting consumption patterns (including preference formation, purchasing, using and disposing of artefacts) do not only have significant environmental impacts, but penetrate all spheres of life. Consumer technology has severe social impacts, provides options for action as well as obstacles to it, and thus increasingly shapes the kind of activities chosen (if not the motives behind them). The mutual enforcement of individualisation and (auto-) mobility illustrates this point: a car, besides being a sink for resources and a source of pollutants has the effect of a 'social presence dilution machine'. It permits its owner not to stay put in a certain neighbourhood for living, shopping, consuming and leisure, but to reach out over a significantly larger distance, covering more people. This way, the car owner can and must be more selective when deciding where to shop, whom to meet and where to go – on the one hand, a gift of choices enhancing individual freedom, on the other a mechanism that contributes to the disintegration of society into different and rather unconnected sub-cultures. Individualism and sub-culture development are at the same time driving forces for increasing mobility demands.

The symbolic value of consumer goods is frequently more important than their initial function as 'service delivery machines' (Schmidt-Bleek and Tischner 1995), providing an important contribution to the subjective quality of life (Spangenberg and Lorek 2003), but also fuelling competitive consumption ('keeping up with the Joneses'). As a consequence, today too many people buy things they don't need with money they don't have to impress people they don't like, regardless of the costs involved and the environmental impact caused. The willingness to consume is a social as well as a psychological phenomenon, and its impacts are environmental as well as social and economic ones. However, what is really the role of products and their consumption in our societies is still far from fully understood. Whereas rather obviously in a capitalist economy the profit motive is driving the dynamics of growth and innovation on the production side, is money the overall driver for our societies, or just a lubricant? Is it commodities, technical artefacts and gadgets, or individual attitudes that make consumption the current key means in the pursuit of happiness? Are humans amoral utility maximisers, social integration seekers, or fun addicts? What is the driving force on the consumption side? Are we watching the rise and fall of the consumer society (Jackson 2002)? Which kind of consumption contributes to the quality of life, and which one does not (Daly 2001)? How can we enjoy gains in the quality of life without detrimental effects on the source of all resources, the environment? What in the end is sustainable consumption, what is overconsumption (Miljöverndepartementet 1995)? What needs to be sustained – life satisfaction, disposable income, or the total standard of living from bought and donated goods and services (Spangenberg 2002)?

3.4.1 The Driving Forces

Products and services are consumed because buying, owning and/or using them has a personal value for which a monetary value is paid or another kind of material or immaterial compensation is offered. In determining what is consumed, different spheres of influence overlap. Developers, producers, retailers, other exchange partners, and consumers themselves, all have a role to play (Lorek et al. 1999). The relative level of influence of the different actors depends on social and institutional settings determining their power position, on arguments (including the 435 billion dollar turnover of the global advertising industry, but also social relations and peer group pressures) and on the responsiveness of the respective audience to these arguments. The responsiveness itself is influenced by a variety of intrinsic and extrinsic factors.

Intrinsic factors comprise cognitive capacities, psychological factors, spontaneous emotions, individual interests and philosophical, moral or ethical norms. Extrinsic factors include socio-economic aspects like the disposable income and time availability as well as social relations (self-esteem, respect, admiration leading to imitation, peer pressure, fashion, family bargaining). Intrinsic factors determine the preferences, while extrinsic ones reflect the economic, social and legal possibilities, obligations and constraints. As both overlap (for example, individual preferences are shaped by social norms and relations and vice versa) no quantitative determination of the relative importance of each one for the resulting behaviour is possible; they co-evolve. For instance, the need for food is a constant, but with societal change, eating habits, time patterns and so on have changed more rapidly in the last 50 years than in the centuries before, a development made possible by increasing income and available technology. As a result, access to a refrigerator was no immediate need in the 1950s, when buying fresh products from the markets was a widespread habit, but today it is.

While extrinsic factors like disposable income have a significant influence on the availability of consumption options, intrinsic factors shape the choice between the alternatives available. One key factor determining such decisions is the individual assessment if existing alternatives are affordable in terms of purchasing power, time use preferences, resource endowment, and the desire to maintain or improve self-esteem, social status and acceptability (Cogoy 1999). Similar criteria apply to goods not traded on markets, but exchanged with or without equivalent compensation, like all services from unpaid work (caring and supply, housekeeping and education, voluntary and community activities, and so on).

The goods consumed, products or services, paid or unpaid, can be symbols of group identity, reflecting the visions, *Leitbilder*, grand narratives or concrete utopias that a group like a nation, an ethnic group, or a lifestyle-based sub-group has, the idea of quality of life they share and live according to. Exposing a certain good (privately or collectively owned, or borrowed) can thus symbolise the membership of a certain group (or the aspiration to be a member), support for a certain idea, and so on: products do not create identity, but they are indispensable tools to express it. This way, goods serve as a 'projection screen' for otherwise defined values. However, to make them suitable for such projections, they must exhibit a 'blank screen', not being too obviously attached to specific values of their own. This mechanism is one of the reasons why green products or those from fair trade have significant problems reaching customers beyond the niche market they already occupy: they are not suitable for expressing any other identity than the ethical values their production is based upon. Expressing one's own identity as an active act, however, is experienced as extremely positive, since it creates the opportunity to experience one's identity, in this case by exhibiting certain products (an extremely frustrating mechanism for those who wish to join this group, but cannot).

A specific form of distinction is the ownership and exhibition of positional or oligarchic, mostly paid goods. The less people can afford a certain artefact at a given time, the smaller the group of potential owners, the higher its positional value, and the higher the incentive for all others to strive for future ownership as well. Then the good will be no longer positional, rendering the intended positional gain unattainable, which is subsequently promised by another good. Although positional goods need not be monetary, tradable or material – status is a clear positional good, time can be one – Mainwaring (2001) suspects that as a rule of thumb positional goods will be more environmentally damaging than less positional goods, as status is most frequently advertised by exhibiting material goods. Once environmental services become sufficiently scarce and thus more valuable in market-economy terms, environmental intensity as such might become a characteristic of positional goods (Altvater 2002). As societies and economies change, altering the patterns of scarcity and the relation of capital, labour and the environment, the failure of consumers to adapt to changing circumstances can lead to a lock-in, to sclerotic, outdated but quasi-sacred consumption patterns, as is the case, for example, with the 'American way of life'.

Such sclerotic consumption patterns inhibit the adaptation of consumption to ever-changing extrinsic conditions and thus the evolution of societies in general and the one towards sustainability in particular. To a significant degree they are the result of fear-induced and safety-oriented value systems emerging from the experience or social stress and deprivation, causing a desire for an idealised past (Giddens 1996), a retroprojective idealism.

3.4.2   The Evolution of Preferences

Whereas in the pursuit of happiness during the 1950s and 1960s the quantity of consumption was taken as a measure of its quality, in the 1970s its social attributes, in the 1980s its price and in the 1990s its fun factor defined its added value for the quality of life. At the turn of century the consumption drive is slowing down and the hunt for bargains is heating up, the risks of life (stock exchange losses, social security cuts, terrorism and war) dominate the public mood, and the quality of life seems likely to re-emerge as a core motive in the first decade of the new century. However, only time will tell whether this will result in another turn in the 300-year-old competition of paradigms between sustainability and expansionism (Grober 2002). A move from the high-throughput consumption society attitude of 'to buy is to be' to the wealthy, value-based, durability promoting 'to have is to be' is possible if not plausible, and the rather philosophical attitude of 'to be is to have' is lurking in the visions of a sustainable knowledge society where social status is more based on knowledge than on the possession of material goods.

However, such a turn to sustainable consumption and production is neither to be expected without deliberately investing significant political, scientific, technological and educational efforts, nor is it easy to achieve. Nonetheless it is possible: less resource squandering products and services are feasible, as an overwhelming list of examples illustrates (von Weizsäcker et al. 1997; Schmidt-Bleek 1999). However, individual preferences alone will not do the job: sustainable consumption today is the art of 'right' behaviour within 'wrong' structures. In this perspective, the strategic challenge of sustainable development policy is to use, to find or even to create opportunities to leave the established socio-economic trajectories and change course towards a new paradigm. This can be based on the values expressed by ordinary people when asked for their most prominent wishes and aspirations: health, fitness, paid work, social security, education and information, a social environment providing acknowledgement and contact, and last but not least a healthy environment. Unlimited consumption, wealth or just only a high income level are not on the wish list – they are means for security and well-being, but no ends in themselves (Dahm et al. 2002).

3.5 MEASURING HOUSEHOLD RESPONSIBILITY

Industrialised, market-based capitalist societies have embarked on a very specific development path in their pursuit of happiness: accumulating material artefacts is considered as increasing wealth, and wealth has become synonymous with well-being. Little wonder then that the richer individuals and societies become, the heavier is their pressure on the environment, and all hopes that the environmental pressure would sooner or later rather automatically decline 'once we can afford it' – the so-called Environmental Kuznets Hypothesis – have turned out to be just wishful thinking (Fischer-Kowalski and Amann 2001; Lorek and Spangenberg 2001b).

With economic globalisation, this process has reached a new quality. Mergers and acquisitions have led to an immense capital concentration, and the expected synergies from these friendly or hostile takeovers can only be realised if the standardisation of core components is extended to all products of the respective transnational corporation. So, for instance, the car frames and the motors are the same in Skoda, Volkswagen, Seat and Audi cars, in Fords and Volvos, and only the outer skin, the design is different. The same applies to computers, shoes and banking services: to exploit the economies of scale, standardisation is applied, resulting in what looks like a broad variety of products at first glance, but is based on a rather narrow range of basic models and components. Product diversity is created as *pluralism by design*, a secondary or *virtual diversity* of essentially identical products. Contemporary consumers are confronted with the broadest choice of products human history has seen, but still their choice is limited to the virtual diversity the market offers.

3.5.1 Getting the Framework Right

What can households do to contribute to a stepwise but massive reduction in environmental space use, given the significant but limited influence *of* consumers, and the plethora of influences *on* them? On the one hand, household production and consumption play a role, but also the upstream impact of consumer demand and the downstream consequences of their consumption and disposal attitudes. Most frequently, when applying the household economics approach favoured by consumer organisations, environmental NGOs and – for instance in Germany – environmental agencies, these up- and downstream influences and thus responsibilities are quite neglected. The other extreme is the system of national accounts (SNA), allocating all impacts to the sectors of final demand (admittedly, the SNA is not intended to measure responsibilities, but – as for welfare – it is frequently misinterpreted in this sense). As households through their consumption of traded goods and public services are directly and indirectly consuming all that is accounted for as final demand (except for a trade surplus, allocated to foreign consumers), in this view households are responsible for all environmental impacts. This kind of assessment is the basis for the calculation of per capita material flow data, resulting in figures like the average material consumption in industrialised countries (80 tons per capita × year) or the average freshwater use (500 tons per capita × year) (Schmidt-Bleek 2003).

None of the extremes adequately reflects the influence and capabilities of consumers; nonetheless they are frequently used and – even worse – mixed without explaining their methodological differences (for instance in the OECD consumption statistics (e.g., OECD 1999). A more appropriate methodology must be sought somewhere in the middle ground. One way to do so is to use the all-encompassing SNA approach and the corresponding monetary and physical input–output tables to assess the environmental space consumption of *all* consumption clusters and thus to identify the most relevant ones. In a second step, those clusters can be named that are under

control of or at least significantly influenced by consumers' decisions. Thus
the relative influence of households can be determined and their overall
environmental responsibility characterised (if not measured) (Spangenberg
and Lorek 2002).

3.5.2   The Role of Households

For Germany, ten consumption clusters have been identified, covering
more than 90 per cent of the environmental space use; six of them, each
representing a share of more than 5 per cent are considered environmentally
relevant (see Table 3.3). Half of these clusters represent state consumption,
that is, processes that can hardly be influenced by consumers to increase the
environmental profile of the services generated. Only three clusters remain
that are both environmentally relevant and open to significant household
influence: construction and housing, transport, and nutrition (the food
chain). Each of them presents more than 20 per cent of environmental space
use, and together they represent about three-quarters of all environmental
pressures in terms of environmental space consumption (Lorek et al.
1999).

Obviously, effective environmental sustainability efforts should focus
on these clusters, offering extrinsic frameworks supportive to change,
and providing an appropriate contextualisation for a positive integration
into the intrinsic motivations. When doing so, however, the potential high
psychological or symbolic value of the clusters of minor environmental
relevance must be taken into account as well.

Table 3.3   Where households can make a difference

Consumption clusters	Influence of private households	Environmental relevance
Clothing	x	
Education/Training		x
Nutrition/Foodchain	x	x
Health care		x
Construction/Housing	x	x
Hygiene	x	
Cleaning	x	
Recreation	x	
Social life		x
Mobility/Transport	x	x

Source: Lorek et al. 1999.

In a similar fashion, within these three clusters a total number of 14 activities have been identified, which are dominating the environmental impact, and environmentally benign alternatives identified. This provides households with obvious choices for or against 'green consumption' in the environmentally most relevant cases, without suppressing the willingness to change by information overload. For instance, in construction/housing to build a new house or to inhabit an existing one is a key decision, as is the insulation and the resulting energy consumption level. For nutrition, the preference for local and seasonal products plays a role, plus the current overconsumption of meat. Regarding mobility, commuting is losing its dominant role, and leisure flights are the most rapidly growing pressure. Such decisions, however, are influenced by different actors in rather differentiated ways. These actors include households on the demand side, and planners, architects, producers, advertisers, retailers, regulators and others on the supply side.

Such lists can be used to describe the most environmentally relevant consumption decisions one by one, relating them to the relative weight of different actors, for example, on an ordinal scale from '0' to '++' in an 'actor matrix' (Lorek and Spangenberg 2001a). For these decisions, households have a significant responsibility – however, how much this is, for example, as compared to public authorities, producers and retailers and so on cannot be quantified. The reason is simple: although it is possible to calculate the resource consumption for each alternative of choices, the pattern of influence and thus of responsibility varies between individuals, over time and between regions, cultures and gender. No simple percentage figure will ever be able to reflect this dynamics, let alone the overlapping spheres of influence of different actors. As a policy guidance, this characterisation visualises which actors are most relevant for the sustainability of household consumption decisions, and offers an opportunity for voluntary agreements as well as for formal regulation.

The indicators developed this way have also been used to compare the relative environmental impact of consumers from different income strata (Lorek and Spangenberg 2001b): affluent people have higher impacts regarding housing and mobility, while on nutrition data are lacking. So rather obviously, the celebrities from the yellow press are as bad an example for sustainable consumption as one can imagine, but the rich and the beautiful still shape the aspirations of the middle class. As long as they are not substituted *by* society as a role model *for* society, this constitutes a specific responsibility and – as long as no voluntary action is taken – a justification for specific policy measures to orient the well-off towards sustainable consumption.

The change needed goes far beyond, but includes promoting eco-efficiency of goods and services in a lifecycle perspective as one key objective of sustainable consumption. For Germany for instance, the Statistical Office reported an increase of energy productivity of 24 per cent during the last decade, 2.2 per cent per annum – a significant improvement, but not enough: 2.4 per cent would have been necessary to meet the 30 per cent reduction target the government had set. Regarding material flows, the result was less promising; from 1990 to 2001 the total resource consumption (without hidden flows) declined by 2 per cent, a far cry from dematerialisation. Even worse, the area of soil sealed off by settlements and infrastructure increased by 8 per cent, 123 hectares daily (Dembrowski 2001). The lack of eco-efficiency is an economic challenge as much as an environmental one: Hartmut Fischer (2002) of Arthur D. Little has estimated the annual cost of the German resource consumption of 11 tons domestic mineral extraction (DMI) plus 9 tons energy carriers to amount to 730 billion euros or 20 000 euros per household. Saving a mere 25 per cent of this material use would result in 180 billion euros of savings, and in the creation of an additional 700 000 paid jobs.

Volume of flows (logarithmic scale)

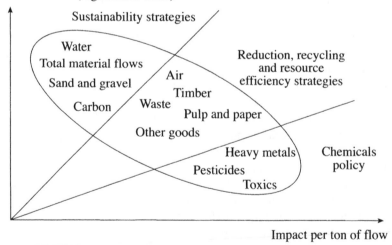

Impact per ton of flow

Source: Palm 2002, adapted from Fischer-Kowalski and Hüttler 1999.

Figure 3.4   Impacts of resource consumption and mediation strategies

When quantifying eco-efficiency, the impacts from production, use and disposal of products are taken into account as environmental costs, and the volume of services delivered as benefits. Unfortunately, the definition of services in these formulas is ambiguous, partly based on more traditional concepts of insatiable desires for a maximum of utility (Giarini 1992) and partly extended to include factors exogenous to the neo-classical model like the satisfaction from ethical motives (Stagl and O'Hara 2001). In either case, a certain act of consumption and the use of time, work and resources needed to make it happen are allocated to one specific purpose (not least to avoid double counting when trying to quantify household impacts). The environmental impact of the consumption act is then allocated to this motive when calculating the environmental burden stemming from fulfilling specific needs or wants. For example, 100 kilometres of transport is considered a service, and the impact of providing it by car or by rail can be compared (Schmidt-Bleek 1999). However, consumption decisions are hardly ever monocausal, but incorporate and react to a variety of influences and interests, all mutually influencing and modifying each other. Consequently, the utility from consumption is not homogeneous and cannot be derived by aggregating single purchases (Keen 2001). To the contrary: utility is a characteristic attributed to goods by the consumers, based on the (expected) capability to provide user satisfaction, and thus as diverse as the needs and preferences, situations and attitudes of consumers. The indicators and consumption clusters suggested avoid this problem by measuring absolute flows, not relative impacts, and thus have no need to quantify 'services'.

Nonetheless, there are trade-offs between environmental criteria and social (and possible economic and institutional) sustainability objectives. As a result, compromises must be sought between goods that have no common denominator regarding their value except for the subjective values attributed to them by individuals based in their personal and usually uninformed preferences. Any meaningful compromising cannot be based on willingness to pay analysis, cost–benefit analysis (CBA) and similar one-dimensional assessments, but must take into account incomprehensible categories based on personal assessments, at best through collective discussions on norms and values. Consequently, multi-criteria decision aid (MCDA) is the method to choose, as it permits combining quantitative and qualitative, numerical and narrative, otherwise incomprehensible valuations, while cost–benefit analysis would not deliver adequate results. Unlike CBA, MCDA does not claim to identify an optimum solution but to provide a better structured and more transparent basis for compromising. In the end, a political process with civil society participation is needed to identify an acceptable compromise. Such politically defined objectives are no substitute for the everyday expression of preferences on the market, but provide an important complement to them, as consumers and citizens, although the same people may express different preferences according to their different roles, endorsing for example, price level increases through eco-taxes they would not have accepted voluntarily in the marketplace. So households may respond to their consumption-based environmental responsibilities not through their role as consumers in the

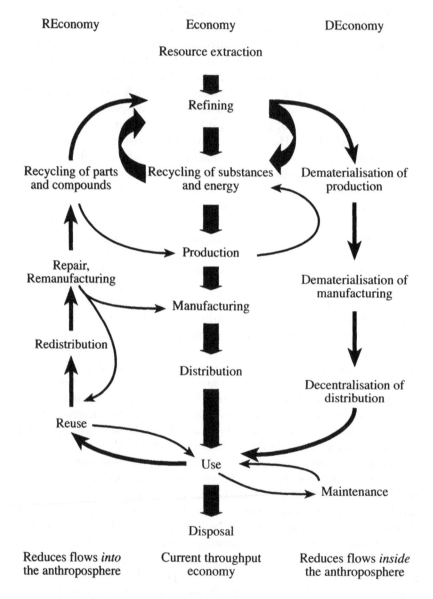

Figure 3.5   Sustainable consumption changes production patterns

marketplace, but rather rationally by endorsing restrictions in the way of consumption (and thus ruling out free rider effects) in their role as citizens (a nightmare to take into account for neoclassical economics).

3.6   CONCLUSION

Sustainable consumption is part of an overall paradigm shift towards sustainable societies, and such a paradigm shift needs to include all relevant actors. Households and individuals are involved in different positions, as citizens, as paid and unpaid workers in production and reproduction, and as consumers. Calling for change of consumer behaviour in isolation is urging for the 'right' behaviour within 'wrong' structures: the necessary change of consumption patterns must be part of a broader transformation. So, for instance, what is needed is short-term public policy regarding hazardous substances, medium-term eco-efficiency strategies and long-term dematerialisation, including a sustainable reorganisation of the total infrastructure of our societies and economies (see Figure 3.4). In all these processes, households will have to play a role, as consumers and as citizens.

Such a gradual but massive reduction of resource use is possible without impairing the standard of living, but only if significant changes in the production patterns take place. On the one hand, the total volume of resource flows must be minimised (dematerialisation), and on the other hand the share of resources extracted anew from the environment must be reduced (recovery and recycling). This transforms the *Economy* as we know it into a *DEconomy*, and complements it with a *REconomy*, as illustrated in Figure 3.5 (Striewski 2003). Both processes are complementary, demand significant investment, create a high number of new, highly qualified jobs (overcompensating those lost in the restructuring process, see for example, Hans-Böckler-Stiftung 2001). They require research, the development of new, dematerialised and recyclable products, learning how to enjoy them and how to dispose them properly as an input to the REconomy. All in all, this makes up for a different kind of *knowledge society*, where people know how to handle consciously the items of everyday use. Identifying and using this kind of bifurcation, departing from the high throughput, Fordist mass consumption society towards a low throughput, quality consumption-based one is the ultimate objective of environmental sustainability policies.

In this context it must be stressed again that sustainable consumption is not lowering the standard of living, but increasing its quality and thus the quality of life. We are just beginning to learn that lesson.

NOTE

1. Figures from Germany, with one oil or gas field considered one point of entry.

REFERENCES

Adriaanse, Albert S., Stefan Bringezu, Allen Hammond, Yuichi Moriguchi, Eric Rodenburg, Donald Rogich and Helmut Schütz (1997), *Resource Flows: The Material Basis of Industrial Economies*, Washington, DC: World Resources Institute.
Altvater, E. (2002), 'Mehr systemische Intelligenz, bitte!', *Politische Ökologie* (76), 24–6.
Bossel, H. (2000), 'Policy assessment and simulation of actor orientation for sustainable development', *Ecological Economics*, **35** (3), 337–55.
Bringezu, Stefan and Helmut Schütz (2001), 'Material use indicators for the European Union, 1980–1997', *Eurostat Working Papers* 111, Luxembourg: Eurostat.
Buitenkamp, Maria, Henk Venner and Teo Warns (1992), *Sustainable Netherlands*, Amsterdam: Vereniging Milieudefensie.
Cogoy, M. (1995), 'Market and non-market determinants of private consumption and their impacts on the environment', *Ecological Economics*, **13**, 169–80.
Cogoy, M. (1999), 'The consumer as a social and environmental actor', *Ecological Economics*, **28** (3), 385–98.
Dahm, Daniel, Rainer Fretschner, Josef Hilbert and Gerhard Scherhorn (2002), 'Gemeinschaftsarbeit im Wohlfahrtsmix der Zukunft: unverzichtbar', in Gerhard Bosch, Peter Hennicke, Josef Hilbert, Kora Kristof and Gerhard Scherhorn (eds), *Die Zukunft von Dienstleistungen. Ihre Auswirkung auf Arbeit. Umwelt und Lebensqualität*, Frankfurt, New York: Campus, pp. 162–83.
Daly, Herman E. (1991), *Steady State Economics*, Washington: Covelo.
Daly, H. E. (2001), 'Unwirtschaftliches Wachstum und Globalisierung in einer vollen Welt', *Natur und Kultur*, **2** (2), 3–22.
Dembrowski, H. (2001), 'Umweltschutz kommt langsamer voran als versprochen', *Frankfurter Rundschau*, (31 October), 17.
Döppe, Tobias, Stefan Giljum, Mark Hammer, Friedrich Hinterberger, Fred Luks, Doris Schnepf and Joachim H. Spangenberg (2003), *Freier Handel, nachhaltiger Handel – ein Widerspruch? Hintergrundpapier für die Debatte nach Johannesburg*, Berlin: Heinrich-Böll-Stiftung.
Ecological Economics (2000), Special Issue 'Beyond homo oeconomicus'.
EuroStat (2001), *Material use indicators for the European Union, 1980–1997*, EuroStat Working Papers 2/2001/B12, prepared for D6 Enrichment and EuroStat by Stefan Bringezu and Helmut Sobütz, Luxembourg: EuroStat.
Fischer, H. (2002), 'Leute rauswerfen kann jeder', *DIE ZEIT*, 26, 28.
Fischer-Kowalski, M. and C. Amann (2001), 'Beyond IPAT and Kuznets curves: Globalization as a vital factor in analysing the environmental impact of socio-economic metabolism', *Population and Environment*, **23** (1), 7–47.
Fischer-Kowalski, M. and W. Hüttler (1999), 'Society's metabolism. The intellectual history of materials flow analysis, Part II, 1970–1998', *Journal of Industrial Ecology*, **2** (4), 107–36.

Giarini, Orio (1992), 'The modern economy as a service economy: The production of utilization value', in Paul Ekins and Manfred Max-Neef (eds), *Real-Life Economics. Understanding Wealth Creation*, London: Routledge, pp. 136–46.

Giddens, Anthony (1996). 'Risiko, Vertrauen und Reflexivität', in Ulrich Beck, Anthony Giddens and Scott Lash, *Reflexive Modernisierung – Eine Kontroverse*, Frankfurt am Main: Suhrkamp, pp. 316–37.

Giddings, B., B. Hopwood and G. O'Brien (2002), 'Environment, economy and society: Fitting them together into sustainable development', *Sustainable Development*, **10** (4), 187–96.

Giljum, S. and K. Hubacek (2003), 'Applying physical input–output analysis to estimate land appropriation (ecological footprints) of international trade activities', *Ecological Economics*, **44** (1), 137–52.

Grober, U. (2002), 'Tiefe Wurzeln: Eine kleine Begriffsgeschichte von "sustainable development – Nachhaltigkeit"', *Natur und Kultur*, **3** (1), 116–28.

Hans-Böckler-Stiftung (ed.) (2001), *Pathways Towards a Sustainable Future*, Düsseldorf: Hans Böckler-Stiftung.

Jackson, T. (2002), 'Paradies-Verbraucher? Aufstieg und Fall der Konsumgesellschaft', *Natur und Kultur*, **3** (2), 55–74.

Keen, Steve (2001), *Debunking Economics. The Naked Emperor of the Social Sciences*, Annandale, Australia: Pluto Press.

Lorek, S. and J.H. Spangenberg (2001a), 'Indicators for environmentally sustainable household consumption', *International Journal on Sustainable Development*, **4** (1), 101–20.

Lorek, Sylvia and Joachim H. Spangenberg (2001b), 'Reichtum und Umwelt', in Jörg Stadlinger (ed.), *Reichtum heute*, Münster: Westfälisches Dampfboot, pp. 155–70.

Lorek, Sylvia, Joachim H. Spangenberg and Christoph Felten (1999), *Prioritäten, Tendenzen und Indikatoren umweltrelevanten Konsumverhaltens (Priorities, Tendencies and Indicators of Environmentally Relevant Consumption Patterns)*, Final Report UBA Research Project 209 01 216/03, Wuppertal: Wuppertal Institute, p. 125.

Mainwaring, L. (2001), 'Environmental values and the frame of reference', *Ecological Economics*, **38** (3), 391–401.

Max-Neef, Manfred (1991), *Human Scale Development*, New York, London: Routledge.

Miljöverndepartementet (Norwegian Ministry of Environment) (1995), *Report from the Oslo Ministerial Roundtable Conference on Sustainable Production and Consumption*, Oslo, 6–10 February 1995, Oslo: Miljöverndepartementet.

OECD (1999), *Towards More Sustainable Household Consumption Patterns – Indicators to Measure Progress*, Paris: OECD.

OECD (2001), *Environmental Indicators to Measure Decoupling of Environmental Pressure from Economic Growth*, ENV/EPOC(2001)26, Paris: OECD.

Opschoor, Hans and Leo Reijnders (1991), 'Towards sustainable development indicators', in Onno J. Kuik and Harmen Verbruggen (eds), *In Search of Indicators of Sustainable Development*, Dordrecht: Kluwer Academic Publishers, pp. 7–27.

Packard, Vance (1960), *The Waste Makers*, Harmondsworth: Penguin Books.

Palm, Viveca Kristina (2002), *Material Flow Accounting in Sweden*, Workshop on Material Flows, Resource Efficiency and Indicators, Copenhagen: Technical University of Denmark.

Pedersen, Ole Gravgård (2002), *DMI and TMR Indicators for Denmark 1981, 1990 and 1997 An Assessment of the Material Requirements of the Danish Economy*, Copenhagen: Statistics Denmark.

Reisch, Lucia A. and Gerhard Scherhorn (1999), 'Sustainable consumption', in S. Bhagwan Dahiya (ed.), *The Current State of Economic Science*, vol. 2, Rohtak/ India: Spellbound Publications, pp. 657–90.

Robert, K.-H., F. Schmidt-Bleek, J. Aloisi de Lardarel, G. Basile, J. L. Jansen, R. Kuehr, T.P. Price, M. Suzuki, P. Hawkena and M. Wackernagel (2002), 'Strategic sustainable development – selection, design and synergies of applied tools', *Journal of Cleaner Production*, **10**, 197–214.

Røpke, I. (1999), 'The dynamics of willingness to consume', *Ecological Economics*, **28** (3), 399–420.

Røpke, I. (2001), 'The environmental impact of changing consumption patterns: a survey', *International Journal of Environment and Pollution*, **15** (2), 127–45.

Schmidt-Bleek, Friedrich (1994), *Wieviel Umwelt braucht der Mensch? MIPS. das Maß für ökologisches Wirtschaften*, Berlin, Basel, Boston: Birkhäuser.

Schmidt-Bleek, Friedrich (1999), *The Fossil Makers*, http://www.factor10-institute. org.

Schmidt-Bleek, Friedrich (2003), *Querschnittspapier Faktor 10, Anregungen und Empfehlungen für die Republik Österreich*, 5 October, Wien: Faktor 10 Institut Austria.

Schmidt-Bleek, Friedrich and Ursula Tischner (1995), *Produktentwicklung, Nutzen gestalten, Natur schonen*, WIFI Brochure No. 270, Vienna: Wirtschaftskammer.

Spangenberg, J.H. (1994), 'Mensch und Müll. Widerspruch', *Münchener Zeitschrift für Philosophie*, **14** (25), 51–7.

Spangenberg, Joachim H. (1996), 'Klimawirksamkeit abfallwirtschaftlicher Maßnahmen', in Klaus Wiemer and Michael Kern, *Abfallwirtschaft – Neues aus Forschung und Praxis. Biologische Abfallbehandlung III*, Witzenhausen: Baeza-Verlag, pp. 63–78.

Spangenberg, J.H. (2002), 'Environmental space and the prism of sustainability: frameworks for indicators measuring sustainable development', *Ecological Indicators*, **2** (4), 295–309.

Spangenberg, J.H. and S. Lorek (2002), 'Environmentally sustainable household consumption: From aggregate environmental pressures to priority fields of action', *Ecological Economics*, **43** (2–3), 127–40.

Spangenberg, Joachim H. and Sylvia Lorek (2003), *Lebensqualität/Konsum und Umwelt: intelligente Lösungen statt unnötiger Gegensätze*, Bonn: Friedrich Ebert Stiftung.

Spangenberg, Joachim H., Aldo Femia, Friedrich Hinterberger and Helmut Schütz (1999), *Material Flow-based Indicators in Environmental Reporting*, Luxembourg: Office for Official Publications of the European Communities.

Stagl, S. and S. U. O'Hara (2001), 'Preferences, needs and sustainability', *International Journal of Sustainable Development*, **4** (1), 4–21.

Striewski, Sandra (2003), 'Optimieren des "Hin-Wegs" – Etablieren des "Rück-Wegs"', in Joachim H. Spangenberg (ed.), *Vision 2020. Arbeit. Umwelt. Gerechtigkeit – Strategien für ein zukunftsfähiges Deutschland*, München: Ökom, pp. 145–64.

Sturm, K.-D. (2001), 'Persistente Ignoranz', *punktum* (9), 21–2.

The Economist (2000), Special Edition, Jan. 2000.

UNDESA UN Department of Economic and Social Affairs (1998), *Measuring Changes in Consumption and Production Patterns – A Set of Indicators*, New York: United Nations.
United Nations (ed.) (1993), *The Earth Summit: Agenda 21. The United Nations Programme of Action from Rio*, New York: United Nations.
van der Voet, E. R. Kleijn, R. Heule, M. Ishikawa and E. Verkijlen (2002), 'Predicting future emissions based on characteristics of stocks', *Ecological Economics*, **41** (2), 223–34.
von Weizsäcker, Ernst U., Amory B. Lovins and L. Hunter Lovins (1997), *Factor Four. Doubling Wealth – Halving Resource Use*, London: Earthscan.
WCED (World Commission on Environment and Development) (1987), *Our Common Future*, Oxford: Oxford University Press.
Wille, J. (2003), 'Ein "Saustall" soll ausgemistet werden', *Frankfurter Rundschau*, (87), 17.

4. Work-related consumption drivers and consumption at work

Inge Røpke

4.1 INTRODUCTION

The main message in this chapter[1] is that the discussion on sustainable consumption should also incorporate the consumption that occurs in relation to work and, more generally, the relationship between consumption at work and consumption at home. Basically, production and consumption are intertwined. The traditional conceptualization of the distinction between production and consumption is questionable and is a barrier to the development of more sustainable life patterns. Here, I start by considering how domestic consumption can be encouraged by work-related factors – an outline inspired by an empirical study on families' acquisition of new consumption goods. This issue leads to an increased awareness that consumption activities also occur in the workplace; examples are given illustrating that production and consumption are intertwined. In the next section I discuss in more detail the conceptual distinction between production and consumption. I conclude with reflections on how to proceed with consumption studies to provide the basis for promoting more sustainable life patterns.

4.2 WORK-RELATED CONSUMPTION DRIVERS

During the period 1999–2001 Jeppe Læssøe and I did a research project on households' first-time acquisition of new consumer goods (reported in Røpke 2001, 2003; Læssøe 2003). The purpose was first to reveal some of the consumption dynamics at the micro-level that compel most consumers in the affluent countries to contribute to the increasing consumption in the short term. The second purpose was to investigate how respondent families use such new technologies, and how these technologies are integrated into gradual changes of everyday life – thereby influencing the consumption dynamics and the environmental impacts of everyday life in the longer term. The study was explorative, and the material consisted of nine in-depth interviews with Danish families with resident children. The study identified different driving forces behind the acquisition of new products and different aspects of the domestication process. The findings were organized in a theoretical framework that emerged through the analysis (Røpke 2003). Here, I do not intend to repeat all the findings of this project, but to elaborate on one striking finding. The material contained extensive evidence on work-related consumption drivers, and below I combine this evidence with information from other sources.

The theoretical framework used to organize the findings from the project outlined the different phases and aspects of the acquisition and domestication process for a new consumer good. Work-related issues emerged relating to several of these phases and aspects.

Firstly, *new ideas* regarding consumer goods that might enrich the home environment sometimes appear in relation to the workplace. For instance, a respondent reported that she became used to the answer-phone at her workplace and developed a wish for one at home. Other examples concern mobile phones, before they were commonplace; computers, related equipment and new software; and also goods that are usually conceived as domestic consumer goods, such as a microwave oven in the kitchen of the workplace, new food items in the canteen and so on. From the history of the diffusion of air conditioning, it is known that new standards of indoor climate can be introduced at workplaces, and when people get used to the new conditions they promote domestic changes (Shove 2003). Currently in Denmark, air conditioning in company cars seems to spill over into private cars.

Inspiration from the workplace can be particularly relevant in the case of the so-called really new products that are not easily classified in terms of well-known product categories. Moreau et al. (2001) and Aggarwal et al. (1998) discuss the problems related to marketing and diffusion of really new products, where many consumers fail to see how a given innovation might provide benefits, where they experience significant learning costs, and where consumer resistance is often far greater than in the case of mere improvements and extensions. Our small empirical study indicates that workplace experience can contribute to breaking down barriers in relation to the acceptance of such new products.

Secondly, the *motives* for acquiring consumer goods can be work related. Sometimes the workplace directly demands acquisitions or the purchase of services, for example, in relation to a dress code or demands regarding hairstyle that the employees have to fulfil. It can also be necessary to be a car owner, to have a mobile phone or to have Internet access or other equipment to do a specific job. In other cases, people may try to improve their chances of either keeping the job they have or of having new career opportunities by following courses in their spare time or by improving their skills at the home computer. For instance, one of the female respondents reported investing in both computer and courses, because she wanted to return to the labour market after staying at home when her children were young.

Thirdly, domestic consumption is sometimes made possible by *work-related gifts*. Employers can have an interest in providing their staff with equipment; it may be a requirement for working at home or for performing the tasks related to mobile work, or it may be useful for improving the skills of the employees. For instance, a photocopier repair engineer reported that his firm had first given him a pager and later decided to buy him a mobile phone. In other cases, employers had subsidized the purchase of computers for remote working or for training at home. Besides such 'functional' gifts, employers also provide fringe benefits that can be important to retain good employees. Due to tax regulations such fringe benefits can be worth more to the employee than the cost to the employer and thus be a cheaper way to pay wages. The variety of products provided as fringe benefits is impressive: mobile phones and cordless phones, tickets for football matches and concerts, travel tickets, luxury food items and so on. In relation to domestic consumption, the work-related gift can be important in the formation of consumption patterns; it constitutes a way to *bypass the traditional arena* for purchasing decisions in the family. In modern Danish families, which are nearly all double-income families, larger purchases are usually negotiated, so it can be useful to be able to bypass this family arena when a family member wants to promote special desires.

Fourthly, the trends above can imply *consequential consumption*. For instance, the increase in remote work demands space for the computer and other equipment and possibly a separate room, stimulating the long-term trend towards more housing space. Such consequences can be seen as a practical version of the so-called Diderot effect (McCracken 1988). Usually, this effect refers to the dramatic effect in a household setting that can follow from the introduction of a new special good, because the consumer has to buy new things to match the style or exclusiveness of the new good. Of course, a computer for remote work might require those aesthetic or symbolic changes, but the practical consequences of such new equipment seem to be more important (or interpreted in terms related to the traditional Diderot effect: sometimes the resistance against aesthetic changes in the living room 'demands' more space in other rooms).

Another more indirect consequence identified in the study is the diffusion of consumer goods in the wake of work-related gifts or acquisitions that make older goods redundant. These are then given away to relatives and friends, who can then bypass the traditional arena for purchasing decisions in their families and learn the new consumption habits.

Obviously, the consumption drivers described above are concrete and close to everyday experiences. Maybe this explains why these drivers seem to be underexposed in sociological and anthropological consumption theories that deal with consumption drivers in more abstract terms.

4.3 CONSUMPTION AT WORK

The phenomenon that work-related factors encourage domestic consumption indicates that consumption activities occur at work. When looking at activities that usually occur at home and are considered as consumption, it is easy to find examples of the same activities happening at the workplace:

- The daily tea, coffee and lunches may be paid by the employer, as may the less frequent office parties, celebrations and so on.
- On business trips, restaurant dinners, for example, are an integrated part of work. The trip may be to interesting places giving opportunities for tourist experiences; likewise, the restaurant dinners can offer opportunities for new or unusual taste experiences.
- The equipment at the workplace can be used for private purposes, such as making phone calls, finding homepages, sending mail and using the photocopier, tools and cars.
- The working conditions can be improved through increasing standards in furnishings, the fitting up of rooms, larger offices and so on.
- Time for sport, physical exercise, massage and so forth, can be integrated in the working hours.

The different forms of 'consumption at work' arise from different reasons. Sometimes the consumption directly arises from the tasks of the employee. For instance, it might be part of the job of marketing people to 'soften up' customers by inviting them to dinners; likewise participating in conferences abroad is part of the work for university academics. The increasing internationalization of both business and academic networks enhances this phenomenon; it implies an increase in travel and so forth. Another reason for consumption at work relates to attempts to attract employees. Apart from the fringe benefits that usually imply domestic consumption, the standards at the workplace regarding lunches, physical surroundings and so on, influence its attractiveness. This is enhanced by the trend towards more fluid borders between the private and the work sphere: not only do people work more at home, they also integrate more

Problematizing consumption

social and leisure activities with work (Hochschild 1997). When the IT bubble was at its most prominent, this trend was demonstrated in a radical form by the integration of sports or other activities during working hours. But as the burst of the bubble showed, the trend can also be reversed – and the consumption level at work can also be reduced. Overall, consumption at work probably increases over time and is seen in a continual interplay between domestic standards and standards at work. However, counteracting forces are also effective in times of economic recession, in sectors under pressure (not least in the public sector), and when 'fashion' dictates such experiments as open-plan offices.

Usually, the phrase 'consumption at work' is not used – basically, it seems to be a contradiction in terms. What occurs at or in relation to the workplace cannot be considered as consumption: the travelling, restaurant visits, lunches and comfortable surroundings are considered as production costs, whether they are 'necessary' or not for the production. The higher up the hierarchy of a firm a person is, the larger the office, the bigger the desk, the more luxurious the furnishing of the room, the more expensive the restaurant dinners on business trips and so on. This is part of the production costs of having high-status staff. The distinction between production costs and consumption is thus based on the convention that consumption belongs to the home and private life, whereas all activities related to work are production costs. The convention can also be expressed in terms of market transactions: consumption is only what is bought with wages (or other income). However, this simple rule is modified by tax regulations concerning the taxation of fringe benefits – remuneration in the form of goods, such as company cars, free telephone, for example, illustrating that the distinction is not as obvious as it might seem.

4.4 CONCEPTUAL DISCUSSION

As the examples above illustrate, the distinction between production and consumption is not clear-cut. The traditional distinction has been questioned in relation to national income accounting: some researchers have concentrated on the production activities occurring at home and have suggested including an estimated value of this informal production in the national product. This issue has been one of the focal points in feminist economic research (for example, Waring 1990), and in ecological economics the point is reflected in the Index for Sustainable Economic Welfare (ISEW) suggested by Daly and Cobb (1989), as the ISEW includes a contribution to welfare from informal work. The focus on 'consumption at work' in this chapter can thus be seen as complementary to these discussions on the production at home.

The history of national income accounting also illustrates the contested distinction between productive and unproductive activities (Miller 1986). Part of the rationale behind national accounting is to account for the activities that contributed to the productive power of a nation. But which activities should then be included? Miller (1986, p. 92) cites *An Introduction to National Income Analysis* (Beckerman 1968, p. 7): 'This distinction between productive activities and all other transactions is absolutely central to the basic concepts of national accounting...' but '...the dividing line between what is and what isn't a productive activity is not at all clear since it is essentially arbitrary'. This arbitrariness emphasizes that the conceptual distinction between production and consumption must be related to the purpose of the specific analysis to be undertaken. Thus the environmental motivation behind this chapter guides the decision about which considerations to include.

The distinction between consumption and production has also been discussed in relation to neoclassical microeconomics. With the concept of utility at the core of the theory, production could be interpreted as the provision of utility, whereas consumption could be about enjoying utility. However, this distinction does not necessarily imply that economic activities can be grouped into two separate categories. In analysing household behaviour, Winston (1982, Chapter 9) argues that a distinction should be made between utility sources: process utility is the flow of satisfaction from doing an activity, while goal utility is the satisfaction from having done an activity. Household activities or consumption activities can provide process and goal utility, positive or negative, and in Winston's time-specific model, households will choose the combination of consumption activities that maximizes the value of time measured in utility. Likewise, work can provide both process and goal utility, so the only essential difference between work and consumption activities is that work pays a money wage as well, and thus also gives rise to indirect utility. Therefore, households will choose between work and consumption again by maximizing the value of time. This framework implies that the provision and enjoyment of utility cannot be used to distinguish production from consumption. This distinction is only a distinction between two different categories of the market model: what happens in firms is called production, and what happens in households is called consumption. In the following it is discussed whether the concepts of production and consumption can be given meaning independently of a market framework and in a way that is interesting and relevant from an environmental viewpoint.

4.4.1   Inspiration from Ecology

As the questioning of the traditional distinction between production
and consumption is basically motivated by environmental concerns, it is
obvious to ask how an environmental perspective, and in particular an
ecological economic perspective, can inform the conceptual discussion.
The basic idea of ecological economics is that socio-economic systems are
embedded in natural systems and that the processes occurring in the socio-
economic systems can be conceptualized not only in social and economic
terms, but also in terms from the natural sciences such as flows of energy
and matter. A socio-economic system as a whole can be understood as an
'organism' with metabolism, as the self-organizing structure is based on a
continuous flow of energy and matter through the system. The question is
whether the concepts of production and consumption make sense inside
this framework. Turning to ecology and the analysis of ecosystems, in
introductions it is usually pointed out that plants are the basic primary
producers: through the process of photosynthesis plants can utilize the
energy input coming from outside the system and thus provide the basis
of living for all other organisms of the system through the food chain.
Thus, all other organisms, including human beings, can be considered to
be 'the consumers' of the system. Human economic activities appropriate
the products of photosynthesis, not only the newly provided products, but
also the historical production in the form of fossil fuels, and transform
low entropy energy to high entropy. Through this process the mass of
human bodies and 'the techno-mass' can be increased. In a few cases
human economic activities can imply more than simple appropriation
of photosynthesis, as some activities can increase the photosynthesis of
the plants – for example, by building terraces in mountainous areas or by
irrigation – and other activities can 'capture' solar energy in other ways,
for example, through the building of windmills, which can utilize the wind
energy generated by the heat from the sun. In this perspective, it could make
sense to talk about human production, when humans succeed in increasing
the utilization of solar energy compared to a situation without human
intervention. Obviously, such an interpretation is far from the traditional
distinction between production and consumption.

When looking closer at ecological insights, however, this distinction
between production and consumption can also be problematized. An
ecosystem functions as a complex whole, where 'the producers' are dependent
on 'the consumers' and vice versa. The different parts of the ecosystem
interact through complex feedback mechanisms, so all parts can be said to
'produce' something for other parts. The same idea applies to the system of
the Earth as a whole, as proposed by James Lovelock's Gaia hypothesis.

When the distinction between production and consumption is made for the human economy, the point of departure is the perspective of a single species. Likewise, zoological studies of a single species can focus on how this species procures food and eats it – how the species maintains metabolism. The concept of procurement can resemble the concept of production, but the dependence on the availability of food in the surroundings is illustrated more clearly in the procurement concept. When an ecological perspective is added to the zoological studies, it is emphasized even more that no species can procure its food independently of the system of which it is a part. This goes for humans as well: we can procure our food from the environment and, as mentioned above, we can even influence the conditions for procurement in a conscious way (for example, by improving the utilization of the solar energy on which we are ultimately dependent), but we cannot create anything edible out of nothing. The human species has succeeded in utilizing an extremely broad variety of food sources; we have learned to render edible different food items that are not immediately edible. Although we cannot create anything edible out of nothing, our procurement activities are so complex that we sometimes forget the material basis for them. Maybe this is why we tend to talk about production instead of procurement, despite the fact that in ecological terms we do nothing more than procure.

4.4.2 Inspiration from Economics

From the perspective of the human species, is it relevant to distinguish between procurement activities (and give them the name of production) and consumption activities? The question is discussed in the context of a broader discussion of the basic economic model behind the concepts. Whereas the ecological perspective above mainly questions the whole idea of regarding humans as producers, the more economically inspired discussion below focuses more on the meaning of the consumption concept: what does consumption actually mean? The basic economic concepts are modelled on the provision and eating of food: first food must be provided, and then it can be eaten. The activities can be integrated, as when berries are picked and eaten immediately, but in most cases the activities are separate. Embedded in this food model are several features that have been discussed in ecological economics (based on some important predecessors):

- The model is based on a basic means–ends rationality. The distinction between production and consumption is based on the basic 'thought figure' of means and ends: we produce (work) in order to consume.
- Human welfare is related to the consumption of goods.
- When goods are consumed, they disappear.

- When a society can produce more than 'necessary', it can command
  a surplus.

I will summarize some of the contributions discussing these features
before returning to the main question of the distinction between production
and consumption. In a paper from 1945 Kenneth Boulding discusses the
consumption concept in economic theory (his agenda in the paper is to
use the discussion as a basis for dealing with macroeconomic issues, which
fall outside the scope of this chapter). He starts by citing Adam Smith's
dictum that 'consumption is the sole end and purpose of production', and
then explains that despite the significance of the consumption concept in
economic theory, the meaning of the concept is unclear; one of the reasons
being the lack of clarity about the concepts of demand and consumer's
expenditure. Boulding states: 'Up to the time of Marshall the meaning of
the word "consumption" was fairly clear. It meant, what it literally means,
the destruction of commodities – i.e. of valuable things – in the way in which
they were intended to be destroyed' (pp. 1–2). And production meant 'the
exact opposite of consumption, namely, the creation of valuable things'
(p. 2). Production and consumption are related through the stock of valuable
things: production builds up the stock; consumption reduces it, and the
rate of accumulation is equal to the difference between the two flows. This
concept of consumption was confused, when Marshall turned directly from
the discussion of consumption to the discussion of demand, and when the
Keynesians defined consumption as 'consumer's expenditure'. In Boulding's
opinion, when he buys a loaf of bread from the baker, the transaction
itself is not consumption: consumption does not take place until he eats
the loaf of bread (p. 4). Until then he has just exchanged a liquid asset for
one that is illiquid.

Boulding thus wants to keep to the clear definition of consumption as
being destruction of valuable goods, and with this definition it is not obvious
that consumption is something desirable. It would be more beneficial if life
could be maintained without destroying valuable things or by doing so at a
slower pace. Boulding elaborates on this in a later paper (1949), where he
draws upon Irving Fisher's concepts of capital and income (Fisher 1906).
Fisher coined the phrase 'psychic income': 'psychic income is that which is
derived from the possession or use of capital, and is the significant welfare
concept' (Boulding 1949, p. 83). In accordance with this, Boulding argues
'that it is the capital stock from which we derive satisfactions, not from
the additions to it (production) or the subtractions from it (consumption);
that consumption, far from being a desideratum, is a deplorable property
of the capital stock which necessitates the equally deplorable activities of
production' (p. 79). Herman Daly, who is also inspired by Fisher, later argues

along the same lines in relation to his steady state economics: the final benefit of economic activity is to provide service, which is 'the satisfaction experienced when wants are satisfied' (the 'psychic income'); service is yielded by the stock, which is the total inventory of 'all physical things capable of satisfying human wants and subject to ownership'; and the stock is maintained and renewed by the throughput, which is the physical flow of matter and energy 'from nature's sources, through the human economy, and back to nature's sinks' (Daly 1991, pp. 35ff, discussed in Røpke 1997). Daly does not apply the concepts of production and consumption here, but it would make sense to use them in the same way as Boulding does: production is about adding to the stock, whereas consumption subtracts from it – and there is no direct relation between consumption in this sense and service/'psychic income'/welfare.

As Boulding explains, 'The illusion that consumption – and its correlative, income – is desirable probably stems from too great an occupation with what Frank Knight calls "one-use goods", such as food and fuel, where the utilisation and consumption of the good are tightly bound together in a single act or event' (1949, p. 80). For multi-use goods it is obvious that we would benefit if they did not depreciate, so we could enjoy the services of these things without the necessity of consuming or producing them. It is more complicated with food, however, after discussing food at length, Boulding concludes, 'in the case of the overwhelming mass of commodities it is not consumption but utilisation which is the source of satisfaction' (1949, p. 80).

Ayres and Kneese (1969) also refer to Knight and Fisher in the seminal paper, where they explain that externalities cannot be considered to be exceptional, as disposal of residuals is an inevitable part of consumption and production processes. They argue that production and consumption processes are often conceived 'in a manner that is somewhat at variance with the fundamental law of conservation of mass' (p. 283). They cite Knight for the point that when food and eating are taken as the typical economic activities, the error is often made of relating value or utility to the good instead of the service, and then they argue that 'Almost all of standard economic theory is in reality concerned with services. Material objects are merely the vehicles which carry some of these services... Yet we persist in referring to the "final consumption" of goods as though material objects such as fuels, materials, and finished goods somehow disappeared into the void' (p. 284). In a related note they add: 'We are tempted to suggest that the word consumption be dropped entirely from the economist's vocabulary as being basically deceptive. It is difficult to think of a suitable substitute, however. At least, the word consumption should not be used in connection with goods, but only with regard to services or flows of "utility"'. Whereas

Ayres and Kneese refer to exactly the same confusion as Boulding, they suggest the opposite solution: instead of reserving the consumption concept for the physical destruction process, they want to reserve it for what Boulding would call the 'psychic income' or the welfare.

The authors cited above are all aware that human production is about procurement – where energy and material flows from nature are organized to build up stock, and where residuals are returned to nature (Boulding later elaborates on this in his seminal spaceship paper (1966), but he also touches upon this issue in the 1949 paper (p. 82). In the spaceship paper he notes that his older consumption papers produced no response whatsoever). The considerations regarding consumption deal with the need to distinguish between stocks and flows, between material goods and the services that can be obtained from these goods, and between destruction of valuable goods and welfare, and it is emphasized that the consumption concept is highly ambiguous, so the use of the concept should always be accompanied by a more specific definition related to the context.

So far the basic means–ends rationality has not been questioned, but Boulding's 1949 paper includes ideas that open up this discussion. Firstly, he emphasizes the 'healthy pleasure in "making things" which is derived from a fundamental "creative urge" in human nature', so there is some satisfaction that arises from the act of production itself (Boulding 1949, p. 80). From this perspective 'there is a value in consumption... in that consumption may be necessary in order to clear the ground for productive activity', and later: 'Consumption is the death of capital', and 'death is at the same time a tragic waste and a magnificent opportunity' (Boulding 1949, p. 81). In this sense production is the end and consumption the means. Secondly, Boulding points out that 'a certain part of consumption by humans (food, shelter, medical care, etc.) may be regarded as contributing to the production of further output'. That consumption 'is a "cost of living" – the "maintenance" of human capital', and it is 'not part of the conscious purposes of a society' (Boulding 1949, p. 85). Accordingly, he finishes with a Ricardian concept of 'net revenue': 'that part of the product of a society which it is free to devote to its purposes – e.g. to war, to luxury, or to welfare' (Boulding 1949, p. 85) – a conception basically inspired by a corn economy, where the surplus is defined as the corn remaining after the necessary consumption and the setting aside of seed corn for the next season. However, in a modern economy it is difficult to give this surplus concept a meaningful interpretation, and the idea of considering consumption to be the final purpose of the economic process is problematized.

As the arguments above illustrate, the concept of consumption is highly ambiguous, and it makes little sense to apply a means–ends perspective to production and consumption at the societal level. We produce in order to consume, and consume in order to produce, so it makes more sense to conceive of the economy as a complex whole along the same lines as described for ecosystems above: the different parts of the economy interact through complex feedback mechanisms, so all parts serve other parts. The concepts of production and consumption do not have any generally valid definitions that are useful for all kinds of economic analyses, so the choice of more specific definitions must depend on the purpose of the analysis to be done. With a focus on environmental issues, I believe that we are best served with a dissolution of the traditional conceptions. There is no meaningful conception of production and consumption as separate activities when focusing on the environment. Basically, humans procure – appropriate nature through their economic activities whether they take place at the workplace or in the home – and from an environmental and distributional viewpoint, the richest 20–30 per cent of the world's population presently procures far too much. And what do we get out of that? It seems to me that it is meaningless to conceive 'consumption' as the purpose of the economic activities; likewise it seems meaningless to conceive of any other singular final aim ('psychic income', utility and so on). When we discuss what we get out of the economic activities, we should instead apply several different perspectives to assess the whole 'package': are basic needs met, what is the standard of health, what are the environmental conditions of everyday life, what is the global and local income distribution, what is the social stability, what are the human rights, working conditions and so on, how are ethical demands related to other species and future generations met for example (elaborated in Røpke 1999a).

In conclusion, the concept of consumption and the distinction between production and consumption cannot be given precise and useful definitions in an ecological economic framework. The focus must be directed towards the appropriation of nature through different activities, irrespective of whether these traditionally have been called production or consumption. However, from a sociological viewpoint it can make sense to refer to different domains of everyday life, such as the domains related to work and to the home, respectively. In accordance with everyday speech, we can use the word consumption about the economic activities that take place at home – knowing that it is based on an intuitive understanding and not a precise definition. When I mention consumption at work, I refer to 'appropriative' activities that could just as well belong to the home domain, but that occur at work. Although these activities cannot be given any precise definition, I think that the perspective can be an eye-opener in the discussion on more sustainable production and consumption patterns.

4.4.3   Consumption Studies of Workplaces

From an environmental viewpoint, the focus should be directed towards
the appropriation of nature whether it takes place in relation to work or
home. We are used to distinguishing between two groups of strategies in
relation to sustainable development. One group relates to the workplace
and concerns the efforts to improve the environmental efficiency in the
provision of goods – increased materials and energy productivity resulting
in fewer materials and energy-intensive goods and services, replacement
of dangerous substances and so on. The whole product chain can be
involved in efforts to improve efficiency and, politically, improvements can
be encouraged by many measures from direct regulation and taxation to
green labelling schemes and green procurement providing an outlet for
greener products. The other group of strategies relates to the homes and
everyday life outside the work sphere and concerns issues such as the choice
of environmentally friendly products and services, recycling, energy savings,
and (for a radical minority) reduced consumption – summarized under
the heading of sustainable consumption, which can also be promoted by
political measures. Applying the perspective that consumption can take place
at work, can contribute to a broader discussion about how we appropriate
nature and how strategies for sustainable development can be extended.

The business strategies towards sustainability have a so-called 'blind
spot' when it comes to the standards and working conditions for both
management and employees and, in particular, when it comes to all the costs
that follow from the increasing complexity behind the supply of goods. The
basic conception is that business management is so focused on the reduction
of costs that all superfluous fat will be removed – and of course, employees
should try to get as much as possible in the form of wages and good working
conditions. Over time, productivity increases have been transformed not
only into increased wages and profits, but also into improving material
standards at the workplaces. Obviously, some of these improvements are
highly desirable and still greatly needed when they decrease heavy manual
or dangerous work and so on, but others are part of a general raising of
standards and of the increasing complexity of the production system.

Take the production of research results as an example. Relying on my
own observations through many years in the academic world, I suggest that
research results are much more environmentally expensive to provide today
than 30 years ago. To survive in the academic world today, the researcher
has to demonstrate that s/he has an international network, takes part in
international conferences and workshops, publishes a large number of
papers – which can only be done by reproducing some of the same results
in slightly different versions in different contexts – and applies for money

for international research projects. The internationalization implies that more air travel, hotel and restaurant expenses, mobile equipment and so on will go into the production of research results. Research results might improve by the growing interconnections, but the related activities can also be counterproductive, as they are very time-consuming. Why do researchers do this? To a large extent they are locked in institutions that place these demands on them – and simultaneously the process is softened by the consumption possibilities related to the increased complexity (the chance to see the world for example) and by the meaning and identity related to the 'reputational organizations' of academia that go beyond the pure necessity related to survival in the academic world (Whitley 2000). These trends are not reserved for universities, but can be found in many industrial activities; based on media coverage I guess that, for example, the pharmaceutical industry could provide illustrative examples. The consumption activities in relation to work are seldom discussed in the perspective of sustainable consumption. These activities are seen as production costs, and even environmentally responsible consumers tend to find that consumption in relation to their work is outside their responsibility, or they tend to be less responsible when consumption takes place in relation to work. In a sense, employees can even feel 'forced' to consume at work.

Consumption related to the domain of home and private life has been extensively elucidated by theoretical work in sociology, anthropology and economics. I will end this small piece by suggesting that much of the insight from these studies should be applied in future studies of consumption at work. Something similar to this has already been done in relation to the role of status goods at work, an important issue in relation to personnel management (some of the contributions are reviewed in Reisch 2003), but much more could be done along these lines, discussing questions such as: How do we communicate through consumption at work (along the lines of Douglas and Isherwood 1980)? What does consumption mean for meaning and identity at work (Warde 1994)? Which social institutions and technical infrastructures contribute to lock-in related to consumption patterns at work (Schor 1991; Otnes 1988)? How do consumption standards at work become normalized (Shove 2003)? What is conspicuous consumption at work – and inconspicuous consumption (Shove and Warde 2001)? What do the relative prices mean for the development of consumption patterns at work (Røpke 1999b)? Which role does novelty play in encouraging consumption at work (Campbell 1992; Pantzar 1997)? When we become more aware of all these environmentally demanding processes at work, we might become better at putting more sustainable consumption patterns on the agenda, also in this domain.

NOTE

1. The ideas presented in this chapter were discussed at a seminar at our department and at a workshop on consumption and sustainability at the National Consumer Research Centre in Helsinki. I am grateful to the participants at these meetings for useful comments and suggestions.

REFERENCES

Aggarwal, P., C. Taihoon Cha and D. Wilemon (1998), 'Barriers to the adoption of really-new products and the role of surrogate buyers', *Journal of Consumer Marketing*, **14** (4), 358–71.

Ayres, R. U. and A. V. Kneese (1969), 'Production, consumption and externalities', *The American Economic Review*, **59**, 282–97.

Beckerman, Wilfred (1968), *An Introduction to National Income Analysis*, London: Weidenfeld and Nicolson.

Boulding, K. E. (1945), 'The consumption concept in economic theory', *The American Economic Review*, **35**, 1–14.

Boulding, K. E. (1949), 'Income or welfare', *The Review of Economic Studies*, **17**, 77–86.

Boulding, Kenneth E. (1966), 'The economics of the coming spaceship earth', in Henry Jarrett (ed.), *Environmental Quality in a Growing Economy*, Baltimore, US: Johns Hopkins University Press, pp. 3–14.

Campbell, Colin (1992), 'The desire for the new: its nature and social location as presented in theories of fashion and modern consumerism', in Roger Silverstone and Eric Hirsch (eds), *Consuming Technologies: Media and Information in Domestic Spaces*, London: Routledge, pp. 48–64.

Daly, Herman E. (1991), *Steady-State Economics*, Second Edition with New Essays, Washington DC: Island Press.

Daly, Herman E. and John B. Cobb (1989), *For the Common Good. Redirecting the Economy Toward Community, the Environment, and a Sustainable Future*, Boston, MA: Beacon Press.

Douglas, Mary and Baron Isherwood (1980) (first published 1978), *The World of Goods. Towards an Anthropology of Consumption*, Harmondsworth: Penguin Books.

Fisher, Irving (1906), *Nature of Capital and Income*, New York: Macmillan.

Hochschild, Arlie Russell (1997), *The Time Bind: When Work Becomes Home and Home Becomes Work*, New York: Metropolitan Books.

Læssøe, Jeppe (2003), 'Acquisition and domestication of new household technologies – some dynamics behind growth in material consumption', in Fatos Göksen, Ornulf Seippel, Martin O'Brien, E. Ünal Zenginobuz, Fikret Adaman and Jesper Grolin (eds), *Integrating and Articulating Environments*, Lisse, NL: Swets and Zeitlinger Publishers/A. A. Balkema Publishers, pp. 109–42.

McCracken, Grant (1988), *Culture and Consumption: New Approaches to the Symbolic Character of Consumer Goods and Activities*, Bloomington: Indiana University Press.

Miller, P. (1986), 'Accounting for progress – national accounting and planning in France: A review essay', *Accounting, Organizations and Society*, **11** (1), 83–104.

Moreau, C. P., A. B. Markman and D. R. Lehmann (2001), '"What is it?" Categorization flexibility and consumers' responses to really new products', *Journal of Consumer Research*, **27**, 489–98.

Otnes, Per (1988), 'Housing consumption: collective systems service', in Per Otnes (ed.), *The Sociology of Consumption*, Oslo: Solum Forlag and Humanities Press International, pp. 119–38.

Pantzar, M. (1997), 'Domestication of everyday life technology: Dynamic views on the social histories of artefacts', *Design Issues*, **13** (3), 52–65.

Reisch, Lucia A. (2003), 'Statusspiele: Der Einfluss sozialer Vergleichsprozesse auf wirtschaftliches Verhalten', in Martin Held, Gisela Kubon-Gilke and Richard Sturn (eds), *Grundfragen der normativen und institutionellen Ökonomik: Experimente in der Ökonomik*, Vol. 2, Marburg: Metropolis, pp. 217–40.

Røpke, Inge (1997), 'Economic growth and the environment – or the extinction of the GDP-dinosaur', in Jan van der Straaten and Andrew Tylecote (eds), *Environment, Technology and Economic Growth: The Challenge to Sustainable Development*, Cheltenham, UK and Lyme, US: Edward Elgar, pp. 55–72.

Røpke, Inge (1999a), 'Some themes in the discussion of the quality of life', in Jörg Köhn, John Gowdy, Friedrich Hinterberger and Jan van der Straaten (eds), *Sustainability in Question. The Search for a Conceptual Framework*, Cheltenham, UK and Northampton, MA, US: Edward Elgar, pp. 247–66.

Røpke, I. (1999b), 'The dynamics of willingness to consume', *Ecological Economics*, **28**, 399–420.

Røpke, I. (2001), 'New technology in everyday life – social processes and environmental impact', *Ecological Economics*, **38**, 403–22.

Røpke, I. (2003), 'Consumption dynamics and technological change – exemplified by the mobile phone and related technologies', *Ecological Economics*, **45**, 171–88.

Schor, Juliet B. (1991), *The Overworked American. The Unexpected Decline of Leisure*, New York: BasicBooks.

Shove, Elizabeth (2003), *Comfort, Cleanliness and Convenience. The Social Organization of Normality*, Oxford and New York: Berg.

Shove, Elizabeth and Alan Warde (2001), 'Inconspicuous consumption: The sociology of consumption, lifestyles, and the environment', in Riley E. Dunlap, Frederick H. Buttel, Peter Dickens and August Gisjwijt (eds), *Sociological Theory and the Environment: Classical Foundations, Contemporary Insights*, Lanham, MD: Rowman and Littlefield.

Warde, A. (1994), 'Consumption, identity-formation and uncertainty', *Sociology*, **28** (4), 877–98.

Waring, Marilyn (1990), *If Women Counted: A New Feminist Economics*, First Edition 1988, New York: HarperCollins.

Whitley, Richard (2000) (Second Edition, First Edition 1984), *The Intellectual and Social Organization of the Sciences*, Oxford, UK: Oxford University Press.

Winston, Gordon C. (1982), *The Timing of Economic Activities. Firms, Households, and Markets in Time-specific Analysis*, Cambridge, UK: Cambridge University Press.

PART II

Explaining consumption

5. Beyond insatiability – needs theory, consumption and sustainability

Tim Jackson, Wander Jager and Sigrid Stagl

5.1 THE DISCOURSE ON HUMAN NEEDS

Ever since the Brundtland Report, the language of human needs has been etched deeply into the conceptual framework of sustainable development (WCED 1987).[1] For even longer than that, the concept of 'needs' has played an important role in our understanding of consumer behaviour and has been a key input to the disciplines of economic psychology, consumer research and marketing (Kassarjian and Robertson 1968). Philosophers from Plato onwards have discussed the relevance of human needs to conceptions of the 'good life' and the role of governance (Haines 1985). More recently, the concept of needs has provided the foundation for an extended ecological and social critique of conventional development (Max-Neef 1991).

In spite of these various manifestations, the discourse on human needs remains a fiercely contested one (Douglas et al. 1998). Some argue that human needs can provide an organizing framework within which to articulate themes about development, progress, quality of life and human happiness. Others point to the failures of development strategies grounded on the idea of 'basic needs' and suggest the need for alternative conceptualizations based on 'capabilities' and 'functionings'. Others again insist that needs are an irrelevant distraction from the pursuit of development and that conventional economic concepts of revealed preference and rational choice are more reliable instruments for understanding consumption and for negotiating sustainability.

One of the aims of this chapter is to provide a review of these different discourses. In particular, the chapter identifies three main avenues of thought in relation to needs theories and explores the relationship between them. The first avenue flows from the discipline of economics, which tends to downplay if not deny outright the legitimacy of any distinction between needs and wants or preferences. A consequence of this position is an assumption of

consumer *insatiability* that dominates economic thought and is supposed
to characterize modern society.

A second major discourse affords the concept of needs a key structural
role in conceptions of human well-being. We discuss the historical pedigree
of this idea and outline some of the modern needs-theoretic conceptions
of human development that have been articulated in the literature. We
also describe briefly the ecological and social critique of conventional
development that flows from this construction. From the perspective of
sustainability, perhaps the most interesting aspect of this critique is the
suggestion that assumptions of insatiability are not only ecologically
problematic but also psychologically and socially suspect. The needs-based
construction appears to offer a kind of double dividend to sustainable
development: the possibility of living better by consuming less.

At the same time, the continuing debate about 'needs' and 'wants' bears
witness to the contentious nature of this conclusion (Campbell 1998). Nor
is opposition to needs theory confined to economists. The third avenue of
thought we examine in this chapter flows from a variety of rather modern
intellectual positions, drawing from sociology, cultural anthropology and
social philosophy, which regard the entire needs-based discourse as rhetorical,
naive and moralistic. We outline the main contentions of this position and
discuss its lessons for the project of sustainable development.

The tension between the different positions outlined here already suggests
that a kind of dialectic inhabits the discourse on needs. The later part of the
chapter explores this dialectic in more detail and attempts to articulate key
lessons from needs theory for debates about lifestyle choice and sustainable
consumption.

5.2   ECONOMICS AND THE DOCTRINE OF INSATIABILITY

Classical economics accepted a formal role for needs in which *individual
utility* was taken to be a measure of 'needs satisfaction' (Smith 1776). But
subsequent developments in economics have assigned an increasingly
marginal role to the concept of human needs. Modern neoclassical
economics is generally either casually dismissive or else wilfully silent on
the subject.[2] Marshall (1961), for example, eschews all discussion of needs
as superfluous, since human choices are more effectively cast in terms of
wants. Heyne (1983, p. 16) insists that 'needs turn out to be mere wants when
we inspect them closely', and in an extraordinary passage suggests that even
thirst, in economic terms, cannot be regarded as indicative of any human
need: 'Do we need water?' he asks rhetorically: 'No. The best way to turn a

drought into a catastrophe is to pretend that water is a need.' In economics, as Allen (1982, p. 23) points out, need is a 'non-word': 'Economics can say much which is useful about desires, preferences and demands,' he insists. 'But the assertion of absolute economic "need" – in contrast to desire, preference and demand – is nonsense'. Equally striking in the conventional formulation is that economics also fails to say much about the nature of preference itself. It interests itself primarily in questions of allocation of resources, and generally refuses resolutely to distinguish between different kinds of preferences or the motivations for the use of these resources. All transactions in the market are assumed to represent the rational decisions of informed consumers, attempting to maximize individual utility in the face of the available choices and their own resource constraints.

Consumer choice theory, after Samuelson (1938), has restricted itself essentially to deriving demand functions for consumer goods on the basis of 'revealed preferences' in the market. Thus, the best we can say about consumer preferences is what we can infer about them from the patterns of expenditure on consumer goods in the market. If the demand for a particular brand of car or washing-machine or video-recorder is high, then we can infer that consumers, in general, prefer that brand over other brands. The reasons for this preference remain opaque within economics, as do the reasons for choosing Sports Utility Vehicles, tumble-dryers and DVD players over, say, eco-holidays or leisure activities (Schor 1992).

Some economic analyses do attempt to distinguish between necessities and luxuries on the basis of the price (or income) elasticity of demand for these goods. Necessities are those goods that consumers attempt to procure no matter how high the price or how constrained their income; luxuries are those they are prepared to forego when the price goes up or economic hardship beckons (Begg et al. 2003). This limited economic unpacking of the dimensions of consumer choice – which is flatly rejected by others (Lebergott 1993 for example) – just about exhausts any attempt either to distinguish between different kinds or levels of consumer preferences or to unravel consumer motivations in the demand for specific goods. Different categories of consumer needs are collapsed by economics into a 'flat plain of wants' (Georgescu-Roegen 1973; Lutz and Lux 1988).

There are some modest exceptions to this tendency.[3] In an essay entitled 'Economic possibilities for our grandchildren', Keynes distinguished between two classes of needs: 'those needs which are absolute in the sense that we feel them whatever the situation of our fellow human beings may be, and those which are relative only in that their satisfaction lifts us above, makes us feel superior to our fellows' (Keynes 1931, p. 326). In the same essay, Keynes looked forward to a point in time – 'much sooner perhaps

than we all of us are aware of' – when absolute needs had all been satisfied
and we could devote our energies to non-economic purposes.

For the most part, however, the modern economics textbook does not
even include the word 'need' in its subject index, choosing instead to cast
its arguments in terms of wants, tastes or consumer preferences (Begg et
al. 2003). Where, occasionally, the concept of need is introduced, it will
invariably appear only to be dismissed very quickly in favour of wants or
preferences. Moreover, as McConnell (1981, p. 23) is eager to point out
'these material wants are for practical purposes *insatiable* or *unlimited.*
This means that material wants for goods and services are incapable of
being completely satisfied' (emphasis in original). It is not difficult to find
similar positions on needs in many economic texts. Anderton (2000, p. 3)
for example, introduces the question of human needs on the first page of
his undergraduate textbook on economics: 'Human needs are finite…' he
concedes. '[But] no-one would choose to live at the level of basic human
needs if he [sic] could enjoy a higher standard of living. This is because
human wants are infinite.' He goes on to use the insatiability of human wants
as the motivation for what he calls the 'basic economic problem', namely
the allocation of scarce resources in the face of infinite wants. In this way,
insatiability becomes not just a defining feature of consumer behaviour, but
a core ideological assumption within economics, in some sense motivating
the discipline itself and the social importance of the economist.

Perhaps more importantly, the concept of insatiability underlies the
entire edifice of the consumer society. Modern economies are themselves
structurally committed to a continuing growth in the national income. In
the words of the former British Prime Minister, Edward Heath – cited in
Douthwaite (1992 p. 20): 'The alternative to expansion is not an England
of quiet market towns, linked only by trains puffing slowly and peacefully
through green meadows. The alternative is slums, dangerous roads, old
factories, cramped schools and stunted lives.' Increasing consumption is seen
as synonymous with an improving standard of living.[4] Growth in consumer
demand is regarded as a vital prerequisite for a continuing improvement
in the quality of our lives. Indeed, in the light of the structural instability
of modern economies, the insatiability of consumer demand assumes the
character almost of a moral imperative. 'Mrs Bush and I want to encourage
Americans to go out shopping' advised President Bush in the aftermath of
the terrorist attacks on 11 September 2001 (Carney and Dickerson 2001,
p. 4). As Baudrillard (1970), Bauman (1998) and others have argued, the
moral imperative to consume has replaced the work ethic as a defining
feature of modern consumer societies. The modern citizen 'must constantly
be ready to actualize all of his potential, all of his capacity for consumption',
writes Baudrillard (1970, p. 80). 'If he forgets, he will be gently reminded

that he has no right not to be happy.' Clearly the time foreseen by Keynes when 'needs of the first class' are all satisfied and economic expansion is no longer necessary has not yet arrived!

Interestingly, and in spite of the reticence of economic theorists to unravel the structure and nature of underlying human motivations, practitioners of economics have been more adventurous in adopting both the language of needs and its theoretical constructs in developing a 'science' of consumer behaviour. The fields of consumer research, economic psychology, marketing studies and motivation research – Ernest Dichter's 'science of desire' (Dichter 1964) – have all provided a rather rich foundation for producers, retailers, marketers and advertisers wanting to know how to design and sell products that consumers will buy. These attempts to develop an understanding of consumer motivations have drawn quite specifically from the needs-theoretic framework that formal economics has rejected. It is to these needs-theoretic approaches that we now turn.

5.3   NEEDS THEORY

If we reject the economists' antipathy to needs and accept that the concept has some kind of place in understanding human motivations, we are immediately faced with a variety of questions: What are needs? How does the concept of needs relate to concepts such as motivation, attitude, value and behaviour? What kinds of needs exist? Is it possible to derive some kind of taxonomy of needs? How might this taxonomy inform our understanding of human well-being? Can needs tell us anything at all about consumption and consumer behaviours? What are the relationships between needs and consumer goods? Modern needs theories emerged precisely in response to these kinds of questions.

One of the problems with the concept of needs is that the word itself is used in a variety of different idiomatic usages, both as a verb and as a noun. Gasper (1996) identifies three distinct generic meanings of the noun 'need'. The first of these refers to underlying internal forces that drive or guide our actions. For example, a need for safety might refer to the underlying drive that people have to protect themselves and the motivation that this provides them with to build houses, buy clothes, enact punitive legislation against criminals and so on. Needs in this category are supposed to have a different ontological status from wants or preferences in two senses. Firstly, they are considered non-negotiable; and secondly, the failure to satisfy such a need has a detrimental effect on the overall health of the individual. The second meaning of the term refers to needs as an (external) environmental requirement for achieving an end. Thus, houses, clothing and effective legal systems might in themselves, in this idiomatic usage, be construed as needs.[5] Theories in this area tend to focus on the conditions under which individuals *feel* safe, or happy or contented (Scitovsky 1976; Argyle 1987 for example). A third usage of the term refers to needs as justified requirements for performing behaviour. Corresponding theory is concerned with the moral and ethical status of specific social characteristics, such as the ability to engage in autonomous action (Doyal and Gough 1991, for example).

Although all three of these usages are interesting in their own right, the one that corresponds most closely to the way in which needs are construed in most modern needs-theoretical frameworks is the first. Not surprisingly – since this usage is concerned primarily with links between motivation, values and behaviour – these theoretical frameworks have been developed primarily within various branches of psychology. One of the earliest 'modern' needs theories emerged in the social psychology of William McDougall (1928), who identified 18 human needs, which he characterized as innate propensities or instincts. Examples from his typology are the need to seek (and perhaps to store) food, the need to explore strange places or things, the need to cry aloud for assistance when our efforts are utterly baffled, the need to laugh at the defects and failings of our fellow creatures and so on. McDougall's listing of what people need represents an early attempt to state universal motivational forces.

Perhaps the most familiar of the modern needs theories is the one that emerged through the humanistic psychology of Abraham Maslow in the mid-twentieth century. Maslow (1954) devised a now well-known hierarchical ordering of needs, in which he argued that needs low in the hierarchy must be at least partially satisfied before needs higher in the hierarchy may become important sources of motivation. From the bottom to the top of his needs-pyramid, represented in Figure 6.1, Maslow (1954) distinguishes physiological and safety needs, needs to belong and be loved, and then 'higher' cognitive, aesthetic and moral needs. The lower order needs in this hierarchy, Maslow called material needs; the middle order needs were referred to as social needs; and the higher order needs, Maslow called growth or 'self-actualization' needs.

The hierarchical nature of needs has a long pedigree. Plato, for instance, declared in *The Republic* that 'the first and chief of our needs is the provision of food for the existence of life... the second is housing, the third is raiment'. There is, moreover, a sense in which some kind of hierarchy is self-evident. If the need for food is not met, the organism dies, and the satisfaction of any other kinds of needs becomes irrelevant. At the same time, however, there are some potential difficulties with this hierarchical view. It seems to suggest, for example, that personal development is dependent on reaching a certain level of material wealth, and there is plenty of evidence against

Figure 5.1   Maslow's hierarchy of needs

this. For example, individuals have been known to compromise even their most basic survival needs to the satisfaction of moral, psychological or spiritual needs. So, for example, the taboo against eating human flesh has often prevented people from taking measures for their own survival; the desire to fulfil a certain visual stereotype has led many people to starve themselves, sometimes literally to death; and Levenstein (1988, ix) describes how American prisoners in the Korean War died rather than stomach the (perfectly nutritional) local cuisine.

The hierarchical approach to human needs has also drawn criticism because it appears to deny access to the satisfaction of higher needs in less developed country populations and legitimizes a distribution of power in favour of those who specialize in so-called 'higher' needs – such as intellectuals and ascetics (Galtung 1990) – in developed country populations.

In fact, in his later writings, Maslow himself revised the hierarchy to place two different sets of needs on a more or less equal footing, reflecting what he saw as a clear 'duality' in human nature (Maslow 1968). According to this later view, we are not, as human beings, uniquely motivated by material concerns for physical survival. There is a part of the human psyche that hankers after esteem and transcendence, even as the person's basic material needs remain unfulfilled.

A further critique of the Maslovian approach is that it over-emphasizes the individualistic nature of needs satisfaction and understates the importance of society, culture and the natural environment, by treating these as secondary in importance to individual motivation. Within this kind of framework it is rather difficult to say anything constructive about the political and social importance of debates about long-term environmental issues such as global climate change (for example) because, for the moment at least, they barely register directly on the question of individual human well-being at all. As Douglas et al. (1998) point out, long-term global environmental issues tend to be sidelined because 'it is too easy to claim that there is another more urgent need to satisfy' (p. 211).

Some more recent theories of human needs have attempted to correct for these kinds of deficiency. Galtung (1980) proposed a four-fold typology of needs involving a two-dimensional matrix composed of material and non-material needs in one dimension, with actor-dependent and structure-dependent satisfaction in the other. Mallmann (1980) proposes another two-dimensional typology which juxtaposes ten needs categories against a three-fold categorization of types of satisfiers: personal, social and ecological. This same idea is extended further in a typology derived by Max-Neef (1991, 1992), which sets nine 'axiological' needs – subsistence, protection, affection, understanding, participation, identity, leisure, creation and freedom – against four 'existential' categories: being, doing, having and interacting (Table 5.1). Whereas the first seven needs have existed since the origins of *Homo habilis*, and, undoubtedly, since the appearance of *Homo sapiens*, the latter two are assumed to have been developed later in the evolutionary process.

There are clearly some resonances between Max-Neef's 'axiological' categories and Maslow's early categorization. In particular, the needs for subsistence and protection correspond closely with Maslow's 'material needs', while participation and affection, for example, are closely linked to Maslow's social needs. Although some of Maslow's 'growth needs' appear to be absent in the later framework, Max-Neef has hypothesized a tenth need for 'transcendence' that fulfils some of these characteristics. Max-Neef argues that this need is today felt only by some, but that it may evolve, somewhere in the future, into a universal need.

Perhaps the most critical aspect of modern needs theories is the importance assigned to the distinction between needs and satisfiers. Needs are conceived dualistically in Max-Neef's framework as a 'deprivation' on the one hand and a 'potential' on the other. A need is a deprivation in the sense of something being lacking; it is a potential to the extent that it

Table 5.1 *A categorization of needs/satisfiers according to Max-Neef (1991, 1992)*

	Being	Having	Doing	Interacting
Subsistence	(1) Physical health, mental health, equilibrium, sense of humour, adaptability	(2) Food, shelter, work	(3) Feed, procreate, rest, work	(4) Living environment, social setting
Protection	(5) Care, adaptability, autonomy, equilibrium, solidarity	(6) Insurance systems, savings, social security, health systems, rights, family, work	(7) Cooperate, prevent, plan, take care of, cure, help	(8) Living space, social environment, dwelling
Affection	(9) Self-esteem, solidarity, respect, tolerance, generosity, receptiveness, passion, determination, sensuality, sense of humour	(10) Friendships, family, partnerships, relationships with nature	(11) Make love, caress, express emotions, share, take care of, cultivate, appreciate	(12) Privacy, intimacy, home, spaces of togetherness
Understanding	(13) Critical conscience, receptiveness, curiosity, astonishment, discipline, intuition, rationality	(14) Literature, teachers, method, educational policies, communication policies	(15) Investigate, study, experiment, educate, analyse, meditate	(16) Settings of formative interaction, schools, universities, academies, groups, communities, family
Participation	(17) Adaptability, receptiveness, solidarity, willingness, determination, dedication, respect, passion, sense of humour	(18) Rights, responsibilities, duties, privileges, work	(19) Become affiliated, cooperate, propose, share, dissent, obey, interact, agree on, express opinions	(20) Settings of participative interactions, parties, associations, churches, communities, neighbourhoods, family
Leisure	(21) Curiosity, receptiveness, imagination, recklessness, sense of humour, tranquillity, sensuality	(22) Games, spectacles, clubs, parties, peace of mind	(23) Day-dream, brood, dream, recall old times, give way to fantasies, remember, relax, have fun, play	(24) Privacy, intimacy, spaces of closeness, free-time, surroundings, landscapes
Creation	(25) Passion, determination, intuition, imagination, boldness, rationality, autonomy, inventiveness, curiosity	(26) Abilities, skills, method, work	(27) Work, invent, build, design, compose, interpret	(28) Productive and feedback settings, workshops, cultural groups, audiences, spaces for expression, temporal freedom
Identity	(29) Sense of belonging, consistency, differentiation, self-esteem, assertiveness	(30) Symbols, language, religions, habits, customs, reference groups, sexuality, values, norms, historical memory, work	(31) Commit oneself, integrate oneself, confront, decide on, get to know oneself, recognize oneself, actualize oneself, grow	(32) Social rhythms, everyday settings, settings which one belongs to, maturation stages
Freedom	(33) Autonomy, self-esteem, determination, passion, assertiveness, open-mindedness, boldness, rebelliousness, tolerance	(34) Equal rights	(35) Dissent, choose, be different from, run risks, develop awareness, commit oneself, disobey	(36) Temporal/spatial plasticity

may also serve to motivate or mobilize the subject. Satisfiers, by contrast, represent different forms of being, having, doing and interacting, which contribute to the 'actualization' of these deprivations or potentials.

In physiological terms, the satisfaction or dissatisfaction of human needs can often be expressed in terms of feelings or emotions. As the concept of emotion is associated with general arousal of the sympathetic nervous system (Schachter 1964), and the satisfaction of a need may actually decrease one's level of arousal, it may be preferable to relate the satisfaction (and dissatisfaction) of needs to the concept of feelings. Pleasant (or unpleasant) feelings about something can be conceived as one of the constituent parts of emotion (Frijda and Mesquita 1992). Feelings may be positive or negative (for example, McDougall 1928: pleasure and pain, and Simonov 1970: positive and negative emotions). It is assumed here that the satisfaction of a need yields positive feelings, whereas the dissatisfaction of needs will yield negative feelings. Extending the typology of needs as presented by Max-Neef (1992) with positive and negative feelings yields the list of feelings presented in Table 5.2.

If a need is not satisfied, the related negative feeling (deprivation) will arouse a drive to satisfy this need. For example, if the need for subsistence is not satisfied because of a lack of food, the negative feeling will be hunger, arousing the drive to eat. If confronted with an opportunity to attempt to satisfy the need in question – say an array of foodstuffs – this drive will result in a motivation to use that opportunity. Often, of course, there will be a variety of possible opportunities available for pursuing the satisfaction of such a need. For example, one might equally choose a tuna sandwich, a banana, a gammon steak, some french fries, a 'veggieburger', some combination of these, or something else entirely in attempting to satisfy one's hunger. The eating of one or all of these foods may alleviate the deprivation. The satisfaction of the underlying need will evoke positive feelings. If a need is fully satisfied, no drive will emerge and the motivation to use a relevant opportunity will be low.

In short, food – and the system that provides for access to food – is not in itself conceived as a need in the Max-Neef framework; rather it is conceived as a satisfier of the need for subsistence. Likewise, education may be regarded as a satisfier of the need for understanding. Breast-feeding is simultaneously a satisfier of the infant's need for subsistence, affection, participation and identity – and the mother's need for creation, participation, identity and affection. Housing is a satisfier of the need for protection. Democracy is a satisfier of the need for participation. Sport can be a satisfier of the needs for leisure, participation, identity and creation. Whereas needs are 'finite, few and classifiable', satisfiers are (generally speaking) culturally determined, and numerous (if not infinite) in variety. If we think of the

Table 5.2 A categorization of feelings according to the typology of needs (Max-Neef 1992)

Basic need	Satisfaction of needs: positive feelings	Dissatisfaction of needs: negative feelings
Subsistence	Satiated, repleted	Hungry
Protection	Safe	In danger, anxiety
Affection	Love/being loved	Hate/indifference
Understanding	Intellectual well-being, smart, clever	Intellectual frustration, dumb, stupid
Participation	Belonging, related, involved	Lonesome, isolated, forsaken
Leisure	Playful, relaxed	Boredom/bored, weary, stressed
Creation	Creative, inspired	Uninspired
Identity	Self-assured, confident, positive self-image	Uncertain, insecure, negative self-image
Freedom	Free, independent	Entangled, chained, bounded, captured, tied

matrix shown in Table 5.1 as a means of identifying the way in which needs can be satisfied, then the number of needs is specified by the number of spaces in the matrix. But the satisfiers are as numerous as the things that could fill the spaces of the matrix. So, for example, breast-feeding is not the only way of ensuring that the subsistence needs of the infant are met. Formal education is not the only way of attempting to meet the need for understanding. There is a huge variety of different kinds of food that might contribute to satisfaction of the need for subsistence. Different kinds of housing could aid the protection need.

From the point of view of such a framework, what varies over time and across cultures is not the set of needs (that is, the dimensions of the matrix), but the set of ways in which a particular culture at a particular time chooses to satisfy – or attempt to satisfy – those needs (that is, the contents of the spaces in the matrix). Cultural change, in this perspective, can be construed as the process of dropping one particular satisfier or set of satisfiers in favour of another. The underlying needs have not changed, but the particular forms of being, having, doing and interacting in which the culture engages in order to satisfy those needs may vary extensively.

A second important aspect of modern needs theories – which flows from the distinction between needs and satisfiers – is the critical recognition that not all the ways in which a particular culture or social group attempts to satisfy the spectrum of needs are equally successful. Thus, the so-called 'satisfiers' that would occupy the spaces in the needs satisfaction matrix of a particular group may in reality be more or less successful at actually satisfying the related needs. Max-Neef's formulation distinguishes five different kinds of 'satisfiers':

- Destroyers or violators occupy the paradoxical position of failing completely to satisfy the need towards which they are directed.[6]
- Pseudo-satisfiers generate a false sense of satisfaction of the need.[7]
- Inhibiting satisfiers satisfy one need to which they are directed but tend to inhibit the satisfaction of other needs.
- Singular satisfiers manage to satisfy a single category of need without affecting satisfaction elsewhere.
- Synergistic satisfiers manage simultaneously to satisfy several different kinds of needs.[8]

Of these different kinds of satisfiers, it is perhaps worth commenting a little more on inhibiting satisfiers, which exhibit the important – and quite frequent – characteristic of a 'trade-off' between the satisfaction of different kinds of needs.[9] Examples of inhibiting satisfiers might include cigarettes (which satisfy certain social needs for participation, identity or leisure but which inhibit the needs for subsistence and protection), cars (which satisfy the need for identity, freedom, participation and so on, but which inhibit long-term needs for protection), television (which satisfies the need for leisure but inhibits the need for creation) and so on. In fact, a more thorough typology of goods and satisfiers might well reveal that a large number of goods occupy the role of inhibiting satisfiers. In particular, it would seem likely that a variety of (environmentally) unsustainable goods and behaviours fall into this category where the satisfied need is a short-term need, and the inhibited needs are longer term. In this sense, inhibiting satisfiers can be thought of as 'behavioural traps'.

Though this classification represents a potentially confusing use of language – how can a satisfier also be a violator? – it does capture a level of sophistication that is lacking both in the economic model and in some previous needs theories. In particular it allows for a much more complex and multifaceted model of development than is provided by the unidimensional concept of economic growth. Using the characterization outlined here, the provision of well-being can be represented as the process of satisfying underlying needs. Poverty, by contrast, can be seen as the failure to satisfy needs. Interestingly, this implies that there is no single concept of poverty, defined simply in terms of low per capita income. Instead, we open the possibility of defining a multiplicity of poverties corresponding to failures to satisfy different kinds of needs. The converse of this is that we can no longer expect economic growth necessarily to alleviate poverty, since poverty is no longer defined in purely monetary terms.[10]

Perhaps the most interesting questions raised by the needs-theoretic framework however, concern the role and function of consumption activities in the process of needs satisfaction. What exactly is the relationship between the finite set of objective human needs and the potentially infinite set of individual desires and preferences expressed through the market? What is the relationship between economic goods and services (in the conventional terminology) and 'satisfiers' (in the needs-theoretic language). What kinds of economic goods actually contribute to the satisfaction of human needs and promote human well-being, and which simply serve as pseudo-satisfiers or destroyers of the underlying needs?

In a sense, these questions are amongst the most crucial questions of our time. In a world in which economic consumption is threatening to erode the integrity of the global ecosystems, it is particularly vital to be able to identify which bits of consumption contribute to human needs satisfaction, and which simply operate as pseudo-satisfiers and destroyers. And yet, the truth is that we have barely even scratched the surface in asking such questions, let alone formulated coherent answers for them.

Two things can, however, be said about the relationship between economic goods and needs satisfaction. First, that it is extremely complex; there is certainly no simple one-to-one map between individual consumer goods and individual needs. Secondly, any relation that does exist between consumption and need satisfaction is highly non-linear. A straightforward example illustrates both these points. As we have already noted, foodstuffs are economic goods that can serve, in part, as satisfiers of the needs for subsistence (by ensuring survival) and protection (by maintaining good health). But even in this relatively straightforward example, there are a number of complexities. For a start, in addition to the foods themselves, the satisfaction of the need for subsistence also requires a variety of other inputs (such as an agricultural system, a distribution system, a food preparation system) not all of which are consumer goods per se, and some of which lie outside the economic system altogether.

Perhaps more importantly, not all foodstuffs are equally effective in the satisfaction of the need for subsistence and protection. Nutritional value is not equally distributed across the economic goods of the food sector; and economic value does not always accord closely with nutritional value. Some foods fail to satisfy. Or operate at best as inhibiting satisfiers. Excessive consumption of refined sugars and carbohydrates, for example, has been implicated in a variety of health concerns including chronic hypoglycaemia, tooth decay and heart disease. Actually, even food that is 'good for you', is only good for you up to a certain point. The nutritional value of almost any food shows diminishing returns to scale. Malnourishment is still widespread in poorer countries; but in the Western world obesity is a growing problem contributing to a range of medical problems from reduced muscular fitness to heart disease. In short, there is no simple linear relationship between the consumption of a particular economic good (such as food) and the satisfaction of the underlying need(s).

Sweet foods also present us with another kind of problem. They are not consumed exclusively for reasons of subsistence. Fine and Leopold (1993, p. 169) point out that '(human) food is not fodder; humans do not feed...it is apparent that what is consumed is not obviously determined by physiological or biological needs. Psychological needs also play a role.' Sweet foods, in particular, are well-known to be associated with the attempted satisfaction of psychological needs. Conventionally, for example, chocolate is identified with the satisfaction of a need for comfort or affection. It may eventually turn out to be a pseudo-satisfier of that need; but the point is that what seems, on the surface, to be an economic good related to the satisfaction of clear-cut subsistence need turns out on close examination to bear a rather complex relationship to a variety of needs, some of them social or psychological rather than material in character.

The fundamental point is this: that the relationship between economic goods and needs satisfaction is inherently complex. Material commodities (and economic goods in general) may be adopted as attempted satisfiers for a wide range of underlying needs. Any particular commodity may simultaneously be an attempted satisfier for several different needs. Moreover, the particular choice of economic good or goods associated with the intended satisfaction of the individual need or needs is determined not just by the success or failure of that good in satisfying the underlying needs, but also by a complex variety of factors including personal psychology, social values and norms, cultural influences, institutional structures, industrial interests and marketing strategies. In any particular culture, at any one point in time, a variety of economic goods will be engaged with differing degrees of success in the attempted satisfaction of a range of underlying needs. Some consumer goods may be better than others in meeting those needs. Some cultural strategies may be very successful in meeting needs. Others may fail entirely. And it is this latter insight – that some cultural attempts at needs satisfaction appear to fail – which provides the foundation for a long-standing critique of conventional development that draws heavily on a needs-based perspective.

5.4 SEVEN 'DEADLY' NEEDS – OVER-CONSUMPTION AS A SOCIAL PATHOLOGY

At the heart of many recent (and some earlier) critiques of modern society is the idea that there is something pathological about recent patterns of consumption. Before outlining the conceptual basis for this idea, however, it is worth paying some attention to the historical pedigree of needs-based critiques of society.

In fact, this pedigree is surprisingly long (Springborg 1981). A needs-theoretical approach to human well-being was inherent in the writings of Plato, Aristotle and the hellenistic philosophers; it was a key component of the Enlightenment inquiry into the psychological bases for human behaviour; it provided a crucial input to the early socialist critiques of capitalism in the mid- to late-nineteenth century; and it formed the foundation for an extended critique of contemporary development that emerged through the humanistic psychology of Abraham Maslow and Carl Rogers in the mid-twentieth century and has informed modern environmental critiques today. Some at least of the economic antipathy to the concept of needs can be attributed to the fact that needs theory has been used in this way – namely as the basis for some rather heated debates about civilization, capitalism and the legitimacy of economic progress. Though we are sometimes inclined to believe that such debates are a modern phenomenon, they can be dated (at least) to the Stoic philosophy of the first century BC. Indeed, the Stoic critique of hellenic civilization bears more than a passing resemblance to modern 'green' critiques of progress. Like radical greens, the Stoics aspired to a simple life in harmony with nature, and situated our failure to achieve this ideal in the disjunction between man's (false) subjective desires and his (true) objective needs.

The same distinction between true and false needs lay at the heart of the socialist and humanistic critiques of progress in the nineteenth and twentieth centuries. The most well-known of these perhaps is Marx's distinction between human and inhuman needs and his indictment of capitalism for its creation of a whole raft of false (inhuman) needs and its alienation of humankind from its true (human) needs. But very similar distinctions are present in the writings of Rousseau (1913), who distinguished between (limited) natural and (infinite) artificial needs; in Marcuse (1964), who argued that false needs were the result of man's 'repressive desublimation' in contemporary society, and in Illich (1977), whose searing critique of modern society is founded on the contention that coercive political and economic interests have created 'ever newer strains of hybridized needs' (p. 30) that now lie outside the control of individual citizens.

The humanistic critique was articulated particularly clearly in needs-theoretic terms by Erich Fromm in the 1970s. In *To Have or to Be?*, Fromm (1976) roundly criticized conventional development for neglecting basic philosophical understandings about human well-being. Alarmed at the alienation and passivity of modern society, he identified two main psychological premises on which the economic system is built:

(1) that the aim of life is happiness, that is maximum pleasure, defined as the satisfaction of any desire or subjective need a person may feel (radical hedonism);
(2) that egotism, selfishness, and greed, as the system needs to generate them in order to function, lead to harmony and peace. (p. 3)

Fromm admits that this form of radical hedonism has been practised throughout history, most particularly by the richest proportion of the population; but points out that, prior to the seventeenth century, with only one exception in the philosophy of Aristippus (a pupil of Socrates in the fourth century BC), radical hedonism 'was never the theory of well-being expressed by the great Masters of Living in China, India, the Near East, and Europe' (p. 4). By contrast, he argues that there is an essential distinction – present in the writings of all the great teachers and philosophers concerned with humankind's optimal well-being – between 'needs (desires) which are only subjectively felt and whose satisfaction leads to momentary pleasure' and 'objectively valid needs' which are 'rooted in human nature and whose realisation is conducive to human growth' (ibid.).[11]

Fromm's intention was to argue explicitly against the insatiability doctrine and to undermine the legitimacy of economic arguments about consumer sovereignty. Needs theory plays a central role in this critique. For needs theory suggests quite explicitly that certain universal motivations underlie human behaviour; and by doing so it seems to allow us to tease apart *what is consumed* in the consumer society from *what contributes to human well-being*. The economic perspective claims categorically that the consumption of any commodity contributes positively to needs satisfaction in the sense of an increase in individual (and collective) utility. By contrast, the needs-based perspective distinguishes a variety of different levels of satisfaction or dissatisfaction of the underlying needs that flow from consumption activities and insists that we cannot unreservedly equate every consumption activity with an increase in well-being.

Evidence of this divergence between economic consumption and human well-being was noted by a wide variety of critical observers writing contemporaneously with Fromm. Murray Bookchin (writing under the pseudonym Lewis Herber) argued that in spite of its material affluence, human society had 'reached a level of anonymity, social atomisation and spiritual isolation... virtually unprecedented in human history' (Herber 1963, p. 187). In attempting to discover why 'unprecedented and fast-moving prosperity had left its beneficiaries unsatisfied', Scitovsky (1976) highlighted the addictive nature of consumer behaviour, and its failure to mirror the complexity of human motivation and experience. In a partial answer to Scitovsky's question, Hirsch (1977) characterized significant proportions of consumption as 'positional consumption', that is, as consumption designed to 'position' the consumer in relation to his or her fellow consumers. The trouble with this kind of strategy is that it confronts us with what Hirsch called 'social limits to growth'. As he described the problem, 'it is a case of everyone in the crowd standing on tiptoe and no one getting a better view. Yet at the start of the process some individuals gain a better view by standing on tiptoe, and others are forced to follow if they are to keep their position. If all do follow... everyone expends more resources and ends up with the same position' (Hirsch 1977, p. 49). The seemingly obsessive behaviour of the modern consumer, like most psychopathological addictions, fails to generate increasing returns in terms of satisfaction. It simply means running ever harder and faster in order to stay in the same place.

Critiques such as these have to some extent been supported by empirical evidence on well-being and life satisfaction. In *The Joyless Economy*, Scitovsky could already cite the failure of reported levels of well-being to match the growth in GDP (1976). In 1991, Erik Jacobs and Robert

Worcester found that people were marginally less happy than they had been in 1981 in spite of increased personal income (Worcester 1998). A similar result was reported over a longer period by Myers and Diener (1996). Oswald (1997) found that reported levels of 'satisfaction with life' in the 1990s were only marginally higher than they had been in the mid-1970s. In some countries, including Britain, they were actually lower. As more recent time-series studies of life satisfaction have shown (Figure 5.2), this divergence has continued unabated over the last decade or so (Donovan et al. 2002; Lane 2000; Frey and Stutzer 2000; Veenhoven 2003).

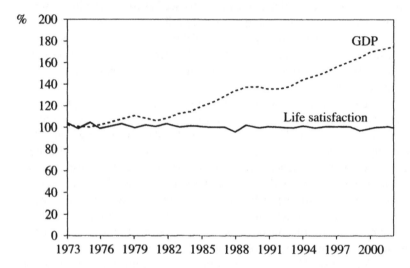

Figure 5.2   Economic growth versus life satisfaction in the UK: 1973–2001

This kind of evidence leaves us with the uncomfortable possibility that at least some of our consumption may not be contributing positively to the satisfaction of any of our needs. More recent support for the same hypothesis has come from a wide variety of studies using psychometric tests to measure the relationship between materialist values, material lifestyles and subjective well-being.[12] These studies draw attention in particular to the apparent failure of material commodities as effective satisfiers of psychological and social needs. Moreover, they place much of the blame for the divergence of life satisfaction from income on precisely this failure. Material acquisitiveness, according to these authors, correlates negatively with subjective well-being.

What the ecological critique of conventional development adds to this litany of discontent is the notion that, in addition to their psychological and social failings, highly materialistic lifestyles are also damaging and potentially disastrous in environmental terms. And here, precisely, lies the 'pathology' from which consumer society appears to be suffering. If ecological damage were incurred as the inevitable result of a broadly successful attempt to increase human well-being, it might well be regarded as an unfortunate but necessary consequence of human development. But that ecological damage should be the result of a series of consumption practices that clearly fail to increase well-being has all the characteristics of a social pathology. Our continued attempts to satisfy the seven social and psychological needs in the Max-Neef framework are not only potentially dangerous in environmental terms, according to this critique, they may not even be successful, in the long run, in meeting the underlying needs. Consumer society, argue these critics, for all its glitter and panache, may simply bequeath us a phenomenal 'double whammy': degraded ecosystems and impoverished lives.

The starkness of this conclusion is mitigated however, by the prospect for improvement that it offers. Environmental imperatives – the demand to reduce the material impact of human activities – are often portrayed and often perceived as constraining human welfare and threatening our quality of life. In contrast, the combined social and ecological critique suggests that existing patterns of consumption already threaten our quality of life, not just because of their impact on the environment, but also because of their failure to satisfy our needs. Reducing the material profligacy of our lives, according to this view, is good for the environment. But it is also good for us. The humanistic position appears to offer us a significant 'double dividend': the possibility of living better by consuming less.

5.5 'A NAIVE AND ABSURD MORALISM'? AGAINST THE RHETORIC OF NEEDS

Given the role played by the language of needs in the long historical debates about human well-being and development, it is not at all surprising to find that needs-theoretical approaches remain highly contentious. Nor is opposition confined to economists wanting to displace the concept of need with the language of wants, preferences and desires. There is also a good deal of scepticism about the whole needs-based project from within disciplines such as sociology, anthropology and cultural studies. Some of this scepticism about needs certainly draws strength from the historical dialectic on well-being. In particular, one strand of thinking is supportive of modern development, opposes the idea that consumer society is in the grip of a pathology, and points to the advances in technical competence and cultural richness that have characterized modern development (McCracken 1997 for example). Interestingly, however, there is also a strand of the argument against needs, which is itself critical of modern society, argues that the 'social logic' of consumerism has left us in the grip of a 'luxurious and spectacular penury' (Baudrillard 1970, p. 68), and yet still insists that 'the desire to moderate consumption or establish a normalizing network of needs, is naive and absurd moralism' (Baudrillard 1968, pp. 24–5).

Critics of needs theory tend to level a variety of charges against the needs-based discourse. Perhaps the most important of these are claims of naivety, rhetoricism and moralism, and we shall look at these charges in more detail in a moment. First, however, we outline one of the key intellectual premises on which most of these critiques rest, namely the insight that, in addition to their functional role, material goods play vital symbolic roles in our lives. Over the second half of the twentieth century, this insight has become an increasingly important defining feature of sociological debates about consumption (Dittmar 1992; Miller 1995). The hypothesis itself has arisen from the confluence of some rather diverse intellectual influences including the semiotics of Charles Morris (1946), the structuralism of Roland Barthes (1973), the social philosophy of Baudrillard (1968, 1970), the social anthropology of Marshall Sahlins (1976) and Mary Douglas (1976), the psychology of Mihalyi Csikszentmihalyi and Eugene Rochberg-Halton (1981) and the consumer and motivation research of Ernest Dichter (1964), Elizabeth Hirschman and Morris Holbrook (1980), Russell Belk (1988) and others.

It would be impossible to do justice to the breadth and scope of this literature here. Nonetheless, the most important lesson from this huge body of work is important for our understanding of critics of the needs-based approach. Material commodities are important to us, not just for what they do, but for what they signify: about us, about our lives, our loves, our desires, about our successes and failings, about our hopes and our dreams. Material goods are not just artefacts. Nor do they offer purely functional benefits. They derive their importance, in part at least, from their symbolic role in mediating and communicating personal, social and cultural meaning not only to others but also to ourselves.

This hypothesis offers a vital clue to our understanding of the social and psychological dimensions of consumer behaviour. In particular, it suggests – contrary to the perspective from humanistic psychology – that material artefacts may after all be legitimate candidates in the search for human well-being, precisely because of their ability to embody symbolic meaning. What looked like irrational or pathological consumer behaviours, claim those sceptical of the humanistic position, become increasingly comprehensible once we view material objects as signs. 'Forget the idea of consumer irrationality', urge Mary Douglas and Baron Isherwood in *The World of Goods*. 'Forget that commodities are good for eating, clothing and shelter; forget their usefulness and try instead the idea that commodities are good for thinking; treat them as a nonverbal medium for the human creative faculty' (Douglas and Isherwood 1979, pp. 40–41).

Douglas and Isherwood draw attention, in particular, to the importance of material goods in providing 'marking services' – social rituals that serve to embed the individual in their social group, cement social relations within the group and play an important role in maintaining information flows between members of the social group. These information flows, claim Douglas and Isherwood, serve a vital purpose in helping both the group and the individual to maintain and improve social resilience in the face of cultural shifts and social shocks. Thus, what is at stake, in asking consumers to forego material consumption is not just the presence or absence of empty, meaningless stuff, or even the invidious display of 'conspicuous consumption' that Veblen (1898) inveighed against. Rather, it is personal identity, social cohesion, cultural capital and the symbolic resources required to create and maintain these.

It is this insight that tends to inform some at least of the antipathy to needs evident in sociology, anthropology and cultural studies. Certainly, it plays a large part in the charge of naivity raised by some of the critics. In particular, according to these critics, the needs-based view appears to underestimate the 'social logic' of consumer society. Symbols are by their nature socially constructed (Dittmar 1992). The task of constructing and maintaining symbolic value is fundamentally a social one (Csikszentmihalyi and Rochberg-Halton 1981). The value attached to symbols is constantly negotiated and renegotiated through social interactions within a specific cultural context (Elliott and Wattanasuwan 1998). In the hands of certain sociologists and social philosophers, this insight has become the basis for a quite specific view of consumer society. According to this view, the individual consumer is 'locked' into a continual process of constructing and reconstructing personal identity in the context of a continually renegotiated universe of social and cultural symbols.

There is clearly a sense in which this model of the perpetual reconstruction of social identity through material goods appears to reinforce the idea that consumer society is in the grip of some kind of social pathology, and indeed some of those critical of the needs perspective – Baudrillard, for instance – do not dispute this point. Bauman (1998, p. 29) points to the convenient resonances between this process of perpetual reconstruction of identity, and the impermanent, transient nature of modern consumer goods. 'Aggregate identities, loosely arranged of the purchasable, not-too-lasting, easily detachable and utterly replaceable tokens currently available in the shops', he writes, 'seem to be exactly what one needs to meet the challenges of contemporary living'. However, this is certainly not a pathology located within the remit or control of the individual consumer, and the idea that he or she could free themselves from the 'iron cage' of consumerism simply by paying a closer attention to a fixed set of individual needs is, for these authors, nothing less than absurd.

In the light of these criticisms, we are confronted with the question of what, if anything, is to be gained by referring to individual needs at all. For some, the answer to this question is clear. The discourse on needs is a rhetorical discourse. In the common usage of the term, to refer to a particular choice as a 'need', rather than simply a want or a preference, appears to offer some form of social justification for that choice, to underline the importance of making it and to claim some form of moral legitimation for it. Campbell (1998) takes this argument even further and identifies two distinct 'rhetorics' employed in the discourse of consumer choice: one is based on needs and the other on wants. Whereas the former is prosecuted through a vocabulary of 'need', 'requirement', 'necessity', and 'deficiency' with accompanying antonyms such as 'satisfaction', 'comfort' or 'utility', the latter employs a vocabulary of 'desire', 'pleasure', and 'love' with accompanying antonyms of 'boredom' or 'indifference'. Campbell locates the origins of these separate discourses within two distinct philosophical traditions. The needs-based discourse, he argues, owes much to the Puritan-inspired utilitarian tradition, whereas the discourse of desire is inherent in the Romantic tradition (and its predecessor of philosophical hedonism), which elevates pleasure over comfort.[13]

Campbell has two principal points to make about this rhetorical division of labour. The first is that the needs-based discourse quite specifically neglects not just the philosophical pedigree of a desire-based discourse, but also its reality as a component of our psychological make-up. As numerous writers from Epicurus to Blake to modern consumer researchers have pointed out (Belk et al. 2003), the dynamic of desire is a fundamental aspect of the human psyche, and Campbell's argument is that this dynamic is not amenable to a neat needs-based characterization. While deprivation and satisfaction may be paradigmatic of a needs-oriented dynamic, Campbell argues that the pursuit of pleasure is not motivated by deprivation and tends to be eroded by guaranteed satisfaction. Moreover, whilst only reality, in Campbell's view, can provide for the satisfaction of needs, 'both illusions and delusions can supply pleasure' (Campbell 1987, p. 61). The second point Campbell makes is that, given this dialectical tension in our make-up between needs and desires, we must regard the employment of a needs-based discourse in practice as a purely rhetorical strategy either to imbue our decisions with moral legitimacy or else to condemn the decisions of others to moral illegitimacy. The declaration that 'I need this or that consumer good', according to Campbell, affords my access to that good priority either over other people's access to it, or over my access to any number of other consumer goods, that I simply desire or prefer.

This latter observation also provides perhaps the strongest charge against the needs-based discourse from its critics, that of moralism. As soon as we attempt to use the language of needs to claim preferentiality for specific consumer choices, we are drawn, either wittingly or unwittingly into a moral discourse. In fact, some at least of the needs-based critics have been quite explicit in their moral condemnation of 'overconsumption'. But is this condemnation valid? The needs sceptics argue not. 'We would like to know how they live, the style and life of these moralists...' declare Douglas and Isherwood (1979, p. 15). 'Overconsumption is more serious and more complicated than personal obesity and moral indignation is not enough for understanding it...The moralists who indignantly condemn overconsumption will eventually have to answer for whom they do not invite to their table, how they wish their daughters to marry, where their old friends are today with whom they started out in their youth.' Though clearly couched in slightly moralistic language itself, this charge has two components to it. The first is that 'moralistic' attempts to regulate one's own consumption may have unforeseen consequences not just for oneself but also for one's dependents and friends. The second is that 'moralistic' attempts to regulate the consumption of others on the basis of some fixed idea about needs are in fact themselves ethically dubious. For the fact of the matter is, according to these critics, that no one person is in a position to identify with authority what the needs of any other person might be. Nearly all the distinctions made between true and false needs are untenable, argues Agnes Heller (cited in Campbell 1998, p. 241) because 'all needs humans recognize as real should also be considered real'.

5.6   FROM NEEDS TO FUNCTIONINGS

A careful reader might be forgiven for feeling slightly frustrated by the way in which the debate about needs somehow slides away from rational inquiry. The arguments about moralism are a case in point. For it seems as though the critiques of needs on grounds of moralism are missing or misinterpreting two critical aspects of modern needs theories. The first is just about noun usage. As we noted earlier there are several distinct usages of the word 'need' as a noun. Whereas needs theory is mainly employing the word in the context of underlying motivations or drives, its critics appear to be attacking another kind of usage, namely the one associated with the external environmental requirement for achieving an end. For needs theory, needs are the underlying physiological, psychological and social functionings that contribute to human well-being. For its critics, needs are the things that humans employ to facilitate these functionings. To specify that humans generally have a number of distinct kinds of underlying drives is not in itself to circumscribe how these drives are to be satisfied. Secondly, modern needs theories do not attempt to prescribe or proscribe specific responses to these drives. From Maslow onwards, needs theories have attempted to offer a categorization of underlying motivations – and not a prescriptive list of what is or is not a legitimate way of satisfying the underlying needs.[14] Moreover, in practice, the Max-Neef framework, for example, is often not used prescriptively or proscriptively at all. Rather it is employed as a tool for reaching inter-subjective agreement on which kinds of satisfiers might best be employed to meet the range of underlying motivations (Max-Neef 1992; Jackson and Marks 1999; Stagl and O'Hara 2001).

Some attempts have been made to avoid this ambiguity in usage – and the disagreements to which it leads – by using a different vocabulary to describe the underlying drives or motivations. This attempt is most prominent, perhaps, in the work of the Nobel prize-winning economist Amartya Sen and his collaborator Martha Nussbaum. In a seminal paper about the standard of living, Sen (1984, 1985, 1992) put forward the idea that individual well-being has to do not solely with income levels, but with the freedoms or 'capabilities' enjoyed by the individual. Capabilities are the potential functionings of people. Functionings are beings and doings. Some examples of functionings are being well-fed, taking part in the community, being sheltered, relating to other people, working on the labour market, caring for others, being healthy and living in harmony with nature (Nussbaum 1998). While functionings are achievements or outcomes, capabilities are the freedom or opportunities to achieve these outcomes (Robeyns 2003).

Sen's focus on capabilities rather than commodities is an attempt to retain a means-based focus (stopping short of the language of needs satisfaction) while noting that some people require a larger commodity endowment than others in order to achieve the same scope of ability to be fully functioning in society (for example, handicapped persons' capability for mobility, or pregnant women's capability for required nutrition). On the one hand, a capability-based approach to consumption differs fundamentally from the utilitarian approach, which considers exclusively the pleasure people get from their consumption choices. Instead, the capabilities view changes the focus from the subjective feeling of pleasure or satisfactions to objective criteria like opportunities for health and participation. It revives the concern with poverty and deprivation, which had been lost in utility theory. On the other hand, its emphasis on opportunities rather than outcomes preserves some of the respect for individual choice, which is one of the key concerns for critics of the needs-based approaches.

The capability approach allows us to distinguish between people who starve and those who are hungry because they choose to fast, and about whom there is no need to worry as long as they have the capability of eating well. Similarly we can distinguish between someone who has to walk because they do not have any other means of mobility and those who choose to walk for environmental reasons. The capability approach directs us to investigate whether societies, and societal consumption patterns, would permit people to live healthy lives, in harmony with each other and with nature.

Nussbaum (2003) has also developed Sen's idea, arguing that capabilities supply guidance superior to that available from consideration of the utility gained from resources. She takes the capability approach further by specifying a definite set of capabilities as the most important ones to protect. This requires taking a more definite stand on which capabilities are important in our ethical judgements and our conceptions of justice. According to Nussbaum, without such a list, the capability approach cannot offer valuable normative guidance on justice. And Robeyns (2003) proposes a method for selecting the relevant capabilities, and applies this method to an analysis of gender inequality in affluent societies. In particular, she emphasizes the importance of the process in specifying a list, such as taking account of the existing literature in the field and having a public discussion on it, to give the list academic and political legitimacy.

Perhaps the most important aspect of the capabilities approach for the arguments in this chapter relates to the 'materiality' of capabilities within different societies. Sen argues that material requirements for physiological functioning tend to be fairly similar in all societies. Crucially however, he claims that the material requirements associated with social and psychological capabilities can vary widely between different societies. Echoing a sentiment expressed much earlier by Adam Smith (1776), he argues that:

> To lead a life without shame, to be able to visit and entertain one's friends, to keep track of what is going on and what others are talking about, and so on, requires a more expensive bundle of goods and services in a society that is generally richer and in which most people have, say, means of transport, affluent clothing, radios or television sets, and so on... The same absolute level of capabilities may thus have a greater relative need for incomes (and commodities). (Sen 1998, p. 298)

The point being made here is in some sense similar to the one that Douglas and Isherwood (1979) made about 'marking services', although expressed in a rather different way. As it is presently organized, modern society has appropriated the symbolic property of commodities to play a vital role in articulating social identity, ensuring social capabilities and maintaining social cohesion. Thus, Sen's framework allows us to re-emphasize the fact that simplistic appeals to consumers to forego material consumption will be unsuccessful. Such appeals are tantamount to demanding that we give up certain key capabilities and freedoms as social beings. Far from being irrational to resist such demands, it would be irrational not to, in such a society.

At the same time, and for all his emphasis on well-being, Sen offers little insight into how it is to be pursued. Thus, he recognizes that whole parts of societies may be trapped in 'hedonic treadmills': while consuming more and more in order to achieve higher well-being this very activity may endanger other dimensions of well-being like living in harmony with nature. And yet he does not offer any insight into how this situation might be corrected. While he asserts that the 'central feature of well-being is to achieve valuable functionings', he provides little guidance in interpreting what 'valuable' means in this context (Dodds 1997). The capabilities approach is merely a normative tool, which can help to frame discussions about lifestyle choices, but it does not allow us to derive goals and criteria directly.

Thus, the capabilities approach also appears to suffer from one of the other criticisms of needs theory, namely that it places considerable emphasis on individual functioning, but fails to unravel for us the 'social logic' of consumption choices, and provides few clues how we might proceed in escaping from hedonic treadmills and creating sustainable societies.

5.7   BEYOND INSATIABILITY – TOWARDS AN ECO-SOCIAL THEORY OF WELL-BEING?

So where exactly does the needs-theoretic approach stand in the face of the criticisms outlined above? How much credit should be given to the charges levelled against it? Is the concept of needs still in any sense useful in attempting to prosecute the project of sustainable development? And if it is not, should the Brundtland definition of sustainability be abandoned as unworkable?

There is, of course, a sense in which the debate about needs may turn out to be just too entrenched, too convoluted, and too laden with political ideology to be amenable at this late stage to useful elucidation. And yet, there is surely also a sense in which the needs-theoretic critique of consumer culture has something useful to say both about the nature of human motivations and about our cultural attempts to improve well-being. In particular, the idea that humans experience some kinds of underlying motivations or drives that are psychological or social in character, and that these kinds of motivations are not always best served by material consumption really does appear to expose a line of fault in conventional development. It also appears to offer something very attractive in terms of negotiating sustainable well-being, namely the possibility that we could significantly reduce material impact without compromising our well-being.

At the same time, critics of needs theory are surely right to point to the key symbolic role of material goods and to the complexity of the social logic within which these symbolic roles are negotiated. We cannot simply dismiss as pathological the importance attributed by consumers to material artefacts. Consumer goods must, in some sense, be regarded not only as functional artefacts, but also as symbolic resources in the fulfilment of vital social and psychological functionings. As such, any attempt to persuade consumers to give them up, without offering alternative resources for the fulfilment of such functionings, could rightly be regarded as naive.

But would it be possible to provide alternative resources? Could we drive a wedge between the requirement for symbolic resources and the demand for material goods? Could we envisage a theory of well-being that accepted the limitations of material resources (both ecologically and psychologically) and offered some other way to facilitate social and psychological functioning? Could such a theory incorporate the dynamic of desire as well as that of needs satisfaction or functioning? Could it offer other forms of symbolic resources to substitute for the use of material artefacts? These questions lie beyond the scope of this chapter but are clearly critical to any attempt to devise an eco-social theory of well-being that might deliver us sustainable development.

NOTES

1. According to the Brundtland Commission, sustainable development is 'development which meets the needs of the present without compromising the ability of future generations to meet their own needs'.
2. This silence reflects a quite deliberate and sometimes explicit agenda – whose roots extend downwards to the ethics of utilitarianism (Russell 2000) and whose branches extend outwards to the politics of neo-liberalism (Berry 1999) – to defend the sovereignty of individual preference over either the interventions of the state or the moral edicts of the church.
3. We should perhaps mention here the attempt by Lancaster (1966) to develop a theory of consumer choice that unravels the simple commodity value of economic goods in terms of the underlying properties or attributes of those goods. Even Lancaster, however, shies away from relating these attributes to specific functionings or motivations on the part of the consumer.
4. A seminal paper by Weitzmann (1976) established a formal equivalence between a non-declining national income and the continued maintenance of (economic) well-being over time.
5. As we note in the later discussion, this second usage of the word 'need' is often substituted by the term 'satisfier' in modern needs theories.

6. A classic example of a 'violator' might be the case of nuclear armaments intended to provide for the protection need.
7. A cornucopious and fat-laden diet may suggest satisfying one's need for subsistence, but endangers this need in the long run due to health problems.
8. An example might be breast-feeding, which simultaneously satisfies the infant's need for subsistence, protection, affection as well as some needs of the mother for participation, affection and so on.
9. A similar point relating to the duality and ambivalences between different kinds of needs is raised by Røpke (1999)
10. This point has also been made in the context of a slightly different conceptual framework for well-being developed by Amartya Sen and his collaborators, to which we return in a later section.
11. This distinction has also been articulated in terms of a distinction between hedonic and eudaemonic well-being (Deci and Ryan 1985).
12. See Kasser (2002) for an overview of some of this literature and an exposition of the needs-theoretic framework that underlies it.
13. This is in some sense an odd perspective on the well-being debate, particularly when set against Fromm's earlier distinction between hedonic well-being – as employed within the conventional economic framework – and eudaemonic well-being as an alternative framework. Moreover, there are places in Campbell's writing where he seems to backtrack on his antipathy for needs, arguing that the pursuit of hedonistic desires may in itself be the result of a 'psychological need' (Campbell 2003). This position is clearly closer to the modern needs theoretic conception than Campbell's earlier writing suggests.
14. Though Campbell (1998) casts Maslow's higher needs (such as self-actualization) as 'wants' in another guise and chastises the hierarchy as an attempt to cut off these higher wants from the lower needs, there is no evidence at all that this reflects Maslow's intention even in the earlier work, and his later work (Maslow 1968) certainly runs directly counter to this intent.

REFERENCES

Allen, William (1982), *Midnight Economist: Broadcast Essays III*, Los Angeles: International Institute for Economic Research.

Anderton, Alain (2000), *Economics* (Third Edition), Ormskirk, UK: Causeway Press.

Argyle, Michael (1987), *The Psychology of Happiness*, London: Methuen.

Barthes, Roland (1973), *Mythologies*, London: Paladin.

Baudrillard, Jean (1968), 'The system of objects', extracted (1988) in *Selected Writings*, Cambridge: Polity Press.

Baudrillard, Jean (1970), *The Consumer Society – Myths and Structures* (reprinted 1998), London: Sage Publications.

Bauman, Zygmunt (1998), *Work, Consumerism and the New Poor*, Buckingham: Open University Press.

Begg, David, Stanley Fischer and Rudiger Dornbusch (2003), *Economics* (Seventh Edition), Maidenhead: McGraw-Hill.

Belk, R. (1988), 'Possessions and the extended self', *Journal of Consumer Research*, **15**, 139–68.

Belk, R., G. Ger and S. Askegaard (2003), 'The fire of desire: A multi-sited inquiry into consumer passion', *Journal of Consumer Research*, **30**, 326–51.

Berry, C. J. (1999), 'Needs and wants', in *The Elgar Companion to Consumer Behaviour and Economic Psychology*, Cheltenham, UK and Northampton, MA, US: Edward Elgar, pp. 401–5.

Campbell, Colin (1987), *The Romantic Ethic and the Spirit of Modern Consumerism*, Oxford: Basil Blackwell.

Campbell, C. (1998), 'Consumption and the rhetorics of need and want', *Journal of Design History*, **11** (3), 235–46.

Campbell, Colin (2003), 'I shop therefore I know that I am: The metaphysical basis of modern consumerism', in Karin Ekstrom and Helen Brembeck (eds), *Elusive Consumption: Tracking New Research Perspectives*, Oxford: Berg.

Carney, J. and J. Dickerson (2001), 'A work in progress', *Time*, 22 October.

Csikszentmihalyi, Mihaly and Eugene Rochberg-Halton (1981), *The Meaning of Things – Domestic Symbols and the Self*, Cambridge, UK and New York: Cambridge University Press.

Deci, Edward L. and Richard Ryan (1985), *Intrinsic Motivation and Self Determination in Human Behaviour*, New York: Plenum Press.

Dichter, Ernest (1964), *The Handbook of Consumer Motivations: The Psychology of Consumption*, New York: McGraw Hill.

Dittmar, Helga (1992), *The Social Psychology of Material Possessions – to Have is to Be*, New York: St Martin's Press.

Dodds, S. (1997), 'Towards a "science of sustainability": Improving the way ecological economics understands human well-being', *Ecological Economics*, **23**, 95–111.

Donovan, Nic, David Halpern and Richard Sargeant (2002), *Life Satisfaction: The State of Knowledge and Implications for Government*, London: Cabinet Office Strategy Unit.

Douglas, Mary (1976), 'Relative poverty, relative communication', in A. Halsey (ed.) *Traditions of Social Policy*, Oxford: Basil Blackwell, pp. 197–215.

Douglas, Mary and Baron Isherwood (1979), *The World of Goods – Towards an Anthropology of Consumption*, reprinted (1996), London and New York: Routledge.

Douglas, Mary, Des Gasper, Steven Ney and Michael Thompson (1998), 'Human needs and wants', in Steve Rayner and Ed Malone (eds), *Human Choice and Climate Change*, Volume 1, Chapter 3, Washington DC: Battelle Press.

Douthwaite, Richard (1992), *The Growth Illusion: How Economic Growth has Enriched the Few, Impoverished the Many and Endangered the Planet*, Bideford, Devon: Green Books.

Doyal, Len and Ian Gough (1991), *A Theory of Human Needs*, London: Macmillan.

Elliott, R. and K. Wattanasuwan (1998), 'Brands as resources for the symbolic construction of identity', *International Journal of Advertising*, **17** (2), 131–45.

Fine, Ben and Ellen Leopold (1993), *The World of Consumption*, London and New York: Routledge.

Frey, B. and A. Stutzer (2000), 'Happiness, economy and institutions', *The Economic Journal*, 110, 918–38.

Frijda, N. and B. Mesquita (1992), 'Emoties, natuur of cultuur' ('Emotions, nature or culture'), *Nederlands Tijdschrift voor de Psychologie en Haar Grensgebieden*, **47** (1), 3–14. (in Dutch).

Fromm, Erich (1976), *To Have or to Be?*, London: Jonathan Cape.

Galtung, Johann (1980), 'The basic needs approach', in Katrin Lederer (ed.) *Human Needs – A Contribution to the Current Debate*, Cambridge, MA: Oelgeschlager, Gunn and Hain, pp. 55–125.

Galtung, Johann (1990), 'International development in human perspective', in J. Burton (ed.) *Conflict: Human Needs Theory*, New York: St Martin's Press.

Gasper, Des (1996), 'Needs and basic needs. A clarification of meanings, levels and different streams of work', Working Paper Series No. 210, The Hague, The Netherlands: Institute of Social Studies.

Georgescu-Roegen, Nicholas (1973), 'Utility and value in economic thought', in P. Wiener (ed.) *Dictionary of the History of Ideas*, Vol 4, Charles Scribner & Sons, New York, p. 451.

Haines, William (1985), 'The hierarchy of needs in classical theory', Paper presented at the Eastern Economic Association Meeting, New York, March 1985.

Herber, Lewis (1963), *Our Synthetic Environment*, London: Jonathan Cape.

Heyne, Paul (1983), *The Economic Way of Thinking*, Chicago: Science Research Associates.

Hirsch, Fred (1977), *Social Limits to Growth*, Revised Edition (1995), London and New York: Routledge.

Hirschman, Elizabeth and Martin Holbrook (eds) (1980), *Symbolic Consumer Behaviour*, Proceedings of the Conference on Consumer Aesthetics and Symbolic Consumption, New York: Association for Consumer Research.

Illich, Ivan (1977), *Towards a History of Needs*, New York: Pantheon Books.

Jackson, T. and N. Marks (1999), 'Consumption, sustainable welfare and human needs – with reference to UK expenditure patterns 1954–1994', *Ecological Economics*, **28** (3), 421–42.

Kassarjian, Harold and Thomas Robertson (1968), *Perspectives in Consumer Behaviour*, Abingdon: Scott, Foresman.

Kasser, Tim (2002), *The High Price of Materialism*, Cambridge, MA: MIT Press.

Keynes, John Maynard (1931), 'Economic possibilities for our grandchildren', in John Maynard Keynes (ed.), *Essays in Persuasion*, London: Macmillan, pp. 321–32.

Lancaster, K. (1966), 'A new approach to consumer theory', *Journal of Political Economy*, **174**, 132–57.

Lane, Robert (2000), *The Loss of Happiness in Market Economies*, New Haven and London: Yale University Press.

Lebergott, Stanley (1993), *Pursuing Happiness – American Consumers in the Twentieth Century*, Princeton: Princeton University Press.

Levenstein, Harvey (1988), *Revolution at the Table: The Transformation of the American Diet*, Oxford: Oxford University Press.

Lutz, Mark and Kenneth Lux (1988), *Humanistic Economics – the New Challenge*, New York: Bootstrap Press.

Mallmann, Carlos (1980), 'Society, needs and rights', in Katrin Lederer (ed.), *Human Needs – A Contribution to the Current Debate*, Cambridge, MA: Oelgeschlager, Gunn and Hain, pp. 37–54.

Marcuse, H. (1964), *One Dimensional Man*, London: Routledge, Kegan and Paul.

Marshall, Alfred (1961), *Principles of Economics* (Ninth Edition), London: Macmillan.

Maslow, Abraham (1954), *Motivation and Personality*, New York: Harper & Row.

Maslow, Abraham (1968), *Towards a Psychology of Being*, New York: van Nostrand Reinhold.

Max-Neef, Manfred (1991), *Human-Scale Development – Conception, Application and Further Reflection*, London: Apex Press.

Max-Neef, Manfred (1992), 'Development and human needs', in Paul Ekins and Manfred Max-Neef (eds), *Real-life Economics: Understanding Wealth Creation*, London and New York: Routledge, pp. 197–213.

McConnell, Campbell (1981), *Economics*, Eighth Edition, New York: McGraw Hill.

McCracken, Grant (1997), *Plenitude*, Book 1, *Culture by Commotion Trilogy*, Toronto: Periph Fluide.

McDougall, William (1928), 'Emotion and feeling distinguished', in Martin L. Reymert (ed.), *Feelings and Emotions*, Worcester, MA: Clark University Press.

Miller, Daniel (ed.), (1995), *Acknowledging Consumption – A Review of New Studies*, London and New York: Routledge.

Morris, Charles (1946), *Signs, Language and Behaviour*, New York: George Braziller.

Myers, D. and E. Diener (1996), 'The pursuit of happiness', *Scientific American*, No. 274, 54–6.

Nussbaum, Martha (1998), 'The good as discipline, the good as freedom', in David A. Crocker and Toby Linden (eds), *Ethics of Consumption*, New York: Rowman and Littlefield, pp. 312–41.

Nussbaum, M. (2003), 'Capabilities as fundamental entitlements: Sen and social justice', *Feminist Economics*, **9** (2–3), 33–59.

Oswald, A. (1997), 'Happiness and economic performance', *Economic Journal*, **107**, 1815–31.

Robeyns, I. (2003), 'Sen's capability approach and gender inequality: Selecting relevant capabilities', *Feminist Economics*, **9** (2–3), 61–92.

Røpke, Inge (1999), 'Some themes in the discussion of quality of life', in Jorg Köhn, John Gowdy, Fritz Hinterberger, Jan van der Straaten (eds), *Sustainability in Question*, Cheltenham, UK and Northampton, MA, US: Edward Elgar, pp. 247–66.

Rousseau, Jean-Jacques (1913 [1762]), *The Social Contract and Discourses*, London: Dent, Everyman.

Russell, Bertrand (2000 [1975]), *A History of Western Philosophical Thought*, Harmondsworth: Penguin.

Sahlins, Marshall (1976), *Culture and Practical Reason*, Chicago: University of Chicago Press.

Samuelson, P. (1938), 'A note on the pure theory of consumer behaviour', *Economica*, **5**, 61–71.

Schachter, Stanley (1964), 'The interaction of cognitive and physiological determinants of emotional state', in Leonard Berkowitz (ed.), *Advances in Experimental Social Psychology*, Vol. 1, New York: Academic Press, pp. 49–79.

Schor, Juliet (1992), *The Overworked American – The Unexpected Decline of Leisure*, New York, BasicBooks.

Scitovsky, Tibor (1976), *The Joyless Economy*, Oxford: Oxford University Press.

Sen, A. (1984), 'The living standard', *Oxford Economic Papers*, **36** (supplement), 74–90.

Sen, Amartya (1985), *Commodities and Capabilities*, Amsterdam: Elsevier.

Sen, Amartya (1992), *Inequality Reexamined*, New York and Cambridge, MA: Russell Sage and Harvard University Press.

Sen, Amartya (1998), 'The living standard', in David Crocker and Toby Linden (eds), *The Ethics of Consumption*, New York: Rowman and Littlefield, pp. 287–311.

Simonov, Pavel Vasilyevich (1970), 'The information theory of emotion', in M. B. Arnold (ed.), *Feelings and Emotions: The Loyola Symposium*, New York, London: Academic Press.

Smith, Adam (1776), *An Inquiry into the Nature and Causes of the Wealth of Nations*, reprinted in R. Campbell and Andrew S. Skinner (eds) (1976), Oxford University Press, Oxford.

Springborg, Patricia (1981), *The Problem of Human Needs and the Critique of Civilisation*, London: George Allen and Unwin.

Stagl, S. and S. O'Hara (2001), 'Preferences, needs and sustainability', *International Journal of Sustainable Development*, **4** (1), 4–21.

Veblen, Thorstein (1898), *The Theory of the Leisure Class*, reprinted 1998, Great Minds Series, London: Prometheus Books.

Veenhoven, Ruut (2003), World Database of Happiness, Catalogue of Happiness Queries, www.eur.nl/fsw/research/happiness.

WCED (1987), *Our Common Future*, The Brundtland Report of the World Commission on Environment and Development, Oxford University Press, Oxford.

Weitzman, M. (1976), 'On the welfare significance of the national product in a dynamic economy', *Quarterly Journal of Economics*, **90**, 156–62.

Worcester, R. (1998), 'More than money', in I. Christie and L. Nash (eds), *The Good Life*, London: Demos.

6. Changing human behaviour and lifestyle: A challenge for sustainable consumption?

Elizabeth Shove

Over the last decade or so, there has been a wealth of social and natural scientific debate about the environmental consequences of contemporary consumption and there is, by now, something of a consensus. It is clear that lifestyles, especially in the West, will have to change if there is to be any chance of averting the long-term consequences of resource depletion, global warming, the loss of biodiversity, the production of waste or the pollution and destruction of valued 'natural' environments. To put Brundtland's famous definition[1] another way round, future generations will encounter a much degraded world if present trends continue. Apparent agreement on this point disguises important theoretical divisions regarding the conceptualisation of behaviour, lifestyle and consumption. Are 'lifestyles' in some sense 'chosen' or are they better seen as 'ways of life', that is, as part of the social fabric (Harrison and Davies 1998)? What is the relation between 'behaviour' – what people do – and what they think? Is consumption an expression of taste, or a moment in a complex system of social, cultural and material reproduction (Shove and Warde 2002)? The task of sifting through these differences is of more than academic interest. As I suggest below, policies designed to promote sustainable consumption are generally founded upon an extraordinarily narrow understanding of human behaviour. It is not too difficult to explain why this might be so, after all, some theoretical positions are much more amenable to policy-making (as it is presently configured) than others. The danger, however, is that this understandable confluence of theory and practice obscures, sometimes even denies, important forms of social and environmental change. In this chapter I want to give a sense of these limitations and of the kinds of social-theoretical development still required if environmental policy is to make an effective and durable contribution to the challenge of establishing and institutionalising more sustainable ways of life.

The chapter* is organised in four sections. The first outlines and characterises three distinctive approaches to consumption as an environmental issue. The second reviews and compares these accounts and the ideas that lie behind them. Section three introduces a new challenge. Meanings of comfort, like expectations of mobility or of food provisioning, have changed dramatically in recent years. As a result, people expect to wear much the same sorts of clothing indoors all year round: they do not expect to sweat nor do they expect to wear bulky sweaters. This inconspicuous trend constitutes a really significant environmental problem. Maintaining conditions that we now count as comfortable, all over the world, requires the use of unsustainably resource-intensive systems of heating and cooling *and* the development of new social conventions and habits. That the production of household air-conditioners in China increased from 220 000 in 1990 to 18 226 700 in 2000 and has been rising by more than 20 per cent per annum (Friedl 2002) is just one indication of the scale and rate of change in this sector. How can such developments be analysed in terms of 'consumption'? I use this case to reflect on the qualities and limits of contemporary approaches for analysing and maybe modifying patterns of consumption that are widespread yet routinely invisible, that are both social and technical, and that seem to have an unstoppable logic of their own. I argue that it is necessary to broaden the reach and scope both of social-environmental theory and of policy if we are to comprehend global transitions of this kind. I finish by reflecting on the types of enquiry and forms of intervention that might be inspired as a result.

6.1 CONCEPTUALISING (ENVIRONMENTALLY SIGNIFICANT) CONSUMPTION, CHOICE AND CHANGE

There are many ways in which one might classify the literature on environmental consumption. The strategy I have chosen distinguishes between positions that view consumers as (1) decision-makers exercising environmental choice, (2) as citizens influencing the range of environmental options on offer, or (3) as practitioners involved in reproducing variously resource-intensive ways of life. These are not watertight categories nor are they all mutually exclusive. Each is nonetheless sustained by supporting strands of social, psychological, political and economic theory. The following sub-sections provide a brief sketch of these three positions and of the research and policy agendas associated with them.

6.1.1   Consumers as Decision-makers: Exercising Environmental Choice

According to the authors of a UK government report entitled *Sustainable Development: Opportunities for Change* 'consumers can have a huge impact on sustainable development through their influence as purchasers. But they need help to make choices' (DETR 1998, p. 28) Observations of this kind have prompted research into the economic and psychological determinants of consumer decision-making in order to figure out how to persuade people 'to change their behaviour' (Ekins 2003). Put more broadly, the aim of a current UK Economic and Social Research Council funded programme on 'Environment and Human Behaviour' is to discover why 'people behave as they do towards the natural environment' and to determine the 'factors that drive or influence human behaviour' (Ekins 2003).

Such formulations of 'the problem' have three related features in common. First, they suppose individual behaviour to be responsive, hence the search for social, economic or psychological stimuli with which to trigger desired outcomes. Second, they imply a method of enquiry that revolves around the isolation and analysis of relevant 'factors'. Finally, they assume that human behaviour can be modified by restructuring the flow of information and incentives, or through education (Ekins 2003). By definition, approaches of this kind pay scant attention to the formulation of options from which consumers 'choose', they do not recognize consumption to be a shared, cultural or collective enterprise, and they take little account of the multiple situations and contexts in which it takes place.

People are primarily addressed as autonomous 'shoppers' whose choices, in the aggregate, determine the fate and future of the planet. Brown and Cameron justify a 'focus primarily on individual behavior because programs and policies aimed at reducing consumption ultimately must alter the consumption decisions made by individuals' (Brown and Cameron 2000, p. 28). This makes some sense. It is, after all, true that much environmental damage could be avoided if we all made 'green' our brand of choice: if we all opted for the most efficient washing machine possible, for locally produced food or for public rather than private transport. In following this line of argument, commentators have been drawn into a maze of motivational psychology and economics in which consumers' actions are explained with reference to a cocktail of competing concepts like those of altruism, status-seeking, identity and rational calculation. While 'the consumer' is credited with considerable power (including that of obliterating or ensuring sustainability), such analyses usually preserve a place for what Packard referred to as the 'hidden persuaders' (Packard 1957). The notion that commercial organisations and advertisers have managed to convince people to consume more lends weight to the view that similar techniques might be used to turn evidently fickle desires in other directions. On the other hand, and as advocates of environmental education are quick to point out, deeper values may be at stake. Brown and Cameron, amongst others, argue that the extent to which promotional efforts succeed, and the degree to which people are willing to 'curb their consumption levels for the greater good of the community' (Brown and Cameron 2000, p. 31) depends upon the existence or otherwise of an underlying bedrock of environmental commitment.

The tacit assumption that consumers' decisions reflect their core beliefs has important consequences. One is to justify efforts to challenge the prevailing ethos of consumerism and the construction of 'false' needs. These take more and less radical forms. Reisch is, for example, of the view that necessary 'changes in deeply rooted values and lifestyles' will only occur when and if 'people become enlightened consumers who learn to identify those goods whose consumption adds little or nothing to welfare' (Reisch 2001, p. 369). The sub-plot here is that understandings of welfare and 'real' needs have become distorted and that the route to personal fulfilment is through less rather than more consumption. Other writers pin their hopes on a collective appreciation of the fact that we are all in the same boat (World Commission on Environment and Development 1987).

Although beliefs are expected to translate into action, they do not always do so. This apparently puzzling discrepancy has prompted further research into competing value systems and needs (Uusitalo 1990; Moisander 1995) and into the institutional, financial or informational 'barriers' that prevent people from being as 'green' as they say they want to be. While they may be swayed by other considerations, the ability to compare the 'true' environmental costs of different courses of action is, it seems, a necessary first step if consumers are to reduce the size of their ecological footprint (Wackernagel and Rees 1995). Following this logic, governments and other agencies have invested heavily in overcoming the barrier of 'popular ignorance' (Ekins 2003) and in providing consumers with the information (labels, advice, and so on) they need to act upon their environmental commitments. In the UK, for example, utilities have been involved in designing and seeking to quantify the effect of educational programmes, as part of the Energy Efficiency Standards of Performance (now called the Energy Efficiency Commitment) scheme. Powergen's Bright Sparks programme is typical. This scheme involved giving school children 'a free, low-energy lamp and a questionnaire on energy use to take home. Families were able to buy a second lamp at the reduced price of £3, with £1.50 of this going to the school.' According to Powergen's promotional material, 'The project increased energy awareness among children aged between seven and 11, saved energy and is reducing electricity bills by £3.1 million. Over 47,000 customers are benefiting' (Powergen 2003).

All this rests upon a pervasive model of individual choice and agency, the assumption being that consumers can reduce the weight of their personal environmental 'rucksack' if that is what they choose to do. Popular representations of environmental pioneers and voluntary downshifters confirm this impression of freedom (Center for a New American Dream 2003).[2]

To summarise and simplify, consumers are positioned as key 'switches' in the environmental system. Turned in one direction and the 'metabolism' of society is endangered, turned another way and it is potentially preserved (Noorman and Uiterkamp 1998). Efforts to isolate the determinants of consumer behaviour tend to rely upon economic theories of rational action. Similarly, lifestyles are believed to reflect personal preferences and commitments, whether to 'the environment', or to goals like those of well-being, identity and status. This kind of reasoning justifies strategies that inform consumers of the consequences of their actions and exhort them to behave differently. This might mean encouraging them to buy a low energy freezer or to spend their holidays at eco-friendly resorts. Sometimes the need for freezing or foreign holiday-making is itself called into question. Either way the individual (and his or her motivations) constitutes the primary unit of analysis, and persuasion – which might also include taxation or regulation – the dominant policy tool.

6.1.2 Consumers as Citizens: Influencing the Environmental Options on Offer

The approaches represented in this second section differ in that consumers figure as the instigators of, not the obstacles to, environmental reform. Assuming that ecological concerns are in fact diffused through society, writers like Spaargaren and van Vliet search for examples of bottom-up 'environmental innovation initiated by the wish of the consumer' (Spaargaren and van Vliet 2000, p. 70). In this account, consumers figure as political actors, able to vote with more than their feet in support of collective projects like those of environmental reform. It is this that justifies reference to them as active 'citizens', not just shoppers.

The notion that motivated citizens will seek to reduce the resource intensity of production is an important, even necessary, part of ecological modernisation theory. Arguments of this sort are usually illustrated with reference to selective case studies of grassroots greening. Taking such an approach, Georg (1999) describes three 'citizen initiatives for "social management of environmental change"'. These cases are used to show how small groups of citizens attempt to 'develop technologies and create social structures that can minimize the environmental degradation associated with the Western way of life' (Georg 1999, p. 456). In the context of this discussion, the key point is that consumers are involved in developing alternative (lower impact) modes of provision and in reproducing new routines associated with them. They have a hand in shaping options as well as exercising choice between them and as van Vliet puts it, 'they participate in the organisation of production–consumption cycles' (van Vliet 2002, p. 53). Developing these ideas, van Vliet illustrates different modes of involvement, distinguishing, for example, between situations in which consumers opt for 'green' electricity tariffs or in which they are themselves providers – owning and using photovoltaic systems and maybe selling 'green' power back to the grid.

A further feature of these examples, and of Spaargaren's earlier work on the ecological modernisation of consumption, is the presumption that people actively and reflexively monitor the environmental profiles of different sectors of their life (Spaargaren 1997). In the examples Georg discusses, eco-villagers soon learn that 'environmentally informed behaviour is expected of them' (Georg 1999, p. 462), and they soon learn what that involves. In the longer run, environmental criteria are expected to seep into the fabric of everyday life such that actors, 'at the level of practical consciousness, the level of the automatic pilot, – "stay in touch" with certain rules of the game, i.e. with a set of criteria for ecologically rational behaviour' (Spaargaren 1997, p. 151).

Proponents of ecological modernisation theory argue that capitalist society can be restructured around ecological goals and that with new technologies and forms of organisation in place, goods and services can be delivered sustainably. This is a particularly attractive message in that there is no hint of restraint, no 'cutting back', and no questioning of contemporary conventions and ways of life. Instead, the challenge is to 'internalise' environmental considerations and position 'ecological rationality as a key variable in social decision-making' (Hajer 1996, p. 252).

This second cluster of ideas shares a number of distinctive features. Most obviously, there is more to consumption than shopping, hence Spaargaren's recommendation that policy ought 'not limit itself to consumer behaviour "on the market" but should also be directed at intermediary organizations and systems which can have a direct influence on changes in household consumption patterns' (1997, p. 193). Put another way, consumers are implicated in what is produced and how. Second, it seems that the 'rules of the game', including the rules of consumption, are formulated and reproduced within social groups. Unlike the first position, this approach acknowledges the cultural and historical construction of choice and preference. On the other hand, both assume that values drive behaviour and that it is necessary to make the environmental consequences of different courses of action visible and explicit. In both there is an implicit emphasis on resources rather than services, the difference being that this second approach expects environmental innovation to be a 'bottom-up' process, perhaps involving the development of new (often more localised), systems of provision. For policy, the challenge is not one of 'top-down' persuasion but of helping consumers find ecologically rational ways of achieving the taken-for-granted goals of daily life.

6.1.3   Consumers as Practitioners: Reproducing More and Less Sustainable Ways of Life

The third family of ideas revolves around the proposition that patterns of consumption follow from the routine accomplishment of what people take to be 'normal' ways of life. As Røpke puts it, 'consumption is woven into everyday life' (1999, p. 403) and must be analysed as such. Those who concentrate on the specification and redefinition of 'normality', rather than on consumption per se, have different accounts of how practices are organised and of the relation between agency and structure. While Cogoy concludes that 'consumption has much to do with the way in which individuals organize their lives' (Cogoy 1999, p. 386), he also observes that 'The fact that most consumers consider spatial mobility or a holiday trip as important contributions to the enjoyment of their lives is not a law of nature, but a cultural phenomenon' (p. 387). In this analysis, people's routines and expectations reflect systems of social and cultural order. Taking a stronger line, Reisch argues that 'the non-stop society *forces* consumers to adopt lifestyles which are unsustainable' (Reisch 2001, p. 374 – my emphasis).

The idea that people are obliged to consume in order to be part of society raises a host of further questions about the relation between consumption and the production and reproduction of social difference, and about how the symbolic significance of specific forms of consumption evolves (Bourdieu 1984; Douglas and Isherwood 1996). These dynamics are important in explaining how concepts of well-being and the 'good life' take the form they do, how are they institutionalised, and with what environmental consequence. They are also important in defining what Redclift refers to as the 'underlying social commitments which drive our consumption, and contribute to waste' (1996, p. 146).

As Redclift observes, normal and acceptable standards, practices and ways of life are rarely articulated or questioned either in social environmental theory or in policy. As a result, contemporary formulations are 'afforded value by being naturalized. Their value is not interrogated' (p. 146). By bringing these issues back into the limelight, he clears the way for a much more challenging interpretation of what environmental policy could and should involve. Such a move foregrounds politically contentious questions about the conventions and assumptions around which society is organised. Redclift uses the example of automobility to illustrate his point: 'the right to individual motorized mobility is', he writes, 'enshrined in the way we regard the motor car. Challenging this commitment may mean redefining the relationship between where we live and work. It will require an altogether more radical way of "managing" the environment' (p. 140). Echoing such an approach, Cogoy also concludes that 'environmental policies are unlikely to be successful if they do not address the question of power distribution and control over time in contemporary society' (1999, p. 395).

Quite what it would mean to 'address the question of power distribution' is itself open to debate. Yet the general conclusion holds: environmental policies that do not *challenge* the status quo – in terms of divisions of labour, resources and time, or social and cultural representations of the good life – have the perverse effect of legitimising ultimately unsustainable patterns of consumption. This criticism can be levelled at the first two positions described above, both of which deal with matters of efficiency (focusing, for instance, on the ecological modernisation of systems of provision, on environmental management and technological innovation) whilst sidestepping debate about the ways of life that are thereby reproduced.

Though sometimes useful, the distinction between efficiency (achieving the same standards of service with fewer resources) and sufficiency (meaning different, less demanding concepts of service) introduces further questions about the relation between technology, consumption and demand. The idea that new technologies might increase resource efficiencies to such an extent that present patterns of consumption become sustainable requires a conceptual separation between means and ends in a way that is itself problematic.

Turning to a different body of literature, there is some support for the view that technological change is important not (only) because of the resource efficiencies that it might promise, but because tools and infrastructures shape (whilst also being shaped by) taken for granted conventions, practices and ways of life (Shove et al. 1998). Rip and Kemp introduce the notion of a 'regime' to describe how 'technical groups and their social environments create stabilized interdependencies that shape further action (1998, p. 338). As they define it, regime change involves the reconfiguration of a 'seamless web' of social, organisational and technological elements. There are two observations to draw from this. First, and as Rip and Kemp explain, 'the idea of a seamless web … implies that the evolution of technology and the evolution of society cannot be separated, and should be thought of in terms of coevolution' (p. 337). In other words, technological 'fixes' to environmental problems are themselves infused with concepts of sufficient and normal practice. Second, and more important, these ideas suggest that patterns of sustainable consumption require and depend upon the development of correspondingly sustainable socio-technical regimes.

Lessons and insights derived from historical studies of the socio-technical co-evolution of electric power (Hughes 1983), telecommunications (Fischer 1992) or automobility are clearly relevant for those wanting to engender comparably wide ranging transitions toward sustainability. Geels (2002), Elzen et al. (2002) and others have taken up the challenge of showing how 'transition theory' might be applied and of figuring out what policy-makers might do to foster the development of socio-technical regimes that have less environmentally damaging consequences than those of today.

In practical terms, this means identifying critical moments or turning points at which socio-technical trajectories might be nudged, if not 'steered' in a different direction. It means looking for opportunities to modulate pathways of transition through considered forms of strategic intervention and it means facilitating interaction between the many actors involved in configuring sectors, services and institutions. Strategies of this kind need not announce themselves as explicitly 'environmental' nor is there any need for consumers and practitioners to 'see' the environment in what they do (Shove 1997). After all, it is not a matter of persuading people to change their behaviour, one by one, but of configuring socio-technical systems such that the environmental burden of 'normal' practice is less.

The approaches gathered together in this third bundle do not make easy bedfellows yet they are alike in emphasising the socio-technical, political and historical structuring of everyday life, with all that entails for patterns of consumption.

6.2   THE THREE POSITIONS COMPARED

Table 6.1 summarizes the positions described above with reference to four 'defining' characteristics. These have to do with (1) the representation of consumers and consumption, (2) the conditions under which more sustainable forms of consumption are expected to arise, (3) the types of policy-making that seem to be required, and (4) the terms in which advances toward sustainability might be recognised.

This table helps identify points of similarity and contrast. As it makes clear, the first two positions suppose that lifestyles can be 'changed' by force of political, moral and environmental commitment, or through economic and other forms of persuasion. By contrast, the third understands changing conventions of everyday life, lifestyles if you will, to be the result of collective, contingent and emergent processes of socio-technical co-evolution. Although the first two positions have some features in common

Table 6.1 Three positions compared

	Representation of consumers and consumption	Conditions of sustainable consumption	Relevant forms of policy intervention	Appropriate measures of sustainable consumption
(1) Consumers as decision-makers	Consumers are viewed as autonomous decision-makers motivated by 'rational' economic or psychological (symbolic or positional) 'factors'	Consumers decide to make 'green' their brand of choice They do so because of new forms of ecological-economic valuation, and/or new interpretations of symbolic significance	Develop and promote more resource-efficient products and technologies Persuade consumers to adopt them by means of information, advice and price	Ecological footprints and other measures of per-capita consumption
(2) Consumers as citizens	Recognize that consumers' choices are structured and that as citizens they have a hand in determining options on offer	Ecologically committed consumers are actively involved in shaping the options on offer and in formulating new or modified institutions and modes of provision	Develop and promote more efficient products and technologies Respond to consumer pressure to develop new institutional forms through which to fulfil existing 'needs'	Ecological footprints and other measures of per-capita consumption together with an assessment of the ecological modernisation of infrastructures, systems and modes of provision
(3) Consumers as practitioners	Consumption is viewed as consequence of practice and analysed as such	The reconfiguration of normal practice and the social, symbolic and technical co-evolution of taken-for-granted routines, habits, and expectations of everyday life	Influencing understand-ings of normal practice, perhaps by 'steering' socio-technical systems in transition, promoting diversity or trying to foster socio-technical con-figurations that work (for the environment)	Assessment of the environmental costs of sustaining normal standards, conventions and expectations and associated (sociotechnical) systems of provision

they differ in the representation of consumer–provider relations, the latter supposing that these are complex, dynamic and themselves an important part of the story.

There are other differences of emphasis and orientation, but in terms of method, the table arguably represents a successive broadening of the frame of reference from (1) individual behaviour to (2) social institutions to (3) the socio-technical fabric of society itself. Some might claim that each 'position' consequently affords a different view of reality, each providing a partial but complementary picture of what consumption is about and how it changes. Others would take a harder line. Advocates of the first position often argue that nothing can happen unless and until individuals decide to act in different ways. From this perspective, the second and third positions describe the backdrop of 'factors' against which autonomous individuals make real decisions that affect the world. By shifting the emphasis just a little, the background becomes the foreground, and the rule-sets and grammars of social convention take centre stage. In practice, such a move involves much more than a simple switch of focus. If we believe that 'the structural properties of social systems are both the medium and outcome of the practices they recursively organize' (Giddens 1984, p. 25), the first two interpretations are not just partial, they are quite simply misleading.

There is nothing to be gained by backing away from hard line conclusions of this sort, or from papering over fundamental differences of theory and approach. Especially not given that differences of orientation generate contrasting interpretations of relevant and appropriate forms of policy intervention. Such is the dominance of economics in policy-making, and such the need to turn truly complex issues into tractable problems (Liberatore 1994) that the positions sketched above do not get anything like equal treatment. The remainder of the chapter considers the practical and political implications of this imbalance. What are the consequences of relying on some but not other forms of social theory? Which issues come to the fore, which are obscured, and with what effect?

It is easy to see why national governments and international agencies routinely adopt the theoretical baggage of the first and sometimes the second paradigms. A recent OECD report entitled *Towards Sustainable Household Consumption?: Trends and Policies in OECD Countries* typifies this approach (OECD 2002). Building upon the results of previous workshops, and including a report on *Information and Consumer Decision-making for Sustainable Consumption* (OECD 2001), these documents review the effectiveness of different policy instruments in influencing consumer decision-making. Although this work acknowledges that it is important to shift the 'structure' of consumption, most of the policy suggestions have to do with modifying information and price signals and providing people with consistent messages about the sustainability of their consumption choices.

The sheer familiarity of this kind of analysis should not lure us into thinking that there is no more to be said. There are many reasons why this representation of consumption and behaviour should be challenged, two of which are particularly important for the present discussion. First, and as indicated above, efforts to persuade people to buy environmentally friendly goods and services may legitimise potentially unsustainable conventions and expectations. Second, by focusing so exclusively on the behaviour of individual consumers, policy-makers have no way of detecting, let alone influencing, longer-term transformations of technology, culture and practice. As a result, large reaches of social environmental change quite simply disappear from view.

In the next section I consider recent developments in the global indoor environment in order to illustrate this point and explore ways of conceptualising and modifying long-term swings in what people take to be normal and necessary patterns of consumption.

6.3   CONSUMING COMFORT – RECENT DEVELOP-MENTS IN THE INDOOR ENVIRONMENT

Although people have reported being comfortable at temperatures ranging from 6–31°C. (Goldsmith 1960; Nicol et al. 1999, p. 271), indoor climates are converging. For a number of reasons, some of which are discussed below, people have come to expect the same indoor conditions all year round and all over the globe. In environmental terms, the resources required to maintain these protected bubbles of around 22°C, whatever the weather outside, are considerable and vast amounts of energy are consumed to this end. There is no doubt about it: this is an arena in which energy consumption is escalating fast, and doing so as a consequence of rapid and radical redefinitions of what indoor environments should be like.

Looking back over the last century, comfort-related patterns of human behaviour and lifestyle have changed dramatically. In the UK, few people now wake to traces of frost on the inside of their windows in winter. Sales of hot-water bottles have dropped and the waistcoat has gone out of fashion. In Southern France and Spain, the long lunchtime break is in decline and in April 1999 the Mexican government officially announced the end of the siesta for its 1.6 million employees (Moore 1999). Meanwhile, people who live in air-conditioned homes keep the windows shut in the summer. They keep cool in private, staying inside rather than spending time outdoors on verandas or porches. In short, more exacting concepts of comfort have reconfigured our relation to the 'natural' world, transformed the ways in which we heat and cool our homes and influenced where and with whom we spend our time (Shove 2003).

All the same it is strange to talk about changing conventions of comfort. As defined by physiologists and building scientists, comfort has to do with the physical relationship between a person and his or her environment, comfortable 'neutrality' being that state in which the heat generated by the human body is equal to the heat transferred away. Such a definition naturalises and standardises the 'need' for comfort in a way that it is difficult to argue with. Surely architects and engineers should do their best to meet the thermal-physiological needs of those who live and work in the structures they design. In addition, and because comfort is specified in the universalising terms of human biology, people's needs are (on average) the same, whatever their social status or cultural background. From this point of view, the global convergence of indoor climates is normal, natural and something to be expected. Whilst there is much that might be done to improve the resource efficiency with which comfortable conditions are achieved and maintained, the specification of comfort is not, in itself, in question: not for policy-makers and not for those seeking to produce a more sustainable built environment.

On the other hand, physiologically-based interpretations of comfort and the heat-balance models on which they depend are relatively recent inventions. As Humphreys observes, the management of comfort 'pre-dates by thousands of years the development of the theory of heat exchange' (Humphreys 1995, p. 5). I do not want to go into detail here, but it is arguably the case that contemporary concepts of comfort reflect the air-conditioning industry's interest in promoting a definition that establishes and justifies the 'need' for mechanical heating and cooling. Gail Cooper's historical study in *Air-Conditioning America* (1998) reveals some of the commercial advantages of isolating and quantifying the parameters of an optimal indoor environment. She writes as follows: 'When it was shown that no natural climate could consistently deliver perfect comfort conditions, air-conditioning broke free of its geographic limits. When no town could deliver an ideal climate, all towns became potential markets for air-conditioning' (Cooper 1998, p. 78). Taking this observation a stage further, Oseland and Humphreys (1993) conclude that there is nothing natural or normal about the convergence of indoor climates. The fact that buildings are now heated and cooled to provide the same conditions the world over tells us more about the effective 'marketing' of an idea than it does about the requirements of the human body. If we subscribe to the view that comfort is an essentially social construct, albeit one that is embedded in a socio-technical complex or 'regime' of regulation, engineering, material structure and habit, we see before us the successful globalisation of just one possible formulation. Since other interpretations are possible, it is reasonable and perhaps important to think about how more environmentally forgiving definitions might take root in the future.

Strategies to contain the environmental costs of 'comfort' vary depending upon whether comfort is taken to be a natural state of affairs or a provisional cultural achievement. As the next section shows, they also depend upon how changing patterns of behaviour and lifestyle are conceptualised and understood.

6.4   RECONSIDERING COMFORT AND CONSUMPTION

Whatever the dynamics involved, heating and cooling now accounts for around half the energy used in buildings. Air-conditioning is not one 'technology' and systems come in different forms. Taking these together, a major report on the industry (BSRIA 2002) concludes that the world market for air-conditioning is growing and changing dramatically, especially in East Asia and Southern Europe. To give an indication of the rate of change, sales of air-conditioners in the Chinese market rose by 41 per cent between 2000 and 2001 (Friedl 2002). And in the UK, one commentator, writing for *Building Services and Environmental Engineer*, is of the view that 'it would only take two or three hot summers to create sufficient momentum for it [the UK market] to reach a critical mass. The moveable market would soar, and a spill over into mini-splits would follow fast and, like air conditioning in cars, would be here to stay' (Giles 2003). On these grounds alone, the reproduction of 'comfort' is an increasingly resource-intensive activity. So what might each of the three 'positions' described above have to 'say' about the standardisation of the indoor climate and associated patterns of energy demand? It is useful to think this question through in order to show how well and how badly contemporary theories fare in analysing and addressing trends in behaviour and lifestyle that are of far-reaching environmental significance.

6.4.1   Promoting Efficiency

To the extent that governments deal with questions of comfort at all, they do so in terms of energy consumption and technical efficiency. In the UK, the aim has been to improve the technical performance of heating and cooling systems and to promote passive solar design. Consistent with this approach, clients and consumers are appealed to as decision-makers responsible for the selection of more or less efficient technologies. Challenging 'need' (for example, the 'need' for air-conditioning in the UK) is for the most part beyond the scope of policy-making as conventionally conceived. It is, in any event, a dangerous path to follow given the range of commercial interests at stake and the politically unpalatable consequences of advocating standards that fall short of 'comfort' as it is currently defined. The storm of outrage that followed Edwina Currie's[3] suggestion that those too poor to heat their homes to 'current' standards should wear more woolly clothing demonstrated the risks involved. Subsequent more cautious efforts to persuade householders to turn the heating down for the sake of the global environment have not been strikingly successful. In fact, average temperatures in British homes have been rising steadily over the last 30 years, from around 17 to 21°C.

Although the promotion of efficiency is by far the most common policy response, it is one that internalises and takes for granted those features of indoor climate change that are the most problematic. Caught up in the flow – indeed arguably contributing to it – such efforts do nothing to address the redefinition of need or to challenge the institutionalisation of lifestyles that suppose and rely upon a standardised indoor climate.

In this respect, the focus on individual behaviour and technology is itself restricting. Although the transformation of societal routine can be analysed as a consequence of multiple individual 'choices' – the decision to invest in air-conditioning, the decision to develop some but not other technologies, the decision to design new homes differently *because* they are air-conditioned, and so forth – it is important to recognise that practices intersect. Whether companies that occupy air-conditioned offices abandon the siesta or not depends, above all, on the working hours of those with whom they interact. To give a somewhat different example, it is increasingly difficult to buy a new car that does not come ready equipped with air-conditioning. Likewise, there is no way you can sit out on the veranda in the cool of the evening if your mechanically conditioned home has been built without one. In short, comfort-related lifestyles have evolved but not necessarily because of personal or even corporate 'choice'.

In concentrating on efficiency not service, and on moments but not contexts of decision-making, governments and international agencies find themselves tinkering with the tip of a metaphorical iceberg that is, unknown to them, moving fast and with a momentum of its own.

6.4.2 Restructuring Supply

What might proponents of ecological modernisation theory have to say about global indoor climate change and the patterns of consumption associated with it? As above, questions of 'need' are naturalised but by taking a rather broader look at the systems of provision involved a much wider cast of actors and interests come into view. Working back from design and engineering, requisite levels of heating and cooling might be achieved with the help of passive or active solar systems, renewable energy and/or better, more precise controls. Walt Patterson (2003) argues that the built environment should be analysed as part of the supply infrastructure since its relative efficiency affects the functioning and the resource intensity of the whole. Similarly, new opportunities for intervention and influence emerge when analysts look beyond the end consumer and examine the many ways in which 'demand' is constructed and configured across the entire supply chain of resource production and consumption (van Vliet 2002; Chappells 2003). Although initiatives inspired by this kind of thinking dig deeper into the systems through which 'comfort' is provided, they too fail to engage with transnational currents of social and cultural change. In short, ecologically modernising consumers are expected to influence the way in which services are provided, but not the specification of 'need'. While the first two strategies take the definition of comfort for granted, the third acknowledges the socio-technical structuring of demand.

6.4.3 Reconfiguring Demand

There are many reasons why conventions of comfort and associated practices change within and between societies. But what, if anything, might be done to halt the diffusion of just one tightly specified formulation? At a stroke, this question increases the scope of enquiry and of possible policy intervention. It is true that there are few precedents to follow but there is no reason why environmental policy should not seek to influence 'long term sociotechnical transformations including cultural aspects such as the aspiration to modernity' (Rip and Kemp 1998, p. 392).

Over the longer run, the technical efficiency of specific devices is much less important than the symbolic relationship between the technologies of indoor climate control, modernity and new, consumption-intensive, concepts of comfort. Illustrating this point, Hal Wilhite et al's (1996) study of Japanese advertisements shows that air-conditioning has been bought and sold as a marker of Westernisation. It is not just that there is status attached to having air-conditioning. In addition, its use challenges more traditional body-centred understandings of comfort and has further consequences for meanings and experience of health and well-being, for the clothing that people wear and for the design and use of the home.

As indicated above, the accomplishment of comfort is entwined with the socio-temporal order, with fashion, with property development and design, and with an interlocking 'package' of contributory practices and expectations. The task of deliberately engineering change is correspondingly complex. On the other hand, these interdependencies generate multiple points of intervention, some of which may have the effect of 'tipping' the entire system in a different direction. To go further here, and to put the insights of 'transition theory' into practice, it is important to learn about how regimes of 'thermal monotony' (Heschong 1979) have taken hold over the last century. Assuming that concepts of comfort are malleable, the question is then how, and under what conditions, societies might (re)generate localised – or at least less resource demanding – interpretations and practices. In some cultures this might involve the reintroduction of the siesta. In others the waistcoat might come back into fashion. Alternatively, sensations of thermal variation might come to be valued in their own right.

Although this is unfamiliar territory – especially for environmental policy – there are ideas and theories that may be of help. I have already suggested that the field of science and technology studies has much to offer when thinking about the relation between systems of technology, convention and practice and how these change. This is not the only option. Following Giddens's theory of structuration, a further intellectual challenge is to discover how rules are restructured, how traditions and innovations are reproduced through practice, and where government policy fits into this picture, if at all. There is more work to be done in figuring out how policy intersects with practice yet the overall message is clear. Environmentalists have to find some way of encouraging and promoting social and cultural diversity in the way that comfort is defined.

This implies a complete reversal of current methods. Rather than standardising energy labelling or promoting efficient technology (and the standardised assumptions of need and service associated with it), national and international agencies should be encouraging the proliferation of regional, climate-sensitive, understandings of comfort and the development of a corresponding variety of localised socio-technical regimes. Rather than inadvertently naturalising the meaning of comfort, its definition should be the subject of explicit discussion and debate.

6.5 CONCLUSIONS AND IMPLICATIONS

I want to make four main points in conclusion. First, and most important, I have tried to show that the most popular and pervasive ways of thinking about consumption and the environment are fundamentally limited. Because they focus on individual behaviour, choice and decision-making they fail to detect sweeping changes in the defining features and contours of everyday life. Because the shifting sands of 'normality' lie outside the field of view, they also lie beyond the reach of plausible and possible policy intervention. Serious restrictions follow. It is all very well to concentrate on cars and on the design and development of more fuel-efficient models, but what about the social and technical infrastructures of automobility and the conventions of co-presence upon which normal forms of social interaction now depend? There are two aspects to this. It is not just that the heritage of psychological and economic thought cuts possible programmes of action short, though this is probably so. The second more pernicious effect of this tradition is to naturalise demand by default. In the bigger scheme of things, currently popular policy 'tools' designed to encourage more sustainable forms of consumer behaviour are likely to prove ineffective, if not counterproductive. Because they do little to challenge or stem the standardisation and globalisation of resource-intensive ways of life, it is possible, indeed likely, that many 'environmental' policies legitimise and foster the standardisation of unsustainable habits and expectations.

My second point is that this need not be the case. As I have hinted already, there are other theories, resources and paradigms on which to draw. Recent interest in transition theory, especially in the Netherlands, illustrates the point that government agencies are willing and able to think more broadly about the limits and possibilities of policy intervention. This may involve little more than swapping one illusion of agency (that policy-makers can influence consumer behaviour through persuasion, taxation and regulation) with another (that if only they could find the right moment and form of intervention, whole 'regimes' of sustainability might fall into place). Yet the very idea of a 'system' in 'transition' brings with it a new way of thinking about consumption, lifestyle and behaviour. While a more systemic, more co-evolutionary approach does not necessarily bring the 'big picture' back into view, it does at least ensure that the construction and reproduction of 'demand' (whether that is for comfort, for automobility, for foreign food or for unprecedented 'standards' of personal hygiene) is made explicit and is itself part of the problem.

In reviewing and exploring alternative ways of conceptualising consumption, lifestyle and behaviour I have tried to reveal divisions in theory, method and approach. The cake can be sliced this way and that, yet my third point is that there are paradigmatic differences in the conceptualisation of agency, structure and social change. To some extent, and as one might expect, these mirror disciplinary divides within the social sciences. As one might also expect, some paradigms are more immediately 'relevant' than others to policy and practice, as that is currently configured. Following the argument developed above, the contemporary confluence of ideas about consumer belief, action and behaviour is uniquely dangerous – blinding environmental policy-makers to precisely those issues that demand most urgent attention.

My fourth point, then, is that a different approach is required if there is to be any hope of engaging with, let alone influencing, deeply problematic trends like those relating to comfort or mobility. This means jumping ship and embracing a new agenda, one that has to do with socio-technical transitions and reconfigurations of rules, resources and habits, and a new set of theoretical tools. It also means re-reading the title of this chapter and giving it a different inflection. Is the challenge of sustainable consumption one of changing human behaviour and lifestyle? I would argue 'no', it is not a question of fretting about prices and barriers or of searching for levers that might be pulled to re-engineer consumer decision-making. Is the challenge of sustainable consumption one of changing dominant ways of thinking about human behaviour and lifestyle? To this question, I have no hesitation in answering 'yes'.

NOTES

* This chapter is based on research funded by the Economic and Social Research Council as part of the Environment and Human Behaviour Programme, 'Future Comforts: Reconfiguring Urban Indoor Environments': Award number 221 25 0005.
1. Sustainable development is defined as 'development that meets the needs of the present without compromising the ability of future generations to meet their own needs'. (World Commission on Environment and Development 1987, p. 43).
2. According to the Center for a New American Dream, 'there is a growing trend of Americans who are working to create a new American Dream – by changing the way they consume to improve their quality of life, protect the environment and promote social justice' (Center for a New American Dream 2003).
3. Edwina Currie was a Conservative Party politician in the UK when she made this suggestion in the 1980s.

REFERENCES

Bourdieu, Pierre (1984), *Distinction: A Social Critique of Judgement and Taste*, London: Routledge.
Brown, P.M. and L.D. Cameron (2000), 'What can be done to reduce overconsumption?', *Ecological Economics*, **32** (1), 27–41.
BSRIA (2002), *The World Market for Air Conditioning*, Bracknell: Building Services Research and Information Association.
Center for a New American Dream (2003), http://www.newdream.org/thedream/index.html.
Chappells, Heather (2003), *Re-conceptualising Electricity and Water: Institutions, Infrastructures and the Construction of Demand*, PhD Thesis, Lancaster University.
Cogoy, M. (1999), 'The consumer as a social and environmental actor', *Ecological Economics*, **28** (3), 385–98.
Cooper, Gail (1998), *Air-Conditioning America: Engineers and the Controlled Environment, 1900–1960*, Baltimore: Johns Hopkins University Press.

DETR (1998), *Sustainable Development: Opportunities for Change*, London: HMSO.

Douglas, Mary and Baron Isherwood (1996), *The World of Goods: Towards an Anthropology of Consumption*, London: Routledge.

Ekins, Paul (2003), *Environment and Human Behaviour: A New Opportunities Programme*, http://www.psi.org.uk/ehb/.

Elzen, Boelie, Frank Geels, Peter Hofman and Ken Green (2002), 'Socio-technical scenarios as a tool for transition policy: An example from the traffic and transport domain', Paper for the workshop 'Transitions to Sustainability through System Innovations', Enschede, University of Twente, July 2002.

Fischer, Claude (1992), *America Calling: A Social History of the Telephone*, Berkeley: University of California Press.

Friedl (2002), *Air Conditioning Industry Report*, Friedl Business Information and Partners, executive summary, http://www.friedlnet.com/0021-008.html.

Geels, F. (2002), 'Technological transitions as evolutionary reconfiguration processes: A multi-level perspective and a case study', *Research Policy*, **31**, 1257–74.

Georg, S. (1999), 'The social shaping of household consumption', *Ecological Economics*, **28** (3), 455–66.

Giddens, Antony (1984), *The Constitution of Society*, Cambridge: Polity Press.

Giles, Andrew (2003), 'Air conditioning still waits for the big push', *Building Services and Environmental Engineer*, http://www.bsee.co.uk.

Goldsmith, R. (1960), 'Use of clothing records to demonstrate acclimatisation to cold in man', *Journal of Applied Physiology*, **15** (5), 776–80.

Hajer, Maarten (1996), 'Ecological modernisation as cultural politics', in Scott Lash, Bron Szerzynski and Brian Wynne (eds), *Risk, Environment and Modernity: Towards a New Ecology*, London: Sage, p. 252.

Harrison, Carolyn and Gail Davies (1998), *Lifestyles and the Environment*, Environment and Sustainability Desk Study for the ESRC Global Environmental Change Programme, http://www.sussex.ac.uk/Units/gec/pubs/reps/dslifest.htm.

Heschong, Lisa (1979), *Thermal Delight in Architecture*, Cambridge, MA: MIT Press.

Hughes, Thomas P. (1983), *Networks of Power: Electrification in Western Society, 1880–1930*, Baltimore: Johns Hopkins University Press.

Humphreys, Michael (1995), 'Thermal comfort temperatures and the habits of hobbits', in Fergus Nicol, Michael Humphreys, Oliver Sykes and Sue Roaf (eds), *Standards for Thermal Comfort*, London: E & F N Spon.

Liberatore, Angela (1994), 'Facing global warming: The interactions between science and policy-making in the European Community', in Michael Redclift and Ted Benton (eds), *Social Theory and the Global Environment*, London: Routledge, pp. 190–204.

Moisander, Johanna (1995), 'Consumers' pro-environmental attitudes and their use of public transportation', *European Council for an Energy Efficient Economy, 1995 Summer Study Proceedings*, http://www.eceee.org/library_links/proceedings/1995/abstract/ece95066.lasso.

Moore, M. (1999), 'Mexicans must say adios to the 3-hour siesta', *Washington Post*, 23 March.

Nicol, F., I. Raja, A. Allaudin, and G. Jamy (1999), 'Climatic variations in comfortable temperatures: The Pakistan projects', *Energy and Buildings*, **30**, 261–79.

Noorman, Klaas J. and Ton Schoot Uiterkamp (eds) (1998), *Green Households? Domestic Consumers, Environment and Sustainability*, London: Earthscan.

OECD (2001), *Report of the OECD 'Workshop on Information and Consumer Decision-making for Sustainable Consumption'*, ENV/EPOC/WNEP(2001)16/FINAL, Paris: OECD.

OECD (2002), *Towards Sustainable Household Consumption?: Trends and Policies in OECD Countries*, Paris: OECD.

Oseland, Nigel and Michael Humphreys (1993), *Trends in Thermal Comfort Research*, Watford: Building Research Establishment.

Packard, Vance (1957), *The Hidden Persuaders: On Psychology and Advertising*, London: Longmans, Green and Co.

Patterson, Walt (2003), 'Keeping the lights on', Working Paper No. 1, OverElectric Challenge, London: Royal Institute of International Affairs.

Powergen (2003), http://www.pgen.com/corporate_responsibility/energy_efficiency.asp.

Redclift, Michael (1996), *Wasted: Counting the Costs of Global Consumption*, London: Earthscan.

Reisch, L. (2001), 'Time and wealth: The role of time and temporalities for sustainable patterns of consumption', *Time and Society*, **10** (2/3), 367–85.

Rip, Arie and Rene Kemp (1998), 'Technological change', in Steve Rayner and Elizabeth Malone (eds), *Human Choice and Climate Change: Resources and Technology, Volume 2*, Columbus, Ohio: Battelle Press, pp. 327–92.

Røpke, I. (1999), 'The dynamics of willingness to consume', *Ecological Economics*, **28**, 399–420.

Shove, Elizabeth (1997), 'Revealing the invisible: Sociology, energy and the environment', in Michael Redclift and Graham Woodgate (eds), *The International Handbook of Environmental Sociology*, Cheltenham, UK and Lyme, US: Edward Elgar, pp. 261–74.

Shove, Elizabeth (2003), *Comfort, Cleanliness and Convenience: The Social Organization of Normality*, Oxford: Berg.

Shove, Elizabeth and Alan Warde (2002), 'Inconspicuous consumption: The sociology of consumption, lifestyles and environment', in Riley Dunlap (ed.), *Sociological Theory and the Environment*, Colorado: Rowman and Littlefield, pp. 230–52.

Shove, Elizabeth, Loren Lutzenhiser, Simon Guy, Bruce Hackett, and Harold Wilhite (1998), 'Energy and social systems', in Steve Rayner, and Elizabeth Malone (eds), *Human Choice and Climate Change: Resources and Technology Volume 2*, Columbus, Ohio: Battelle Press, pp. 291–322.

Spaargaren, G. (1997), *The Ecological Modernisation of Production and Consumption: Essays in Environmental Sociology*, Wageningen: Landbouw University.

Spaargaren, G. and B. van Vliet (2000), 'Lifestyles, consumption and the environment: The ecological modernization of domestic consumption', *Environmental Politics* (9), 50–77.

Uusitalo, L. (1990), 'Consumer preferences for environmental quality and other social goals', *Journal of Consumer Policy*, **13** (3), 231–51.

van Vliet, B. (2002), 'Greening the grid: the ecological modernisation of network-bound systems', PhD thesis, Wageningen University, the Netherlands.

Wackernagel, Mathis and William Rees (1995), *Our Ecological Footprint*, Gabriola Island, BC: New Society Publishers.

Wilhite, Harold, Hidetoshi Nakagami and Chiharu Murakoshi (1996), 'The dynamics of changing Japanese energy consumption patterns and their implications for sustainable consumption', *Human Dimensions of Energy Consumption 1996 ACEEE Summer Study on Energy Efficiency in Buildings*, Washington DC: ACEEE, 8.231–8.238.

World Commission on Environment and Development (WCED) (1987), *Our Common Future*, Oxford: Oxford University Press.

7. Domestic electricity consumption – consumers and appliances*

Kirsten Gram-Hanssen

7.1 INTRODUCTION

According to international environmental and sustainability agreements, energy consumption must be reduced, and this has been one of the goals of Danish energy policy since the early 1980s. Nevertheless, today the Danish energy consumption is at the same level as it was ten or 15 years ago. Approximately one-third of the energy is consumed directly by households for heating, appliances and lighting; this has also been stable throughout the years (Danish Energy Authority 2001). This stability, however, spans two different points: (1) buildings and appliances are much more energy efficient today than 15 years ago, and (2) the total number of both houses and appliances has been growing correspondingly. Growth in the total number of houses and appliances follows from two parallel tendencies. One is the demographic tendency towards more single-person households resulting in fewer persons to share each appliance, and secondly a parallel tendency that each household has a growing number of different types of appliance (Gram-Hanssen 2003).

Since the first energy crises in the 1970s there has been focus on research in reduced energy consumption. This started primarily with technical research but from the 1980s onwards the social aspect of energy consumption also gained attention (for international overviews see Lutzenhiser 1993; Wilhite et al. 2000). At least two major approaches are seen in this research. One focuses on quantitative analyses of correlations between socio-economic background variables and the level of energy consumption (for example, Gladhart et al. 1987; Pedersen and Broegaard 1997). In these studies it is demonstrated that energy consumption is heavily dependent on factors such as the number of persons living in the household, at what stage of their lifecycle the inhabitants are, the type and size of house and the income of the household. The other approach is to use qualitative methods to describe how attitudes and routines structure everyday life and thereby the level of energy

132

consumption (for example, Wilhite et al. 1996; Aune 1997; Kuehn 1998). In these studies it is shown that deep-rooted cultural differences (international as well as intercultural and sub-cultural) are behind differences in energy consumption.

Both quantitative and qualitative studies have focused mainly on the obvious and large cultural differences, comparing different social classes in one country or comparing countries with a totally different cultural background. However, it can be difficult to use these results in strategies intended to change behaviour, as these differences represent the strong and not easily changeable physical and social structures in a society. Nevertheless, similar households (according to all relevant background variables) may still have differences in energy consumption of 200–300 per cent. If it can be explained why one family uses double the amount of energy than another family under very similar conditions, this knowledge might lead to new strategies of how to promote energy savings.

On this background a research project was established to investigate differences in energy consumption in similar households.[1] In the following section, the project design and methods of this project are presented. The next section concentrates on results from the questionnaire concerning consumers, appliances and electricity consumption, and it is shown that differences in electricity consumption between similar households relate to the number and the use of appliances and not to their efficiency. In the analysis of the qualitative interviews, focus is therefore on differences in buying and using appliances. To be able to analyse these qualitative results the next paragraphs introduce and consider different theoretical approaches in order to understand the mechanisms behind the consumption. The results are then interpreted in light of the theories. Finally, the conclusion illuminates how this kind of research can be used to comment on campaigns for a more sustainable consumption.

7.2 PROJECT DESIGN AND METHODS

The study took place in Albertslund, a modern suburb of Copenhagen mainly built as a planned development in the 1960s. The municipality is divided into neighbourhoods, many of them with high-density/low-rise buildings, and mostly with very similar buildings within the neighbourhood. The neighbourhoods themselves are also similar. The municipality records supply data (water, heat and electricity) at the neighbourhood and household levels and publishes these data every year in an eco-account. This eco-account is part of an environmental policy aimed at measuring environmental performance in the municipality and at encouraging residents

134 *Explaining consumption*

to save energy. These features, the many similar buildings and the high degree of recorded data, make Albertslund an ideal 'laboratory' for research questions.

Based on data for Albertslund as a whole, seven high-density/low-rise neighbourhoods, with a combined total of 1000 households were selected for detailed analysis. These households were subjected to different investigations, including computer calculations of building heat loss, a questionnaire among residents, qualitative interviews with ten families, and detailed indoor climate monitoring. The questionnaire collected socio-economic and demographic data; questions about appliance ownership, age, energy efficiency level and use; and questions regarding room temperature, ventilation and bathing habits. About 50 per cent of the 1000 households answered the questionnaire, resulting in 534 completed surveys. The survey respondents gave permission for their consumption data to be accessed from the municipality's eco-accounts, allowing a matched set of survey and consumption data. Based on these data, the respondents were separated into three equal-sized groups to define high, medium, and low energy use categories. Five households with low energy use and five with high energy use were chosen for in-depth qualitative interviews (Kvale 1996). The ten interviews explored the interviewees' attitudes, use patterns and everyday life concerning all practices with relation to energy consumption; these interviews were taped and transcribed.

7.3 QUANTITATIVE RESULTS: CONSUMERS, APPLIANCES AND ELECTRICITY CONSUMPTION

Domestic electricity consumption varies greatly, even within neighbourhoods with very similar buildings. An example of this is in Figure 7.1, which shows that some households use ten times more electricity than others.

The main explanation for this variation is related to the number of persons living in the household. Figure 7.2 shows that the electricity consumption per household increases with the number of persons living in it, and Figure 7.3 (based on the same data as Figure 7.2) shows that the electricity consumption per person decreases with the number of persons living in the household. These figures clearly illustrate that the unit of measurement is in itself important. The household is the consumption unit and thus may be the appropriate unit for analytical purposes; however, focusing on consumption per household obscures the important information that fewer persons per household causes a higher level of electricity per person; consequently,

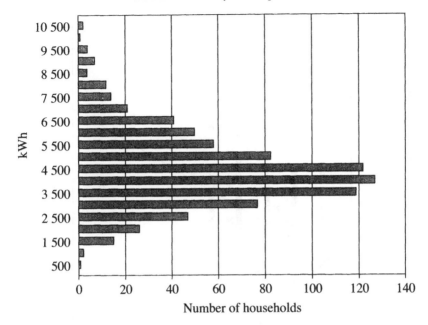

Figure 7.1   *Distribution of annual electricity consumption per household in a neighbourhood with very similar terraced houses. Based on data from Albertslund eco-account (Albertslund Kommune 2001)*

this may be one of the reasons for a higher national level of electricity consumption, as more and more people live alone.

Household size is one of the explanations for variations in electricity consumption among households, yet as also seen in Figure 7.2, households with the same number of people may show variations in electricity consumption of several hundred per cent. A possible explanation for these variations is the level of appliance efficiency in different households. The survey data, however, indicate that the appliance efficiency of light bulbs and refrigerator-freezers does not explain why some households use much more electricity than others (see Tables 7.1 and 7.2).

What seems to explain variations in electricity consumption between similar households, is the possession and the use of appliances. Using the tumble dryer as an example, Table 7.3 shows that there is a strong correlation between whether or not a household has a tumble dryer and the level of electricity consumption; furthermore, Table 7.4 shows a strong correlation between how often the tumble dryer is used if the household has one, and the household's level of electricity consumption. Survey results also show

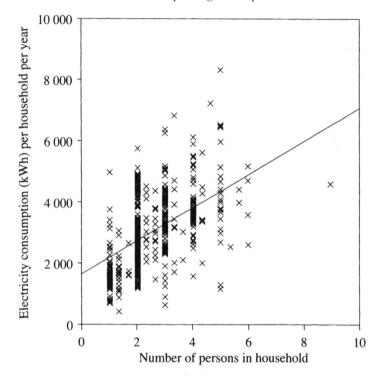

Figure 7.2   *Electricity consumption per household increases with the*
                number of persons (fractional number of persons refers to part-
                time inhabitants) in the household. Based on survey data and
                consumption data from utilities (n = 512)

Table 7.1   *Percentage of electric light in home from CFLs (low-*
              energy bulbs) correlated with electricity consumption (516
              respondents). No positive correlation: gamma = 0.029, not
              significant p = 0.727

Household level of electricity consumption	< 25% CFLs	25–50% CFLs	>50%CFLs	
Low level	74	14	12	100 (n = 170)
Medium level	81	11	8	100 (n = 170)
High level	73	14	13	100 (n = 176)
	(n = 392)	(n = 68)	(n = 56)	(n = 116)

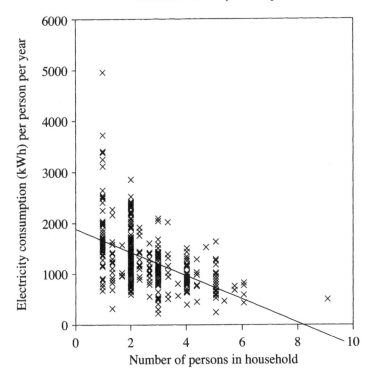

Figure 7.3 *Electricity consumption[2] per person decreases with the number of persons in the household (fractional number of persons refers to part-time inhabitants). Based on the same data as Figure 7.2*

Table 7.2 *Low-energy-consuming refrigerator-freezer in home correlated with electricity consumption (percentage) (214 respondents). No positive correlation: gamma = –0.055, not significant p = 0.628*

Household level of electricity consumption	Low-energy fridge-freezer	No low-energy fridge-freezer	
Low level	53	47	100 (n = 79)
Medium level	62	38	100 (n = 65)
High level	49	51	100 (n = 70)
	(n = 116)	(n = 98)	(n = 214)

that the number of television sets and computers as well as the number of appliances with a standby function strongly correlates to the household's level of electricity consumption.

Table 7.3 Ownership (percentage) of tumble dryer correlated with electricity consumption (504 respondents, gamma = 0.597, significant with p = 0.000)

Household level of electricity consumption	Have tumble dryer	No tumble dryer	
Low level	21	79	100 (n = 163)
Medium level	38	62	100 (n = 167)
High level	68	32	100 (n = 174)
	(n = 216)	(n = 288)	(n = 504)

Table 7.4 Weekly tumble dryer use (percentage) correlated with electricity consumption (199 respondents). Strong positive correlation: gamma = 0.334, significant with p = 0.000

Household level of electricity consumption	One time	Two times	Three times	Four times	4–25 times	
Low level	53	13	13	9	13	100 (n = 32)
Medium level	34	20	14	17	15	100 (n = 59)
High level	21	14	16	21	28	100 (n = 108)
	(n = 60)	(n = 31)	(n = 50)	(n = 23)	(n = 35)	(n = 199)

Note that results based on self-reported survey data, for example, energy efficiency of appliances and the use of appliances, might be inaccurate. However, if the household answers that they have more than 50 per cent or less than 25 per cent of low-energy bulbs, the element of uncertainty can be considered small and thus the data valid. The same applies to the question: Is the tumble dryer used once a week or more than four times a week? Whether the household is classified as a low, medium or high electricity consumer is, however, not based on self-reported data, but on consumption data gathered directly from the utilities.

Survey data show that variations between the level of electricity consumption of these very similar households can be better explained by the number and the use of appliances, than by the level of energy efficiency of the appliances. However, this does not give any indication about why some households own a tumble dryer and others do not, or why some families have one television set and others have five. To answer this question, I will once again return to the survey results, and after a theoretical introduction show some of the qualitative results.

In this project, focus is on variations between very similar households, and the work concerns households in similar types of houses. It is known that people living in the same neighbourhood resemble each other, to some extent, regarding socio-economic background, such as income and education and also to some extent, where the households are in their lifecycles. The seven neighbourhoods studied contain three neighbourhoods with owner-occupied houses and four with rented houses.

Survey results on employment, income and education together with interviews show that inhabitants from these neighbourhoods are generally from the middle and working classes. It also shows, as expected, that the inhabitants of the owner-occupied neighbourhoods are generally better educated and also generally have a higher income than inhabitants of rented houses. Apart from similarities, there are also socio-economic variations within each neighbourhood. Therefore, although focus is on similar households, variations are found in those background variables that are known to correlate with the level of electricity consumption.

If focus is on tumble dryers, it can be seen from Table 7.3 that 57 per cent (288 out of 504 households) of the respondents in this survey do not own a tumble dryer. This is slightly higher than the national figure of 42 per cent (Statistics Denmark 2002). If ownership of a tumble dryer is related to background variables, it is shown that the more people in the household, the more affluent and younger they are, the more likely they are to own a tumble dryer. However, as is always the case with statistics, this probability also covers the finding of people with very low incomes and people in a household of only one or two that has a tumble dryer. This highlights the need to know more about why people do or do not purchase a tumble dryer, and why they buy all other types of appliance.

7.4   QUALITATIVE RESULTS: STATEMENTS ON PURCHASE AND USE

Among these very similar households, some families own a tumble dryer, others do not; some families own four computers, others have none. The interviews reveal that the reason for purchasing, and the way to use computers, tumble dryers and all other types of appliances (1) differs with the type of technology and (2) differs between families.

All interviewed households owned a washing machine, whereas only the five families with high electricity consumption owned a tumble dryer.

Among the interviewees, families with children at home do not have a stronger tendency to own a tumble dryer than couples whose children have left home. Asked why they did not own a tumble dryer, the general answer was, that they did not think they 'needed it'. They did not think it was a problem to hang the clothes on a clothesline, and one of the interviewees even said that it was wonderful when she could hang the laundry outside and that she disliked using dryers. For the families without a tumble dryer, it is not a privation: it is a choice.

Asking the families who owned a tumble dryer why they did, some families answered that it was never a question at all if they should have one or not: they couldn't imagine living without one. Out of environmental concern, one family actually tried to live without a tumble dryer, but thought it was frustrating to have clothes 'hanging all over the house' and it was causing humidity problems. In contrast, an old couple stated that they felt that having a tumble dryer was a luxury, and the husband thinks that his wife 'deserves this luxury'. Apparently, a tumble dryer can be anything from unpleasant to a necessity or a luxury, depending on who was asked.

One thing is to own a tumble dryer, another is how the dryer is used. Its use is often correlated to use of the washing machine, but not always. One family, the family who thought about not having a tumble dryer out of environmental concern, reports that they had previously used the dryer for heating their towels while they were in the bath because they liked to dry themselves with a hot towel. In the interview situation the family feels that they have to apologize for this energy consuming habit, while at the same time they express that they actually loved the hot towels. Another family also uses the dryer a lot, but in this family it is correlated to the amount of laundry. The mother explains that she washes and dries at least three full loads of washing every day. And she goes on to explain that this is only possible because she works at home and thus has time to fill the machine several times a day. All five members of the family change all their clothes daily, this includes sports clothes and towels for daily use. The primary reason is not that the clothes are dirty, but it is the easiest way to clean the floor and to avoid having all the wet towels hanging up to dry and remembering which towel belongs to whom. These stories show that the tumble dryer can be used for things other than for drying clothes that have been washed because they were dirty, for example, for tidying up the house. Most of the interviewees state that most of their clothes aren't really dirty when they are washed. Stories of the tumble dryer thus highlight the fact that once a technology enters into everyday life, it may change its role and be used for many purposes other than that thought of when it was developed and purchased.

The next type of technology that is described is the computer. Among the interviewees, one family, an old couple, does not own a computer, whereas the rest have one or several computers with a varying assortment of accessories. The general impression from the interviews is that there is a strong pressure to own a computer. Some interviewees say that their studies require them to own a computer or that their work encourages it by advantageous sales offers. Others explain that because they have a job where they don't have access to a computer, they want to have one at home so that they don't 'fall behind developments'. Parents describe how their children pester them to get a computer (or one extra) and an old couple tells of how their grown-up children push them to get Internet and email. 'It is because they want to widen our horizon' the parents explain. Irrespective of what kind of family interviewed in these middle- and working-class neighbourhoods, it seems as if they experience a pressure from friends, family and more generally, from 'society' to get a computer. The reasons for having a computer, apart from work and study-related reasons, vary from 'just knowing how to use it' to emailing with friends and family, and widening the horizon through the Internet. However, in many families it seems that the most widespread use of it is for computer games.

Other types of technology may follow other patterns. For lighting, for instance, it appeared to be closely related to style and interior decoration, and different fashions in lighting, such as halogen lamps or PH-lamps, direct the light setting in many homes. There were stories of how dreaming of and buying a new kitchen may also include buying a dishwasher, even though the family had lived for 20 years without missing one. Habits change when new technologies enter the household. An old couple tells of how their grown children teach them to wash more things in the dishwasher; again supporting the idea that the surroundings push towards consumption.

Before going deeper into analysing these qualitative results, a more theoretical approach as to why people buy things needs to be introduced. The field of consumer theory is of interest here.

7.5 THEORETICAL APPROACHES TO CONSUMPTION

The last decade has seen a growing number of publications in the field of consumption theory (for introductions see Miller 1995; Corrigan 1997). These publications come from anthropology, sociology, economy and psychology as well as other disciplines. Academia's growing focus on the consumer may be viewed as a parallel or response to a change in the 'real world'. It is seen that citizens using public institutions are being transformed into consumers as part of the changes in the welfare state at the same time as the maturation of mass consumption, which started with the Fordist production methods 100 years ago, is witnessed. Consumerism is not a new phenomenon, but in terms of economics, ecology and politics in the last decade it has become much more relevant and central in the understanding of society.

Consumer theory deals with experiences, motivations and reasons for why people buy things and why different groups of consumers buy different things. Several authors have given their way of summarizing the different approaches to consumption, many of them emphasizing that the complexity of consumption has to be understood as an integrated framework of different theories – no one theory can explain it all (that is, Gabriel and Lang 1995; Shove and Warde 2001). Featherstone (1991) has described a historical line in consumer research where the research before the 1980s was relatively undeveloped and primarily focused on consumption as an appendage of production. From the 1980s and onwards there has been much more focus on the cultural and communicative aspects of consumption, and here research could be divided into a modern and a post-modern way of understanding consumers. In the following introduction I will use this division between modern and post-modern understandings; however, I will also present approaches that question this strong focus on communication.

Classical studies by Bourdieu and Douglas on consumption focused on the communicative aspects of signals and symbols in relation to social groups, and this has been shown to be relevant in the study of energy consumption (Kuehn 1998). Bourdieu describes consumption and 'good taste' as a way for the higher social classes to distinguish themselves from the lower classes (Bourdieu 1984), and he shows how residential neighbourhoods in this way form part of the symbolic power structure of society (Bourdieu 1996). The notion of 'habitus' is central to Bourdieu's theory (Bourdieu 1998). Habitus comprises the values, norms, attitudes, preferences and behaviour of the individual and it is a deep-rooted and unconscious structure, determined by the social and material conditions of childhood. Habitus is built into the body as a so-called social DNA, and it makes people able to act in everyday life without consciously considering every single mcve made. Bourdieu uses the notion of habitus to define social classes as groups of individuals with the same habitus, and he distinguishes between three classes: the bourgeoisie, petit bourgeoisie and the working class. Taste is to appreciate some goods or some forms of behaviour as opposed to others. Through taste, signals are sent about social belonging; however, it is the taste of the bourgeoisie that defines the taste of all three classes. The taste of the bourgeoisie is closely connected with appreciating what requires much money (economic capital) or a high cultural competence (cultural capital), which the other classes do not possess. In this way the higher social classes distinguish themselves from the lower classes. The taste of the petit bourgeoisie is defined by their trying to emulate the taste and norms of the bourgeoisie, whereas the taste of the working class is defined by the choice of necessity. What is there to choose when there is neither the economic nor the cultural capital to emulate the taste of the bourgeoisie?

In contrast to this description based on a class society is the late- or post-modern understanding. The argument is that a society is approaching where institutions from modern society, such as class, family and community are dissolving and where the individual therefore has to express and create his or her own individual identity (Giddens 1990; Beck 1992). That the individual is freed from these institutions does not mean that there is free choice and equal opportunities or that people behave more individually, in the sense of differently, from each other. On the contrary, one of the paradoxes of the individualized society is that it is based on mass culture and mass consumption as much as ever. What the individualized society means is that individuals hunt to find and express their own identity through consumption choice of everything from clothes to education and partner. Zygmunt Bauman goes one step further talking about the post-modern society, as characterized by consumption, in such a way that he defines those who do not fit in to this society, the expelled, as defined by their inability to consume – the flawed consumers (Bauman 1997).

This discussion on modern versus post-modern consumption theory, however, focuses primarily on the communicative aspects of consumption. Campbell argues against this, stating that these theories depend on the consumer and the observer sharing a common understanding of the 'language' that is used (Campbell 1995). As an alternative to the strong focus on communication, Campbell proposes a theory of pleasure and daydreaming as the wheel that turns the need for consumption; others have shown that this might be a very relevant theory, also in the understanding of energy consumption (Jensen 2002). When Campbell describes what drives the modern consumers to consume to the extent they do, he distinguishes between traditional and modern hedonism (Campbell 1987). Where traditional hedonism is about satisfying needs (such as food and warmth), modern hedonism is about pleasure. Traditional hedonism requires a physical consumption whereas modern hedonism can be related to immaterial activities such as daydreaming and fantasies. When, nevertheless, modern hedonism leads to a higher material level of consumption, it is because pleasurable sensation, in contrast to satisfying needs, is, in principle, insatiable. The driving force of the consumption spiral is daydreams of how life would be with the new product, for example, a new kitchen. When the coveted object is purchased, however, satisfaction seldom follows, on the contrary, it often disappoints. Reality seldom lives up to the dreams, and new daydreams quickly follow as a source of new pleasure and a never-ending consumption spiral has been started.

These theories all concern conspicuous consumption, and it has been argued that this may not be relevant for interpreting consumption of electricity, which is characterized by being invisible and by not being important at all to the consumer in itself but only through the services it provides (Shove and Chappells 2001). However, as described in previous paragraphs, analyses of electricity consumption show that the level of electricity consumption correlates strongly with the number and use of appliances and, as shown in the following section, some of these appliances could be viewed as conspicuous consumption, whereas others cannot.

Consumer theories primarily focus on why to consume, and not on what happens afterwards in relation to the consumed object. Talking about energy consumption, it is relevant not only to understand why people buy new appliances, but also to know how they are used afterwards. The subject area known as 'domestication of technology' deals with this (Lie and Sørensen 1996). Here, the focus is on how technology is used, tamed, and (re)interpreted in everyday life. The theories of domestication of technology thus promote understanding of the mutual construction process between humans and the consumed appliances.

7.6   DISCUSSING FINDINGS AND APPLYING THEORIES

An important question concerning the interviewed families is: Is there something more general to say about why some families use two or three times as much electricity as other families living under similar conditions? In the qualitative interviews one thing seems to separate the high-level users from the low-level users. This is their general attitude towards consumption: if they express that they like consuming, or if they express that they find satisfaction in saving. It is characteristic among the interviewed families with a high level of electricity consumption that most families emphasize that they enjoy consuming. They use expressions like, 'you should be good to yourself', 'I just love to...' and 'I think we deserve to...'. Conversely, the families with a low level of electricity consumption use expressions such as 'we don't think we need to have...' and 'we can do without...'. The reasons that some families find more, or as much, satisfaction in saving as in consuming are diverse. In some of the interviewed families it is a habit that they were raised with. One immigrant family brought up in a less materially affluent society, and an old working-class couple brought up in disadvantaged circumstances describe how their attitude towards saving is something they have learned and carried within them from their childhood. In another family, it is clearly a politically conscious attitude towards the environment that has led to an anti-consumer behaviour. But it is not always so that a disadvantaged childhood or a concern for the environment leads to a 'saving attitude'. On the contrary, there are also examples among the interviewed families that a disadvantaged childhood and youth may lead to the family thinking that they deserve to have more luxury now because they did not have it earlier. And there are examples of families with a conscious and positive attitude towards the environment who think that they ought to save resources, but in their daily practices do not manage to do so because of other priorities.

In this way through the interviews it is shown that the families' general attitude towards consumption is relevant in understanding their level of energy consumption. The next question is then which theoretical understanding can be found for these differences in attitudes towards consumption. Some families enjoy or appreciate saving rather than consuming, and in the interview two different approaches to this saving attitude are given. For the families where the saving attitude is something they bring with them from their childhood it is very straightforward to understand this as a working-class habitus, defined by the choice of necessity as Bourdieu has described it. In this understanding the saving attitude is something people are brought up with and carry within them in a way that in taste and in daily routines they unconsciously prefer not to waste anything, even though they may be able to afford it in their present life. Other families among the interviewees, however, express an opposite reaction to the same background. An old working-class couple tells of how their childhood and youth were marked by poverty. As most other Danes in the last half-century, they have experienced growing wealth and they say that they think they 'deserve a little luxury' now that they can afford it. This family thus contradicts Bourdieu's understanding of the stability of habitus and social classes. Their feelings are better understood through Beck's description of the 'elevator effect'. By this, Beck means that our society today witnesses greater social inequality than ever at the same time as the feeling of class belonging is disappearing because all groups in society have experienced a growing wealth that is more visible than the growing differences (Beck 1992).

Not all families with a saving attitude had a disadvantaged, working-class childhood. In one of the interviewed families the saving attitude had its basis in a conscious environmental choice. However, this did not imply that the explanations this family gave for saving habits primarily or only related to rational environmental arguments. On the contrary, the woman, for instance, said that she actually loved to hang the laundry outside to dry, and with this and other expressions her attitude towards saving may be understood as a special variant of modern hedonism. Some of her daydreams and romantic attitudes (both certainly not all) are directed towards habits that are more environmentally correct than others and in this way she may be able to feel pleasure in saving. Examples from this family, besides the laundry drying, are, for instance, sometimes taking the bicycle instead of the car and keeping a low indoor temperature.

Other families enjoyed consuming, and again it can be asked how theoretically can these families be understood. One of the questions raised in the theoretical introduction relates to the question of whether conspicuous consumption primarily relates to class-based taste communities or to individualized identity-seeking and daydreaming. Some of the technologies consuming energy may be viewed as conspicuous consumption. Fashion in lighting for instance, or new kitchens furnished with all types of white goods are examples that may be analysed as distinction or identity-seeking consumption. The material in this project is deliberately very socially homogeneous and therefore not suitable for investigating whether this consumption should primarily be analysed as based on social class identity or on late-modern individualized identity-seeking. Other studies have focused explicitly on this question. Based on a study of middle- and upper-class detached houses it is argued that the choice of house primarily can be understood in a class-based context, whereas furnishing and indoor decorating has to be viewed as a more individualized and playful activity (Gram-Hanssen and Bech-Danielsen 2002). A study of middle-class families and their kitchens supports the argument that localized class-based taste communities strongly influence taste and identity formation in kitchen arrangements (Southerton 2001).

Many of the energy consuming household technologies cannot be understood as conspicuous consumption. Tumble dryers, as one of the technologies I focused on in this chapter, do not seem to be viewed as related to either status-seeking or daydreaming. One family viewed tumble dryers as a luxury, in the sense of eliminating some manual work. This, however, I understand as some kind of traditional hedonism in relaxing. Most families with a tumble dryer saw it as some kind of ordinary consumption, something that is a necessity. Also, having a computer seems to have become so normal that any kind of distinction in merely owning one has disappeared. Here the point seems more to be that those not having one are stigmatized. Bauman talks about the flawed consumers, as the 'dirt' of the post-modern society (Bauman 1997). In his description he focuses in a much broader sense on those who are unable to participate in the consumer society. This understanding may give meaning also in a narrower sense such as looking solely at consuming computers. Those not having a computer are viewed as outside the community as well as being practically excluded as more and more services and information are only available via the Internet. This was not the case only a few years ago, and computers thus remind us that technologies, as well as other kinds of consumer goods, are not stable in belonging to the groups of either distinctive or ordinary consumption.

Finally the last theoretical observation on the empirical work focuses on the theories of domestication of technology and how they can promote adherence to an understanding of a mutually constructing process between social organization and consumed technologies in everyday life (Lie and Sørensen 1996). The tumble dryer is produced and marketed as a device for drying clothes, but in homes it may be reinterpreted as also being a towel heater or a floor cleaner. This reinterpretation is closely related to the social relations and norms in the individual family as well as to both social and technical structures surrounding the family. This reinterpretation has fundamental consequences for the level of electricity consumption.

7.7 CONCLUSION: FINAL THOUGHTS AND IMPLICATION FOR CAMPAIGNS ON ENERGY SAVING

In this chapter it is shown that the main reason for differences in the level of electricity consumption between families living under similar physical and socio-economic conditions, originates in how many appliances the family owns and how often they are used, not in the energy efficiency of the appliances. This finding has implications for both the theoretical understanding of energy use and for policy instruments for energy saving, including, in particular, energy saving campaigns.

In the theoretical understanding of energy consumption in everyday life others have emphasized that electricity is invisible and not something that is wanted in itself, and therefore not something that should be analysed as consumption in the sociological or anthropological sense. This understanding has to be extended by the finding that electricity consumption is strongly dependent on the number and the use of technologies in the household. Both are subjects that are relevant to analyse for a consumption perspective. Through the theoretical interpretation of the qualitative interviews it is shown that the reasons for buying new appliances and the way the appliances are used follow very different patterns both from one family to another and from one type of technology to another. In this way I have sought to show that we cannot find one explanation in one consumer theory explaining all aspects of electricity consumption, but we can find much inspiration for very different approaches in analysing everyday life, technology and energy consumption. With this conclusion, I am in line with many other recent consumer studies emphasizing that consumer decisions regarding purchase and use are multi-causal, in the sense that they can be understood as simultaneously being habitual, rationally bounded and a symbolic act.

The results presented in this chapter also have implications for energy saving campaigns. Based on the result on efficiency versus number of technologies, it is highly relevant to question the message that both authorities and supply companies are sending in campaigns with the purpose of saving energy. In these campaigns, at least in Denmark, focus is solely on efficiency of appliances and light bulbs, and the message is to buy more of the efficient technologies. From analyses of the interviews, another strategy could be recommended. It has been pointed out here that the families' attitude towards consumption is important. Some families find more satisfaction in saving than in consuming, and this attitude actually influences their level of electricity consumption. However, as the interviews also showed, this 'saving attitude' may be under continuous pressure from friends and family as well as from society in general. Energy saving campaigns with their strong focus on buying more efficient technologies can even be imagined to be part of this pressure. Another strategy in energy saving campaigns could therefore be to show the positive aspect of saving, instead of buying, through positive story-telling about a slightly more modest lifestyle. Authorities and supply companies often state that they cannot moralize about how people should live their lives. The question is: Why are campaigns of buying regarded as less moralizing than campaigns of not buying?

As an illustration of how difficult it is to introduce these stories in the media, let me conclude with my own experiences of how the media have covered the results from this project. One day in May 2003, the growing electricity consumption in Danish households was front-page news in one of the national newspapers; it was also on national television and radio. I was interviewed for all these media and explained that the number and use of appliances are much more important than their energy efficiency, and I said that in general the number of appliances in Danish households is growing fast. Both these messages came through. I also said that this does not mean that all modern families love buying new appliances and that there are, in fact, some families with fewer appliances than average – and not because of necessity. This message, however, was not conveyed in any of the media. On the contrary, all items concluded, one way or another, that ordinary modern families desire more and more appliances, and in this way the media coverage of this project contributed to marginalizing those families who actually do not believe that they need any more machines in their everyday life.

NOTES

* The chapter is based on results from the project 'Energy Consumption in Dwellings – Technical and Behavioural Reasons for Variations' financed by the Danish Energy Authority under the ERP-2000 programme. Senior researchers Ole Michael Jensen, Dan Ove Petersen and Jørn Dinesen, Danish Building and Urban Research contributed to many of the results presented here.
1. The project focused on heat as well as electricity consumption, but this chapter concentrates on findings related to electricity consumption. For a presentation of preliminary findings concerning both heat and electricity see Gram-Hanssen 2002. The project as a whole is reported in Gram-Hanssen 2003.
2. The Danish average electricity consumption is 1568 kWh per person (Danish Building and Urban Research 2003).

REFERENCES

Albertslund Kommune (2001), *Grønt regnskab 2000 for boliger og erhverv*, Albertslund.

Aune, M. (1997), *'Nøktern eller nytende': Energiforbruk og hverdagsliv i norske husholdninger* (Report no. 34), Trondheim: Norwegian University of Science and Technology, Centre for Technology and Society.

Bauman, Zygmunt (1997), *Postmodernity and its Discontents*, Oxford: Blackwell.

Beck, Ulrich (1992), *Risk Society: Towards a New Modernity*, London: Sage.

Bourdieu, Pierre (1984), *Distinction. A Social Critique of the Judgement of Taste*, Cambridge: Polity Press.

Bourdieu, P. (1996), 'Et steds betydning', in *Symbolsk magt*, Oslo: Pax forlag A/S. ('Effets de lieu', in Bourdieu et al., *La misère du Monde*, Seuil, Paris 1993).

Bourdieu, Pierre (1998), *Practical Reason*, Oxford: Blackwell Publisher.

Campbell, Colin (1987), *The Romantic Ethic and the Spirit of Modern Consumerism*, Oxford: Basil Blackwell.

Campbell, Colin (1995), 'The sociology of consumption', in Daniel Miller (ed.), *Acknowledging Consumption. A Review of New Studies*, London and New York: Routledge, pp. 96–126.

Corrigan, Peter (1997), *The Sociology of Consumption. An Introduction*, London: Sage Publications.

Danish Building and Urban Research (2003), *Grønt regnskab for boliger*: Version 3.1. Hørsholm: http://www.by-og-byg.dk/udgivelser/pc-content.cspx.

Danish Energy Authority (2001), *Energistatistik 2000: Danmarks produktion og forbrug af energi*, Copenhagen: Danish Energy Authority.

Featherstone, Mike (1991), *Consumer Culture and Post-modernism*, London: Sage.

Gabriel, Yiannis and Lang, Tim (1995), *The Unmanageable Consumer. Contemporary Consumption and its Fragmentation*, London: Sage.

Giddens, Anthony (1990), *The Consequences of Modernity*, Cambridge: Polity Press.

Gladhart, Peter M., Bonnie Maas Morrison and James J. Zuiches (1987), *Energy and Families: Lifestyles and Energy Consumption in Lansing*, East Lansing, MI: Michigan State University Press.

Gram-Hanssen, Kirsten (2002), 'Technology and culture as explanations for variations in energy consumption', *in Proceedings of ACEEE 2002 Summer Study on Energy Efficiency in Buildings*, 18–23 August, Silomar, Pacific Grove, CA.

Gram-Hanssen, Kirsten (2003), *Boligers energiforbrug – sociale og tekniske forklaringer på forskelle*, By og byg results 029, Hørsholm: Danish Building and Urban Research.

Gram-Hanssen, Kirsten and Claus Bech-Danielsen (2002), 'House, home and identity from a consumption perspective', *Housing, Theory and Society*, **21** (1), 17–26.

Jensen, Jesper O. (2002), *Livsstil, Boform og Ressourceforbrug*, PhD dissertation, Hørsholm: Danish Building and Urban Research.

Kuehn, Susanne (1998), *Livsstilens betydning for energiforbruget* (Sociologisk Instituts PhD serie nr. 6), Copenhagen: Copenhagen University, Dept. of Sociology.

Kvale, Steinar (1996), *Interviews: An Introduction to Qualitative Research Interviewing*, Thousand Oaks, CA: Sage.

Lie, Merete and Knut H. Sørensen (eds) (1996), *Making Technology our Own? Domesticating Technology into Everyday Life*, Oslo: Scandinavian University Press.

Lutzenhiser, L. (1993), 'Social and behavioural aspects of energy use', *Annual Review of Energy and the Environment*, **18**, 247–89.

Miller, Daniel (ed.) (1995), *Acknowledging Consumption. A Review of New Studies*, London and New York: Routledge.

Pedersen, Lene Holm and Eva Broegaard (1997), *Husholdningernes elforbrug: En analyse af attituder og adfærd på energi- og miljøområdet*, Copenhagen: AKF Forlaget.

Shove, Elizabeth and Heather Chappells (2001), 'Ordinary consumption and extraordinary relationships: Utilities and their users', in Jukka Gronow and Alan Warde (eds), *Ordinary Consumption*, Berkshire, UK: Harwood Academic Publishers, pp. 45–58.

Shove, Elizabeth and Alan Warde (2001), 'Inconspicuous consumption: The sociology of consumption, lifestyle and the environment', in Riley E. Dunlap, Frederick H. Buttel, Peter Dickens and August Gijswijt (eds), *Social Theory and the Environment: Classical Foundations, Contemporary Insights*, Lanham, Maryland: Rowman & Littlefield, pp. 230–51.

Southerton, D. (2001), 'Consuming kitchens. Taste, context and identity formation', *Journal of Consumer Culture*, **1** (2), 179–203.

Statistics Denmark (2002), *Danmark i tal 2002*, Copenhagen, located 29/4 2003 at: www.dst.dk/danmark-_i_tal.

Wilhite, Harold, H. Nakagami, T. Masuda, Y, Yamaga and H. Haneda (1996), 'A cross-cultural analysis of household energy use behaviour in Japan and Norway', *Energy Policy*, **24** (9), 795–803.

Wilhite, Harold, Elizabeth Shove, Loren Lutzenhiser and Willett Kempton (2000), 'Twenty years of energy demand management: We know more about individual behavior but how much do we really know about demand?', *Proceedings of ACEEE 2000 Summer Study*, Washington DC.

8. Sustainability in everyday life – a matter of time?*

Mikko Jalas

8.1 INTRODUCTION

Sustainability is a fundamental and far-reaching concept of redirecting social change. It predisposes new institutional arrangements as well as changes in the values of individuals and in the technological trajectories; it materializes in the changing patterns of everyday conducts as well as in the structural changes in economic activities and in the adoption of new, more efficient technology. While the optimism about the scope and the reach of radical technological innovations is widespread and strong, many authors emphasize that relevant changes must involve consumers in a more fundamental manner. In addition to technological innovations such as fuel-efficient cars, the patterns of everyday life need to change. Such changes are implied in various degrees in notions such as sustainable consumption, sustainable lifestyles, sufficiency revolution and alternative models of wealth (for example, Sachs 1999; Reisch 2001). In more concrete terms the thoughts are reflected in the calls for a slower pace of life, work-sharing and shorter working hours (Schor 1991; Sanne 2000) and in more specific suggestions such as reducing long-distance tourism. Altogether, the discussion of sustainable consumption seems to presuppose different kinds of changes in the activities or behaviour of individuals and in their patterns of time use.

Time use researchers claim that analyses of the formal economy are inadequate for studying the real patterns of life in a society. According to them, utility, well-being, social stratification as well as social exclusion are more readily to be observed in the patterns of time use. Thus time use surveys have collected detailed data on the daily life of occupational groups, geographic districts and even entire national populations and documented the everyday life of individuals and households in terms of how time is spent; in what activities, with whom and where.

Within the history of time use surveys, they have been used as tools for social planning as well as indicators of well-being. In this chapter I argue that there are also a number of potential crossings of time use surveys and sustainability concerns. One of the strands builds upon the 'new home economics' and the claims that market commodities are not final sources of utility but rather inputs for household production, in which the units of time substitute the monetary units of the formal economy. Thus, time use surveys would seem to offer a possibility to extend the concept of material flow analysis of the formal economy to the informal sphere of household production and consumption. Time use researchers have also advanced the thought that the changes in economic activity can be better understood by considering human activity outside of the formal economy (Gershuny 1987, 1999). It is thus not only about producing extended accounts of societal metabolism or giving more detailed descriptions of the links between market production and individual well-being. Rather it is argued that time use is an intermediate phenomenon and that time use data can be used to study the potential impacts of institutional changes and policy reforms on monetary consumption.

The applications of time use data cover a large field of interests in the social sciences. It is outside the scope of this chapter to try to cover discussions of labour supply and related taxation, albeit they clearly hinge on the sustainability debate (see Schor 1991 and Sanne 2000). Likewise, the alternative social indicators of well-being, the extended analysis of welfare and criticism of GNP indicators are areas that are left aside. Instead of contributing to these debates I will concentrate on the attempts that have been made to describe and model the demand for, or consumption of, market goods on the basis of time use data.

The chapter continues from hereon first with a short history of time use research and a description of the available data resources. Secondly I will briefly consider the issue of time use and sustainable consumption in general. Thereafter the chapter presents a review of a few studies that address the macro-level links between demand and time use. The concluding remarks summarize the presented arguments as well as point out some current efforts of utilizing time use data in the debate on sustainable consumption.

8.2 SHORT HISTORY OF TIME USE RESEARCH: STUDYING NON-MARKET ACTIVITY AND PLANNING WELL-BEING

8.2.1 Time Use Surveys

An exploration of the potential of time use studies must begin with a description of the methods that are used and data that are available.

Many good reviews on the development of time use survey research exist (see Harvey 1999 and Pentland et al. 1999 for general reviews and Juster and Stafford 1991 and Klevmarken 1999 for reviews of the work done by economists). Within the scope of this chapter, it thus suffices to take up a few important studies that mark the path towards the nationwide representative time use surveys of today.

Systematic attempts to record the way individuals use their time date back to the beginning of the 20th century. Early studies in the US, the UK and in the Soviet Union focused on describing the living conditions of working-class people and rural farmers. The Soviet research tradition was strong during the 1920s and 1930s but faded temporarily in the pre-World War II years. Interestingly one of the major strands of the Soviet work focused on the 'strategic issues of social forecasting and macroeconomic planning of manpower time and productivity' (Harvey 1999). The researchers tried to track the changes in everyday life that were created by the revolutionary reforms of the 1920s in the Soviet Union. Thus, they were, for example, interested in the currently relevant topic of the effects of shorter working hours.

Since the early days of systematic time use surveys many different methods have been used and the scope of the studies has varied from narrow occupational or social groups to representative nationwide studies. The multinational time use project in 1965–67 (Szalai 1972) has been a landmark for the current type of studies. Szalai and his colleagues coordinated a project in which data on 12 countries were collected using a time diary method. The work on the project marked the beginning of the collection of internationally comparable and longitudinal data. Many additional national surveys were conducted during the 1970s and, in time, time use surveys gained a position in national statistical offices.

The time diaries have since been established as the principal method of recording data on time use. They are usually close-ended records of activities in a predetermined time span such as a 24-hour period. Activities are coded according to a standardized activity coding. Commonly the surveys also record secondary activities, the location and the social contacts for each interval of time use. The new European harmonization effort of time use surveys is the most recent major attempt to further develop the methodology. It includes a suggestion of a ten-minute interval for diary recordings, a detailed, hierarchical list of activity codes and a recommendation that the data are collected from all members of the households for two separate days of a week and a weekend (Eurostat 1999a; Fisher and Gershuny 2002).

There have been various attempts to study the subjective meaning of time use in addition to the mere description of the patterns of everyday life according to a pre-given list of activities. These attempts vary from including a subjective measure of the desirability of the reported activities (for example, Robinson 1977; Elchardus 1991) to background variables recording the ways respondents would spend available extra time (for example, the recent Finnish national study) or manage unexpected time shortages. Despite these attempts representative time use studies remain of necessity rather shallow descriptions of patterns of observed time use.

Since the work of the multinational time use project, national studies have been repeated at various intervals, ranging from five- (Japan, Canada) to a more typical ten-year interval. The European harmonization work on time use research has also synchronized studies in Europe. There are hence new data from 13 European countries that have been collected after 1998 (European Communities 2003). In addition to the European activities and the surveys of such industrialized countries as Australia, Canada, Japan and New Zealand, time use studies are also increasingly conducted in developing countries (United Nations 2003).

While the very early studies were, essentially, descriptions of living conditions and leisure practices, more recent studies have had diverse uses. Within the frame of economics, Juster and Stafford (1991) distinguish between two major uses. Firstly, time use data have been used to derive macro-level social and economic accounting systems that include non-market activities. Secondly, the data have been used for the micro-level descriptions and modelling of household activities, the related intra-family division of work and the labour supply of households. Furthermore, the delegate issue of undeclared work and moonlighting has been studied on the bases of time use data (Viby Mogensen 1990).

Despite the prominence of the diary method and the multinational data collection efforts, frequent longitudinal panel data and internationally comparable cross-sectional data on entire populations have remained a wish by time use researchers. However, while there are weaknesses in the data, many writers still claim that the data are under-used (Klevmarken 1999; Juster 1999). At the same time the costly collection of the data continuously calls for new uses. Time use data, as they are currently used, are not integrated to serve national accounting, for example. Rather, the data appear as a curiosity with many potential uses.

8.2.2   Theories on Time Use: Allocation Decisions of a Scarce Resource and Reflections of a Social Structure

Time is such an ambiguous concept that, at a descriptive level, any research into the human impacts on the environment is, by definition, interested in time use; human action implies time use. However, time use researchers have also advanced the thought that the survey data can be used to model potential impacts of various demographic and institutional changes and technological innovations. Such a move beyond descriptive time use statistics presupposes considerations of why people spend their time the way they do and theoretical understanding of the use of time. In the following, two major lines of theorizing are considered insofar as they relate to the topic of this chapter and are implicit in the discussion on sustainable consumption.

According to the tradition of home economics (for example, Becker 1965) families operate as mini-firms; time is an abstract commodity; activities are productive and contribute to higher purposes of life; decisions about time allocation depend on the opportunity costs of time as well as the available household production technology. Such simplifications, while they are crude and alien, nevertheless enable a more comprehensive analysis of the non-monetarized social life and the demand for market goods and services; it can be claimed that the demand for goods and services is dependent on the activity patterns of people. Accordingly, the activities of individuals, be they productive or leisure pursuits, require varying material intermediaries, and the economic theory of time allocation advances the understanding of the individual choices between these variously environmentally relevant activities.

The proliferating sociological and cultural approaches on time use have given rise to a qualitative research on time use and to a variety of different conceptions of time. Thus, time use research is not only occupied with the modelling of rational time allocation on an individual level, but seeks as well to elaborate on the different ways that humans experience and relate to time and on the ways time use is regulated by the society. Sure enough, time use is partly a question of the (rational) decisions of individuals, but not all options are open and not all choices are perceived. Time use 'decisions' are affected by various policies, institutional arrangements and technological innovations as well as by embedded 'cultural' norms. There is, indeed, a strand of sociology working towards a sociology of time (Hassard 1990) and suggesting that the explanations of patterns of time use reside also on the more structural level. Within these writings it has been claimed that time is a social construct and that different cultures thus have different conceptions of time (for example, Sorokin and Merton [1937] 1990; Levine 1997). Also, the more specific changes in temporal orientations that coincide with processes of industrialization and modernization have been mapped (for example, Coser and Coser [1963] 1990; Thompson [1967] 1974; Cross 1993). This long line of sociological work precedes the contemporary interest in the sources of 'work-and-spend' lifestyles (Schor 1991), time-squeeze and harriedness (Southerton 2003) and the excessive material consumption of industrialized countries (Røpke 1999).

This chapter is mainly concerned with the specific attempts of relating activity patterns and monetary consumption and hence dependent on the economists' claim that monetary consumption is an input to the household activities. However, this focus is not to suggest that the second line of theorizing is trivial. On the contrary, the sociological explanations of time use make the first claim interesting. Patterns of time use do not result directly from rational individual decisions and technological innovations, but are impacted by many emergent layers of social reality. Consequently, the wide range of time-related policies and institutions condition the changes in activity patterns and enhance or undermine the shifts towards sustainable consumption.

8.2.3   Sustainability: Lifestyles and Patterns of Time Use

Sustainable consumption is presented as a far-reaching concept that addresses lifestyles and the quantity of demand in the wealthy industrialized countries (Princen 1999). Accordingly the discussion seems to presuppose different kinds of changes in the activities or behaviour of individuals and in their patterns of time use. From the point of view of this discussion, time use survey data constitute a resource that has hardly been tapped, albeit a number of questions seem feasible. Can lifestyles be distinguished in time use data and can the changes in lifestyles be linked to consequent changes in demand for products and services? Is it conceivable that such data could help to better understand the potential for substitution between various products and services, the impacts of time-saving technologies and the causes of time-squeeze and work-and-spend lifestyles? Furthermore, if downshifting (Schor 1991) or wealth-in-time (Reisch 2001) are important concepts in the sustainability debate, can the conditions for such changes be traced in the time use data?

A popular topic of mobile phones might serve to rephrase the questions. The rapid increase in the telecommunication service expenditures has frequently been heralded as a sign of the dematerialization of the economy. However, one might also ask when and where the phones are being used. Do they replace some other activities and does telecommunication as an activity require less material inputs than the alternatives? Can we discern other complementary impacts on the structure of the economy. Furthermore, what are the secondary impacts of increased communication in terms of schedules and the patterns of work and leisure activities?

Some of the questions are to be answered more readily based on time use survey data than others. The data are weak in exploring the deep-rooted cultural and sociological explanations of the empirical patterns of time use and the causes of consumption-oriented lifestyles; it is rather obvious that such questions call for qualitative research approaches on time use and for such concepts that acknowledge the different temporal facets of human experience. However, the survey data are potent in the task of describing the temporal context of increasing material consumption in everyday life. This chapter will trace the pursuits that have been made on a descriptive level concerning the linking of time use and the consumption of natural resources. However, instead of considering the specific findings of particular studies such as Fritsch (1974), Schipper et al. (1989), Mäntylä (1996), Piorkowsky (1997), Heiskanen and Pantzar (1997), Jalas (2002) and van der Werf (2002), I will in the following concentrate on the questions of relating and linking time use and monetary consumption data.

8.3 LINKING TIME USE AND CONSUMPTION

8.3.1 The Inputs of Household Activities

There is an axiomatic assumption within much of the time use research that goods are not direct sources of utility and that consumption is a temporal process; only when goods are combined with human time, is it possible to derive utility from them. In other words individuals and households acquire and use goods to engage in activities. This assumption is stated with various degrees of confidence. Schmidt and Viby Mogensen (1990, p. 19) phrase the idea with little caution; '... every main category of time use corresponds to a particular section of the final demand for goods and services', while Juster et al. (1981a, p. 32) argue more strongly that tangible flows '... can always be associated with some corresponding use of time; it is not possible to conceive of a flow of goods being produced or used without some activity being engaged in by one or more persons. Thus, in principle, the entire market economy as well as the production and use of goods within the household can be understood in terms of the allocation of time across alternative activities.'

Similar to Juster et al. (1981a), Gershuny (1987 and 1999) has been keen on demonstrating that, combined with input–output tables, time use data can be used to model the whole society. He argues that '... if we are to understand the processes of structural change in "the economy" [referring to the "formal economy"], we need to consider evidence about behaviour outside it: we need to know more about the detail of daily life' (1987, p. 57). In the 1987 paper, he shows that the employment effects of the rising service sector and new domestic self-service technology can be better appreciated and evaluated from a time use perspective than what is possible with the monetary data alone. Using input–output tables and suggesting that each household activity has a counterpart in the household expenditures he thus follows the effects of changing patterns of time use in the structure of the economy and in employment. As I have proposed (Jalas, 2005), it is possible to track similar changes in the materials or energy use in the economy; the accounting frame is the same, but energy or materials intensity data are substituted for the labour intensity figures of economic activities.

The link between time use and expenditure data is the fundamental basis for considering economic activity and the associated use of natural resources from a time use perspective. Micro-level studies in the field of home economics have approximated household production functions and the inputs of market goods and services, which are utilized in household activities. However, the visions of macro-level socio-economic accounting require consideration of the complete range of goods and services produced by the economy. Such linking of time use and expenditure data has been called matching (Chadeau and Roy 1986), translation (Gershuny 1987), recategorization (Brodersen 1990b) and allocation (Jalas 2002). Heiskanen and Pantzar (1997) refer to a rearrangement of energy use and expenditure data according to 'end-service' categories.

8.3.2 Categories of Everyday Life

In the following I will review some studies that have attempted the linking of time use data and expenditure data. All of them are based on a priori reasoning of the scheme. Such reasoning is based on the lexical time use categories, which imply a selection of goods and services directly or indirectly; like watching TV implies the use of TV equipment. However, it is obvious that not all goods can be allocated to specific time use categories. Furniture, clothing and housing are used in many activities; they constitute the infrastructure that other activities depend on. The list of activities to consider is not self-evident either. Some lexical categories such as telecommunication, clearly encompass multiple different end uses. Likewise, it is possible to conceive of many different, internally consistent means–ends hierarchies in everyday life. Are cooking and eating mere inputs for other, meaningful activities, or should they be regarded as outputs and thus feature in the accounting system independently? Arbitrariness is, however, the nature of all accounting systems; they categorize reality and establish meanings and relations.

Table 8.1 presents the time use categories of six such studies that have proposed a link between time use and expenditures on a macro-level. The space available does not enable the exposition of all the expenditure categories that the authors suggest to attach to the specific categories of time use. However, the arbitrariness of the time use categories makes them interesting as such. For example, the clear production orientation of Chadeau and Roy (1986) is visible in Table 8.1. After presenting the studies I will briefly comment on the major differences between the studies in terms of allocating expenditure to specific time use.

Juster and his colleagues (1981a, see also 1981b and 1985) ambitiously attempt to construct a frame of how market production ultimately contributes to subjective well-being.[1] They call for a time-based account of well-being arguing that the satisfactions associated with flows of goods are subsumed by the satisfactions derived from the activities associated with those goods; activities yield intrinsic benefits. In formulating the relationship between market production and subjective well-being, they distinguish a link between products and patterns of time use (objective well-being) and another link between the patterns of time use and the experienced subjective well-being. It is the former link between market goods and time use that is precisely of interest in this current text.

Contrary to Juster et al., Gershuny (1987 and 1999) has been tracking the reverse relationship while being interested in how the time use changes impact economic activity and consequent employment. The 1987 paper is interesting as it considers explicitly the causal link from changing patterns of time use to the economic activity and utilizes input–output tables of the national accounting. However, the matching scheme of Gershuny appears as a rather tentative part of the illustrative article.

Chadeau and Roy (1986) are explicitly interested in the productive activities of households. They again reverse the causality that was suggested above and claim that 'What households produce and the way they produce depends to a large extent on what they may acquire on the market' (Chadeau and Roy 1986, p. 387). Despite their focus, the scheme covers the full range of consumption expenditures as they also consider so-called pure final consumption products, which do not '... serve in any further productive process before being actually consumed in the proper sense of the term' (p. 387). However, such a definition lumps together, for example, convenience food, clothes, as well as various leisure-related equipment such as sports gear and entertainment technology, resulting in a very heterogeneous and counterintuitive category. On the other hand, the scheme of Chadeau and Roy (1986) is elaborate in terms of the possibilities and the potential impacts of households outsourcing their productive activities. It distinguishes between substitute products and complementary products as input in productive activities as well as the capital equipment of production.

In the same tradition, the Eurostat (1999b) report summarizes European efforts to establish satellite accounts for household production. For such efforts one of the alternatives is the so-called input method in which household production is valued on the bases of used capital and

Table 8.1 *Suggested activity categories for combining household expenditure and time use data*

Juster et al. (1981a, 1981b)	Chadeau and Roy (1986)*	Gershuny (1987)	Brodersen (1990a) and Viby Mogensen (1990)	Jalas (2002)	Van der Werf (2002)
Education	Making edible goods	Housework	Paid work	Washing and ironing	Work and commuting
Child care	Crop growing, animal husbandry	Cooking meals, washing up.	House-keeping	Cleaning and organizing	Household work
		Eating meals & snacks			
Medical care	Sewing, weaving and knitting	Child care	Maintenance work	Cooking, preserving and dishwashing	Education
Home improvement	Carpentry	Shopping	Care for others	Meals and snacks at home	Sleep
Social	Major construction work	Travel, communications	Purchase of goods and services	Shopping	Personal hygiene
Organizations	Preparing and cooking food	Dressing, toilet, sleep	Education	All transport	Eating
Interpersonal	Preserving, deep freezing	Restaurants	Necessary time	Use of cars in shopping	Hotels, restaurants, cafés
Home maintenance	Dishwashing, laundry, ironing	Pubs & social clubs	Sports and the like	Use of cars in commuting	Reading books
Personal care	House cleaning	Cinema, theatre, social events	Restaurant/café	Eating in restaurants	Reading magazines
Shopping/administration	Shopping	Playing sports	Entertainment	Culture and sports events	TV
Cooking	Repair of clothes	Walks	Watching TV	Reading	Using computers
Market work	Repair of vehicles	Entertaining or visiting friends	Socializing	Using TV and audio equipment	Playing

160

Sports	Repair of other durables	TV, radio, music	Reading	Having a sauna	Culture
Spectator events	Repair and decorating	Reading, studying	Other free time		Sports
Active leisure	Gardening	Conversations, relaxing	Holiday trips		
Passive leisure	Child care	Odd jobs, gardening			
Reading	Personal care	Hobbies and pastimes, knitting and sewing			
Eating	Supervising children	Holidays			
Sleeping	Personal beauty services	Personal services			
	Pet care				
	Travel				
	Household management				
	Telephone calls				

Note: * Due to the space limits not all categories of the original scheme are presented.

161

labour inputs. Thus, such a method requires the reclassification of the final consumption expenditures of the SNA. However, just as the scheme of Chadeau and Roy (1986), this production-oriented scheme does not elaborate on leisure-related consumption activities.

Viby Mogensen (1990) and his colleagues share the interest of Gershuny (1987) in their project in which they trace the potential economic impacts of the changes in everyday life of Danes. The project represents a major effort to expound on the use of time use statistics in macro-level economic analysis. Viby Mogensen and his colleagues take as a starting point that the demand for market goods and services cannot be explained only by income and demographic variables. Rather, they ask whether the trends in time use have significantly impacted and are likely to impact consumption and the structure of the Danish economy. As compared to the earlier attempts such as Juster et al. (1981a), the work of Mogensen et al. can be regarded as less tentative as the matching scheme is applied to a more extensive longitudinal series of data sets containing expenditure and time use data. They have also decided to reduce the fine-grained classification scheme of Chadeau and Roy (1986) to a much more aggregate level of activities and allow for, or admit, a wider range of non-activity-specific expenditure items.

There are more recent papers, which bear a specific interest in tracking the environmental consequences of patterns of time use. Wenke (1999) has been early in suggesting such a system of accounting, but has not worked with empirical data. Jalas (2002) and van der Werf (2002) have both employed input–output tables to study the energy intensity of free-time activities. However, the energy intensity figures of these two studies appear to differ rather significantly. One of the sources of the differences is the treatment of the energy expenditure of housing and heating, but, other than this, the sources of the differences are not readily observable.

Both housing and dwelling expenditures and transportation-related expenditures are environmentally significant (Spangenberg and Lorek 2002), but difficult to treat in the above schemes. Juster et al. (1981a), Eurostat (1999b), though implicitly, and van der Werf (2002) suggest the allocation of housing and dwelling expenditures to the specific activities that take place at home, whereas Gershuny assigns housing-related expenditures surprisingly to housework. Others have argued that the expenditure is not dependent on the hours spent at home.

Travel and transportation expenditures have also been treated differently in the schemes. Van der Werf is specific in allocating different modes of transportation to different activity categories. In his analyses there is thus no separate category for transportation. Brodersen (1990a and 1990b) and Jalas (2002) have used secondary data to allocate the different modes of transportation to specific activity categories. Juster et al. (1981a) are not specific in their treatment of transportation in the activity scheme, and while Chadeau and Roy (1986) acknowledge the different uses of transportation services, they do not provide allocation suggestions, either. The Eurostat report (1999b), which is significant as it is both recent and directly policy-related, allocates travel-related expenditures to an independent productive activity 'Travel' with no further allocation. However, following the logic of a production-oriented scheme, the report suggests treating the purchase of 'transportation services' as final consumption, since there is no 'production' involved. Hence, transportation-related consumption expenditures are separated into two different categories depending on whether they are intermediary consumption or final consumption.

Finally, there is still another point to make. The studies originate from a 20-year period, but hardly make reference to each other. There are no direct references between the papers, except for Brodersen (1990a) and the Eurostat report (1999b) referring to Chadeau and Roy (1986) and Jalas (2002) referring to the work of Brodersen (1990a). This may be due to the fact that many of the papers have been published as parts of edited books or conference proceedings and not as journal articles. Another reason might be the differences in the points of view and in the interests that have brought the authors to consider the linking of the data. Regardless of the reasons, research on the time and consumption nexus, at least as it has been discussed in these papers, has not accumulated to anything more than individual suggestions. It is, however, obvious that the theoretical work of household economists as well as the efforts of extending the boundaries of national accounting bear a close resemblance to the interests of the studies reviewed here and may facilitate more coherent discussions of the same theme.

8.3.3 Can Time Use Data Explain Changes in the Use of Natural Resources?

The underlying assumption of the studies presented above is that goods and services enter as inputs to specific activities. Based on such an assumption they outlined potential and plausible links between the patterns of time use and the demand for goods and services. But establishing the connection between time and consumption at one point of time is not a sufficient condition for being able to link *changes* in time use to *changes* in expenditure. Rather, such a link assumes that the 'technology' of everyday life – the household 'production' technology – is known or essentially remains the same; the same types of goods are used in the same activities in the same amounts.

The assumption of no technological change is counterintuitive. Activities, such as travelling, depend on a changing mix of different technologies. In addition to technological innovations, also social innovations, such as outsourcing domestic activities, impact the type and volume of material goods needed in the various household activities. It is thus obvious that changes in expenditure do not result directly from the changes in the patterns of time use.

A more relevant – in fact a crucial – question for the proposed approach is whether time use changes occur independently of technological change. Regarding this question, the economic theory of time allocation and the sociological theory of time use take a very different stance. Independent time use changes are problematic from the point of view of household economics. Technology, together with opportunity costs, *explains* the changes in time allocation in the theory of Becker (1965). Similarly, Gershuny (1987) suggests that technological innovations such TVs and VCRs have *caused* changes in entertainment-related time use. However, time use is not a mere question of available technologies and rational allocation. Rather, as was argued before, social and cultural factors impact the set of feasible alternatives and thus condition individuals' decisions regarding time use. In the same vein, if products and services are regarded as inputs in non-productive, intrinsically meaningful consumption processes, there are no theoretical objections to assume that the patterns of time use can change independently of such technological innovations that alter material inputs of these activities.

These questions can be empirically approached by analysing the time series data of expenditures and time use. Viby Mogensen and his colleagues (1990) claim that there were no such data existing before their project in the late 1980s in which they analysed three Danish time use surveys of 1964, 1975 and 1987. However, it appears that at least Juster et al. (1981a) should be included in such a list as they present an empirical analysis of time and expenditure data from the two waves of 1965 and 1975. In addition to Juster et al. (1981a) and Viby Mogensen (1990) such an attempt has been repeated by Jalas (2005) while analysing the changes in consumption in Finland based on two waves of data from 1987–88 and from 1999–2000.

What are the results? Viby Mogensen reframes the intuitive limits of time use data in explaining monetary patterns of consumption: 'Altogether it is clear that there is no simple connection between time use and consumption. Many other factors – such as income, housing arrangement, and life cycle placement – play a decisive role as well' (Viby Mogensen 1990, p. 42). In elaborating on the findings in more detail Brodersen (1990b) notes that dwelling expenses rose sharply in the period they analysed – and since dwelling costs were not matched with any activities, the analysis has no power in terms of this major change. The focus of Brodersen is not particularly on the changing technology of the activities – he does not, for example, present expenditure per time use – ratios. However, he states that the changes in DIY expenditures and related maintenance services as well as the transportation-related expenditures follow the respective changes of time use, which indicates that technology, when analysed on such an aggregate level, has not changed in these activities. The major 'technological' change took place in dwelling expenses; they rose significantly, while time use at home declined. Finally, Brodersen suggests a list of difficulties and uncertainties in comparing the data from the different periods. Despite these obstacles, the project, nevertheless, also included an econometric estimation of the potential of time use changes to impact demand. The result of this exercise was that any such impacts on the economy that would cause difficulties in adjusting, are unlikely (Gelting 1990).

Juster et al. (1981a) present an interesting comparison of how the 'goods intensity of activities' (market value of used inputs per time used in the activity) has developed from 1965 to 1975. On average, the intensities have risen with the increases in GDP. However, they have not risen at an equal pace. The authors note that the intensity of household production activity has risen and assign this to the array of household technologies that substitute goods for labour, the so-called time-saving technologies. Also, active leisure and spectator sports clearly required more expenditures per unit of time in 1975. The greatest increases appear with interpersonal communication, which Juster and his colleagues assign to increasing telecommunication expenditures.

While studying the changes in the energy use in Finland, I have included a factor of time use in a decomposition frame in addition to the demographic variables (Jalas, 2005). This study focused on the direct and indirect energy requirements of final consumption in Finland concerning a period from 1987–88 to 1999–2000. The changes in the primary energy demand were decomposed to changes in the following decomposition factors:

- population growth;
- changes in relative shares of population living in different household types;
- changes in time use within the analysed time use categories;
- changes in the energy intensity of these time use categories;
- changes in household infrastructure.

A base-year decomposition indicated that while the population growth and demographic changes towards smaller households both contributed to a significant increase in energy demand, Finns had at the same time shifted their activity patterns towards less energy-intensive activities. Outdoor activities, indoor hobbies, viewing TV and, contrary to the common thinking, also sleeping time, had increased their share of the day during the 1990s in Finland. However, it also appeared that while Finns had engaged in less energy-intensive activities, the energy intensities of the activities had risen. In actual numbers, which, however, need to be interpreted with caution, the technological impact, that is, the energy intensity impact, was greater than the impact of changing patterns of time use.

The results of this energy analysis cannot be directly compared with Juster et al. (1981a) and Viby Mogensen (1990) analyses of expenditures. However, the same factors have impacted the structure of household expenditures and the energy requirements of households. Thus, my results complied in many respects with those of Viby Mogensen (1990) and Brodersen (1990b); demographic changes are important as well as the changes in housing infrastructure. Furthermore, the time-saving household technology could also be noted in the energy analyses as an increase in the energy requirements matched with slightly less time used in the productive household activities (Jalas, 2005).

8.4   CONCLUDING REMARKS

Time use data that are collected in nationwide representative surveys document the course of everyday life in terms of activities, social contacts and location. Such data have been used in the micro-level analysis of household production as well as the macro-level analysis of extended welfare. However, these data have hardly been tapped by the discussions that originate from and orbit around the concept of sustainable consumption.

From the point of view of sustainable consumption, there are a number of potential applications of such data. Within this chapter, I have concentrated on such applications that stem from the assumption that market goods and services are not direct sources of utility, but rather enter household activities as inputs. Hence I suggested two applications of time use data. Firstly, it is conceivable that descriptive material accounting could be extended to cover non-market activities. Such an analysis would provide a more comprehensive view of how natural resources ultimately contribute to human well-being and a fresh point of view to observe the changes in lifestyles and consumption.

Secondly, time use data help to contextualize the normative prescriptions of the less materials-intensive patterns of economic activity. It is obvious that the changes in the structure and volume of demand have a counterpart in the non-market activity of individuals; patterns of time use both condition and have direct implications for the changes in demand. Furthermore, from a policy point of view it is crucial to distinguish that the patterns of time use do not appear as rational decisions based on wages and available household technology. Rather, time is regulated by different policies, social conventions and institutions. Thus, if we accept the claim that sustainable consumption is to a significant degree an issue of changing patterns of consumption and different lifestyles, it is these policies, conventions and institutions that should be addressed.

The linking of expenditure data and time use data is an elementary step in analysing consumption from a time use perspective. This chapter reviewed some of the earlier attempts to establish a macro-level matching or linking of time use and household expenditure data. These previous writings constitute a rather sporadic body of work. Environmental concerns have also only been a tiny, close to non-existent sub-track within the interests that have motivated time use surveys. However, the issue is appearing on the agenda of environmental policy-makers as a number of constituencies are taking an interest in the subject. Based on an assignment from the Japanese Ministry of Trade and Industry (METI) and the Japanese Institute for Advanced Industrial Science and Technology (AIST), Hofstetter and Madjar (2003) have reviewed attempts to link physical resources, time use and indicators of subjective well-being. In their report they suggest further work with Japanese, Danish and UK data. The work of van der Werf is associated with a long history of energy analysis at the Dutch Center for Energy and Environmental Studies (IVEM) (for example, Biesiot and Noorman 1999). Thus, albeit the work of van der Werf represents a rather tentative attempt in using time use data in energy analyses, it is obviously important as being part of the work at IVEM. There is also a Finnish government-financed research proposal to study sustainable consumption and the possibilities of linking time use and expenditure data (Perrels 2003).

Some of the reasons for the apparent fading and the current lack of academic interests in linking time use data and consumption expenditure data are rather obvious. The available data do not enable an empirically-based 'matching' of the two data sets and, as Gershuny (1987) suggests, collecting such data is surely confronted with practical difficulties as well as low response rates. However, many of the obstacles that Viby Mogensen (1990) and his colleagues confronted in their project originated from the differences between the existing data sets. Such obstacles may be overcome by the continuing harmonization of time use research. Furthermore it also appears possible to enhance the possibilities and empirical grounds of linking expenditure and time use data by including more activity-specific variables related to expenditures and household technology in the time use surveys.

There are sound, policy-related reasons for pursuing an improvement in the matching of the two data sets. While Viby Mogensen and his colleagues concluded that changing patterns of time use can hardly cause such changes in demand that would cause difficulties in adjusting, the debate on sustainable

168   *Explaining consumption*

consumption is a subtler issue. Rather than seeking to cause disruptions in the economy, realistic policies on sustainable consumption should probably pursue more incremental changes in the structure and volume of economic activity. For devising applicable policies on sustainable consumption the everyday life perspective of time use survey data may thus be of value in setting the context.

NOTES

* This work has been supported by the Helsinki School of Economics Foundation, the Finnish Ministry of the Environment and the Finnish Graduate School on Environmental Social Sciences. I also wish to thank Eva Heiskanen and Raimo Lovio for their continuing support.
1. The work of Juster and his colleagues has been published in a volume that resulted from a conference of social accounting (1981a) and as a journal paper (Juster et al. 1981b). The majority of the arguments have also been repeated in Juster et al. (1985) and in Dow and Juster (1985). However, the journal article (1981b) and the 1985 papers do not repeat the empirical work on the matching scheme.

REFERENCES

Becker, Gary (1965), 'A theory of the allocation of time', *The Economic Journal*, **75**, 493–517.
Biesiot, Wouter and Klass Jan Noorman (1999), 'Energy requirements of household consumption: a case study of the Netherlands', *Ecological Economics*, **28**, 367–83.
Brodersen, Søren (1990a), 'Reanalysis of the consumer surveys. Classification and method', in Gunnar Viby Mogensen (ed.), *Time and Consumption*, Copenhagen: Danmarks Statistik, pp. 273–90.
Brodersen, Søren (1990b), 'A historical analysis of household expenditure surveys', in Gunnar Viby Mogensen (ed.), *Time and Consumption*, Copenhagen: Danmarks Statistik, pp. 291–331.
Chadeau, Ann and Caroline Roy (1986), 'Relating households' final consumption to household activities: Substitutability or complementarity between market and non-market production', *Review of Income and Wealth*, **32** (4), 387–407.
Coser, Lewis and Rose Coser (1963), 'Time perspective and social structure', reprinted in John Hassard (ed.) (1990), *The Sociology of Time*, London, UK: Macmillan.
Cross, Gary (1993), *Time and Money. The Making of the Consumer Culture*, London, UK: Routledge.
Dow, Greg K. and F. Thomas Juster (1985), 'Goods, time, and well-being: The joint dependence problem', in F. Thomas Juster and Frank P. Stafford (eds), *Time, Goods, and Well-Being*, Ann Arbor, US: The University of Michigan, pp. 397–414.
Elchardus, Mark (1991), 'Rationality and the specialization of meaning. A sociological approach to the allocation of time', in Gerrit Antonides, Wil Arts and

W. Fred van Raaij (eds), *The Consumption of Time and the Timing of Consumption. Proceedings of the International Colloquium, Amsterdam, 6–8 November 1990*, Amsterdam, the Netherlands: Royal Netherlands Academy of Arts and Sciences, pp. 69–86.

European Communities (2003), *Time Use at Different Stages of Life – Results from 13 European Countries*, http://europa.eu.int/comm/eurostat/Public/datashop/print-catalogue/EN?catalogue=Eurostat&collection=12-Working%20papers%20and%20studies&product=KS-CC-03-001-__-N-EN.

Eurostat (1999a), *Survey on Time Use. Activity coding list*, Eurostat DOC E2/TUS/3.6/99, http://www.iser.essex.ac.uk/activities/iatur/pdf/abstract31/word7.pdf.

Eurostat (1999b), *Proposal for a Satellite Account of Household Production*, Final report of the project SC96LO9 Time Use Survey: Development of a European Satellite System of Household Production, Eurostat.

Fisher, Kimberly and Jonathan Gershuny (2002), 'Setting the trend for cross-national European time use research', A paper presented at the *International Association for Time Use Research Annual conference 2002*, Lisbon, 15–18 October, http://pascal.iseg.utl.pt/~cisep/IATUR/abstracts/abstract33.htm.

Fritsch, Albert J. (1974), *The Contrasumers: A Citizen's Guide to Resource Conservation*, New York, US: Praeger.

Gelting, Thomas (1990), 'Projection of time use and consumption', in Gunnar Viby Mogensen (ed.), *Time and Consumption*, Copenhagen: Danmarks Statistik, pp. 359–67.

Gershuny, Jonathan (1987), 'Time use and the dynamics of the service sector', *The Service Industry Journal*, **7** (4), 56–72.

Gershuny, Jonathan (1999), 'Informal economic activity and time use evidence', in Joachim Merz and Manfred Ehling (eds), *Time Use – Research, Data and Policy*, Baden Baden: Nomos, pp. 13–24.

Harvey, Andrew S. (1999), 'Time use research: The roots to the future', in Joachim Merz and Manfred Ehling (eds), *Time Use – Research, Data and Policy*, Baden Baden: Nomos, pp. 123–49.

Hassard, John (ed.) (1990), *The Sociology of Time*, London, UK: Macmillan.

Heiskanen, Eva and Mika Pantzar (1997), 'Towards sustainable consumption: Two new perspectives', *Journal of Consumer Policy*, **20**, 409–42.

Hofstetter, Patrick and Michael Madjar (2003), *Linking Change in Happiness, Time-use, Sustainable Consumption, and Environmental Impacts: An Attempt to Understand Time-rebound Effects – Final Report*, available at http://geocities.com/patrick_hofstetter/#_List_of_publications_(English only) [accessed 4.9.2003].

Jalas, Mikko (2002), 'A time use perspective on the materials intensity of consumption', *Ecological Economics*, **41**, 109–23.

Jalas, Mikko (2005), 'Everyday life – context of the increasing energy demands: Time-use survey data in a decomposition analysis', *Journal of Industrial Ecology*, **9** (1–2).

Juster, F. Thomas (1999), 'The future of research on time use', in Joachim Merz and Manfred Ehling (eds), *Time Use – Research, Data and Policy*, Baden Baden: Nomos, pp. 551–8.

Juster, F. Thomas and Frank P. Stafford (1991), 'The allocation of time: Empirical findings, behavioural models, and problems of measurement', *Journal of Economic Literature*, **XXIX**, 471–522.

Juster, F. Thomas, Paul N. Courant and Greg K. Dow (1981a), 'The theory and measurement of well-being: A suggested framework for accounting and analysis', in F. Thomas Juster and Kenneth C. Land (eds), *Social Accounting Systems: Essays on the State of the Art*, New York, US: Academic Press, pp. 23–94.

Juster, F. Thomas, Paul N. Courant and Greg K. Dow (1981b), 'A theoretical framework for the measurement of well-being', *Review of Income and Wealth*, **27** (1), 1–31.

Juster, F. Thomas, Paul N. Courant and Greg K. Dow (1985), 'A conceptual framework for the analysis of time allocation data', in F. Thomas Juster and Frank P. Stafford (eds), *Time, Goods, and Well-Being*, Ann Arbor, US: The University of Michigan, pp. 113–32.

Klevmarken, Anders (1999), 'Microeconomic analysis of time use data: Did we reach the Promised Land?', in Joachim Merz and Manfred Ehling (eds) *Time Use – Research, Data and Policy*, Baden Baden: Nomos, pp. 423–56.

Levine, Robert (1997), *A Geography of Time*, New York, US: BasicBooks.

Mäntylä, Kaj (1996), 'Energy consumption in spare time activities', *in LINKKI Research Program on Consumer Habits and Energy Conservation – Summary Report*, Helsinki: Helsinki University Printing House, pp. 247–59.

Pentland, Wendy E. and Andrew S. Harvey (1999), 'Future directions', in Wendy E. Pentland, Andrew S. Harvey, M. Powell Lawton and Mary Ann McColl (eds), *Time Use Research in the Social Sciences*, New York, US: Kluwer, pp. 259–68.

Pentland, Wendy E., Andrew S. Harvey, M. Powell Lawton and Mary Ann McColl (eds), Time Use Research in the Social Sciences, New York, US: Kluwer.

Perrels, Adriaan (2003), 'Refining consumption modelling – distinguishing volume and quality choices', A paper presented at the *6th Nordic Conference on the Environmental Social Sciences, 12–14 June 2003, Turku.*

Piorkowsky, Michael-Burkhard (1997), 'Der Einfluss des Freizeitverhaltens auf den Energieverbrauch der Haushalte' ('The impact of free time activities on the energy use of households'), in Jörg Fasholz and Herbert Weber (eds), *17. Hochschultage Energie 1–2 Oktober 1996, Essen. [Proceedings]*, Essen, Germany: Verlag Peter Pomp, pp. 79–89.

Princen, Thomas (1999), 'Consumption and environment: some conceptual issues', *Ecological Economics*, **31**, 347–63.

Reisch, Lucia A. (2001), 'Time and wealth. The role of time and temporalities for sustainable patterns of consumption', *Time and Society*, **10** (2/3), 367–85.

Robinson, John P. (1977), *How Americans Use Time. A Social-Psychological Analysis of Everyday Behavior*, New York, US, London, UK: Praeger Publishers.

Røpke, Inge (1999), 'The dynamics of willingness to consume', *Ecological Economics*, **28**, 399–420.

Sachs, Wolfgang (1999), *Planet Dialectics: Explorations in Environment and Development*, Halifax, Canada, Nova Scotia: Fernwood Publishing; Johannesburg: Witwaterstand University Press; London, UK, New York, US: Zed Books.

Sanne, Christer (2000), 'Dealing with environmental savings in a dynamic economy – how to stop chasing your tail in the pursuit of sustainability', *Energy Policy*, **28**, 487–95.

Schipper, Lee, Sarita Bartlett, Dianne Hawk and Edward Vine (1989), 'Linking lifestyles and energy use: A matter of time', *Annual Review of Energy*, **14**, 273–320.

Schmidt, Erik I. and Gunnar Viby Mogensen (1990), 'The problem', in Gunnar Viby Mogensen (ed.), *Time and Consumption*, Copenhagen: Danmarks Statistik, pp. 13–22.

Schor, Juliet B. (1991), *The Overworked American: The Unexpected Decline of Leisure*, New York, US: BasicBooks.

Sorokin, Pitirim and Robert Merton (1937), 'Social-time: A methodological and functional analysis', reprinted in John Hassard (ed.) (1990), *The Sociology of Time*, London, UK: Macmillan.

Southerton, Dale (2003), 'Squeezing time: Allocating practices, coordinating networks and scheduling society', *Time and Society*, **12** (1), 5–25.

Spangenberg, Joachim H. and Sylvia Lorek (2002), 'Environmentally sustainable household consumption: From aggregate environmental pressures to priority fields of action', *Ecological Economics*, **43**, 127–40.

Szalai, Alexander (ed.) (1972), *The Use of Time: Daily Activities of Urban and Suburban Populations in Twelve Countries*, The Hague: Mouton.

Thompson, Edward P. (1967), 'Time, work-discipline, and industrial capitalism', reprinted in Michael W. Flinn and T. Christopher Smout (eds) (1974), *Essays in Social History*, Oxford: Clarendon Press, pp. 39–77.

United Nations (2003), *Time Use Surveys*, http://unstats.un.org/unsd/methods/timeuse/index.htm [accessed 4.9.2003].

van der Werf, Peter (2002), *Tijdbesteding en Energiegebruik* (*Time Use and Energy Use*, in Dutch), IVEM-doctoraalverslag [Master's] nr. 149, Groningen: University of Groningen.

Viby Mogensen, Gunnar (ed.) (1990), *Time and Consumption*, Copenhagen: Danmarks Statistik.

Wenke, Martin (1999), 'Time use, sustainable consumption and environmental protection measures of private households – some aspects of combining national accounts and time use data', in Joachim Merz and Manfred Ehling (eds), *Time Use – Research, Data and Policy*, Baden Baden: Nomos, pp. 180–94.

PART III

Changing consumption

9. Sustainable consumption as a consumer policy issue

Lucia A. Reisch

9.1 INTRODUCTION

For the first time since consumer policy had emerged as a distinctive policy field in the 1960s in Europe, a normative notion, which goes far beyond direct individual consumer benefits, has been put at the core of a national consumer policy strategy, namely: sustainable consumption and production. To date, sustainable consumption and production have been perceived exclusively as environmental and development policy issues, not as consumer policy issues. The fact that, in Germany, the Federal Ministry of Consumer Protection has now decided to actively promote and support sustainable patterns of consumption has two consequences. Firstly, an increased political attention and public visibility of the issue of sustainable consumption; secondly, a broadened perspective of the subject, since 'the consumer' (however he or she is defined) on micro-level and private consumption on macro-level are explicitly added to the picture, complementing the dominating view of businesses and the state as primarily responsible actors.

This chapter is built on the hypothesis that, with a consumer policy ministry taking the lead in the sustainable consumption debate, an opportunity for a more holistic and more effective approach to promote sustainable consumption has opened up. Since the conceptual thinking together of 'sustainable development' and traditional consumer policy in a concept of 'consumer policy for sustainability' is relatively new – both in academia and in politics – the chapter starts out with an overview on the scope and scale of consumer policy. In a second section, the process and results of a reorientation towards a 'new consumer policy' is presented and discussed. Following this discussion, an integrated view of the consumer is proposed that conceptualizes the consumer as fulfilling three different but interrelated roles in three social systems: the market, civil society and the community. In conclusion, the chapter reflects on the necessary next steps to implementing the concept of a 'sustainable consumer policy' in both academic discourse and politics.

While the chapter discusses its topic against the backcloth of the new German consumer policy strategy, it might provide useful lessons to learn for other countries' sustainable development policies. After all, most OECD countries are faced with similar global trends and the challenge of sustainable development. And for the EU-25 countries, it certainly holds true that the scope of action of national independent consumer policies is steadily shrinking due to increased consumer policy legislation on a European level.

9.2 SCOPE AND SCALE OF CONSUMER POLICY

Concepts of consumer policy are context-bound and history-related. Three constituent characteristics can be identified: consumer policy's relationship with other policy areas (for example, with competition policy and environmental policy), the overall strategic goals and *Leitbilder* it promotes (for example, material wealth or sustainable development), and the generally propagated level of intervention (that is, a state interventionist versus a free market laissez-faire approach) (see Reisch 2004).

Historically, early consumer policy ideas in post-war Germany were dominated by the neo-liberal Freiburg School, which – as the Chicago School in the USA today – regards competition policy as the sole and most effective consumer policy. The notion of *empowered consumers* at the heart of an effective competition regime and an independent consumer policy to promote and safeguard this empowerment was established in the 1960s, when former president John F. Kennedy proclaimed a 'Consumer Bill of Rights' (Lampman 1988). The basic idea is that consumers can only live up to their role as autonomous market players and herewith contribute to functional markets if they are endowed with rights that balance their weaker position in the market place. The four basic rights for consumers, which had been set up in this bill, were also incorporated in the European Community's first Consumer Policy Programme of 1975: the right to safety, that is, the right to be protected against the marketing of goods that are hazardous to health and life; the right to be informed, that is, to be protected against fraudulent, deceitful, or grossly misleading information, advertising, labelling, or other practices, and to be given the facts needed to make an informed choice; the right to choose, that is, to be assured of access to a variety of goods and services at competitive prices; and in those industries in which competition is not workable and government regulation is substituted, an assurance of satisfactory quality and service at a fair price; and the right to be heard, in other words, to be assured that consumer interests will receive full and sympathetic consideration in the formulation of government policy.

These basic rights have gained in relevance in the following decades and are also relevant in the sustainable development debate. For instance, the *right to safety*, armed with strict liability laws, has created comparatively high safety standards for European and US products and has led to intensive controlling schemes, in particular for food and consumer items. However, controlling schemes have two general problems. Firstly, only those health risks that are known – and 'scientifically proven' – are tested for, which means that potentially dangerous chemicals (for example, acrylamid) or potential allergens in genetically modified food items may pass those schemes. Secondly, controlling schemes tend to bear significant costs which, in practice, leads to different safety levels depending on the financial possibilities of the state or nation state managing these schemes. Here, voluntary private controlling schemes run by businesses and private certification bodies can potentially fill the safety gap – but only if consumers are willing to pay for it.

Similarly, the *right to choose* is the key argument in Europe's scepticism against the production and marketing of genetically modified food. Both organic and conventional farmers and their associations fear that once green GM technology is on the fields, it will spread uncontrollably and hence make it impossible to meet the high purity standards that organic food certification bodies (for example, IFOAM) have set. Hence, the consumer will over time lose the option to choose GMO-free food items.

Moreover, the *right to be informed* and the *right to be heard* are both intensely debated against the background of the Rio Declaration of 1992. Already then, three 'principles of access' were formulated: access to information, to public participation and to justice. The Aarhus Convention that came into force in 2001, anchored these three principles as legally binding citizens' environmental rights. Consumer activists today promote the idea of using the Convention as a blueprint for the development of general citizens' consumer rights. With increased access to information from both businesses and state agencies, consumers will be empowered, for example, to receive information not only on product, but also on process qualities such as fair trade labour standards or animal rights issues. On a global level, transparency initiatives such as the Global Reporting Initiative aim at providing consumer-citizens with relevant business information.

During the past decades, three new consumer rights have been propagated by consumer policy actors: the right to representation, the right to adequate and effective legal protection and the right to protection of the private sphere. The latter is a reaction to the tremendously growing misuse of private data (for example, via data mining or spamming) made possible by new developments in information and communication technology (Reisch 2003a). The right to representation was designed to counterbalance the structurally disadvantaged status of the private consumer as a member of an interest group that is potentially difficult to organize due to the 'logic of collective action' in large heterogeneous groups (Olson 1965). The right to legal protection was developed to compensate for the relatively weak position of private consumers as laypersons in legal action as compared to companies as professional and experienced litigants.

In this traditional, protective and somehow defensive consumer rights approach to consumer policy, the primary policy tools are information – which is expected to meet a 'rational consumer' – and legal protection. The overall aim is to increase the material welfare of the consumer in a social market economy. Following basically the perspective of neoclassical economics, the consumer is simplified as a 'black box', which strives towards efficient utility maximization. This view was challenged when the environmental agenda entered consumer policy in the 1980s, and the scope of the policy field was extended to environmental, and soon also development issues. It soon became clear that even good-quality information is not sufficient to achieve behaviour change. Environmental policy promoting 'greener consumption styles' necessarily had to open the 'black box' and introduce an empirically more valid – and hence more complex if not 'unmanageable' – view of the consumer, which recognizes his or her cognitive, emotional, and behavioural limitations and inconsistent, habit-bound, and symbol-driven behaviour. Behavioural science-oriented consumer research, armed with the results of cognitive psychology and – later – experimental economics, had gained momentum since the 1970s and provided the necessary empirical and theoretical knowledge of the consumer as market actor (Reisch 2004).

Consumer policy as conceptualized today operates as direct and indirect, and as market-related and public sector-related policy (Reisch 2004). *Direct consumer policy* deals with legal, safety and economic issues that are consumer-related, including those of health- and nutrition-related consumer protection. It also comprises the fields of consumer research, consumer information and education, and the promotion of consumer associations and cooperative action. The latter is legitimized by the need to compensate for structural weaknesses on the consumer side as regards obtaining information, organizing and representing their interests, and hence to safeguard the market balance between the market players and secure functioning markets. As *indirect consumer policy*, it considers consumer interests in other policy areas such as environmental and social policy, and safeguards public goods and the global commons (for example, consumer education, public transport infrastructure, public services).

Market-related consumer policy comprises the design of the framework for legal certainty, the competitive base of the market, transparency and a clear division of responsibilities within which marketable consumer product-service systems are provided by private and public suppliers in sufficient quantities, in the desired quality and at affordable prices. Consumer policy in the *public sector* includes the promotion and monitoring of the provision of goods and services in non-competitive areas (natural monopolies) in which public (or state-protected) monopolists supply the market, and of public services provided by public agencies.

Policies aiming at supporting sustainable consumption styles and providing supportive infrastructures – 'sustainable consumption policies' – comprise elements of all four: they can be market-related and public sector-related, direct and indirect. Regarding relevant policy fields, consumer policy is *cross-sectoral politics*. In the Coalition Agreement of the German government as of September 2002, consumer policy has been anchored – for the first time ever in a governmental document – as a central, cross-theme, cross-departmental and cross-sectoral task of federal government. In order to gain political momentum, federal consumer policy, that is, in the first place the newly founded Federal Ministry of Consumer Protection, Food and Agriculture, has to clarify its strategic role in relation to the other policy areas, in particular to economic, social and sustainability policies. The first step into that direction has been the national Action Plan for Consumer Protection (Government of the Federal Republic of Germany 2003), which was presented to the public in May 2003. A second step is expected from the national Consumer Policy Strategy, which will soon be released. At European level, and according to its own rhetoric (European Commission 2002), 'systematic integration of consumer interests in all relevant policy areas' is striven for while also taking account of other sectoral interests in consumer policy. While such an overarching European consumer policy strategy conceptualizes consumer issues in a broad sense and as cross-cutting issues in all relevant policy sectors, there is in fact little evidence to date of the integration of EU consumer policy in other areas such as environment, competition or financial issues (DTI 2003).

In all OECD countries, consumer policy has tended to be seen as a relatively low-key area in terms of government priorities (DTI 2003). In Germany, this has slightly changed with the institutionalization of a Federal Ministry for Consumer Protection resulting from the BSE crisis that had hit Germany in the late 1990s. Yet, it is still mostly the defensive management of food scandals and other negative events that increase political visibility and public attention of the ministry's activities – rather than a proactive, creative, continuous cross-cutting quality of life policy. This also holds true for non-governmental consumer policy actors whose relative profile seems to have lessened somewhat in the past decade. However, one has to acknowledge that consumer actors and activism have partly changed their appearance, and might be (unintentionally) disguised in political consumerism (Micheletti, 2003) or citizen movements such as Attac or Greenpeace. The latter, for instance, has founded its own consumer organization in Germany called 'Einkaufsnetz' ('Shopping Net'), which has reached significant attention within only one year, promoting healthy and sustainable consumption patterns. Established consumer organizations are both competing and cooperating with new actors in the policy field, forming campaign-specific actor alliances, non-governmental organizations for specific supply systems (for example, 'Foodwatch' and 'Slow Food' for the food sector), and theme-related alliances (for example, the currently running national 'Fair Feels Good' campaign for fair trade goods). Given their cross-sectoral function and partly public funding, consumer organizations are indeed ideal communicators and initiators of cooperation and communication between and within civil society's actor groups, ministries and businesses.

9.3   REORIENTATION TOWARDS NEW CONSUMER POLICY

In November 2003, the British Ministry of Trade and Industry published a comparative study of consumer policy regimes protecting and empowering consumers within ten OECD countries (DTI 2003). The aim of this report was threefold. Firstly, to compare UK's consumer policy regime with other OECD countries' and to learn lessons from other regimes' good practices, successes and pitfalls. Secondly, to inform the development of a new consumer strategy in the UK, which is due to be completed by Summer 2004. Thirdly, to provide a source of information that will encourage debate amongst the EU and OECD countries about the importance of consumers and the role of consumer policy for economic prosperity and quality of life.

Likewise, attempts to redefine, re-evaluate, and reposition the policy field of consumer policy and to develop timely consumer policy strategies in the light of new challenges and current trends, are on the agenda of several European nation states and the European Community today. The challenges of an enlarged Europe, of the trends towards an information society and knowledge society, the ongoing liberalization, deregulation and privatization of public utilities and governmental services, the issue of global governance, global markets and citizen empowerment, the trend towards increasing social and spatial mobility and towards a general acceleration of life, and, last but certainly not least, the political commitment to promote sustainable development in the North and the South – these are issues consumer policy strategies have to deal with today.

New challenges call for new policies. While the traditional 'consumer rights approach' as presented above continues to play an important role in consumer policy, it has lately been supplemented by two other strategic goals: firstly, consumer policy as a catalyst to boost the economy, and secondly, consumer policy as an engine to promote sustainable development. However, it is obvious that these new goals are neither conflict-free themselves nor can they simply be 'added on' to an existing consumer policy agenda. Rather, they have to be carefully analysed, weighted against each other, and integrated in a new consumer policy strategy. As stated in the introduction, the political 'relaunch' of consumer policy as a policy field, which is currently taking place in Germany, offers a unique opportunity to do that.

The first goal – to boost economic growth – is also mirrored in the DTI report cited above. Here, consumer policy is viewed as a key element to improve productivity and quality of production, to enhance quality of life for all and to secure market opportunities for responsible businesses. This is new since as shown above, in both Europe and the US, consumer policy has been perceived as defensive consumer protection policy, which was typically accompanied by business concerns, rather than a proactive economic policy (Reich 1992). A widely recognized White Paper (DTI 1999) officially formulated the new perspective on consumer policy and inspired other national policies: well-informed and active consumers supported by an effective system of law and enforcement were expected to play a significant part in ensuring healthy competition in which responsive businesses can succeed. It is worth noting that the rationale behind EU harmonization initiatives in consumer policy is to make the Common Market safer for cross-border market transactions and hence boost consumer sales. There is no explicit intent to strengthen social or environmental goals of consumer policy, to counterbalance social disadvantage of vulnerable consumer groups (for example, migrants, children) or to promote environmental quality of life (Micklitz and Weatherill 1993).

The second goal – to promote sustainable consumption – represents an equally profound change in perspective. The basic idea is that the increasing negative externalities of consumption raise the question of *duties* – countervailing the traditional consumer rights approach with proposing moral and legal *obligations*. As laid down in the Action Plan for Consumer Protection and some other official documents of the German Consumer Protection Ministry, while the plurality of lifestyles in modern consumer society is acknowledged and remains unquestioned, public consumer policy aims to support the development of more sustainable lifestyles through actively promoting sustainable consumption patterns at micro-level and providing supportive institutional infrastructure at meso- and macro-level. The inclusion of a sustainability strategy in consumer policy is justified by the key role consumer demand plays in sustainable development worldwide (see Spangenberg in this volume). While highly successful environment policy in the North has made production processes and service packages more environmentally compatible and, to a certain extent, more socially acceptable, growth and rebound effects have more than counterbalanced efficiency-based progress in many areas of consumption (Michaelis and Lorek 2004).

While political statements always have their own story and have to be regarded with distance and caution, the fact remains that an official plead for and active support of sustainable lifestyles by a federal consumer policy ministry is a political innovation that should not be underestimated as pure rhetoric. Following the 1992 UN Conference on Environment and Development in Rio and its multilateral Agenda 21 action plan committing governments to promote sustainable patterns of production and consumption, the idea of 'sustainable consumer policy' was aired (for example, in Hansen and Schrader 1997). The groundwork had already been completed during discourse on 'political' and 'qualitative' consumption that took place as early as in the 1970s/1980s, primarily between consumer organizations, environmental groups and development activists. The Federal Republic of Germany has on many occasions expressed its explicit commitment to the vision of sustainable development and to focusing on this vision in terms of policy-making. The German Council for Sustainable Development, called into being by the German government in 2001, supports the implementation of a National Sustainability Strategy by recommending goals and indicators and by suggesting projects (Government of the Federal Republic of Germany 2002).

However welcome such institutional arrangements in the name of sustainable development may be, in the end, political will can only be measured by the actual decisions and strategies regarding conflicts that a concept of 'sustainable consumer policy' has to cope with. As in any policy or market sector, there are direct and tangible conflicting objectives both on an individual level and on a policy level. Regarding the individual level, the 'interests' of the consumers may range from maximization of personal wealth (as assumed in neoclassical economics), to the optimization of various material and immaterial components of wealth (that is, a balance of wealth in goods, space and time), to a restraint from consumption in favour of higher-priority objectives. Moreover, ethics-motivated objectives might in some cases go hand in hand with economic growth as in the case of efficiency strategies (for example, the purchase of a new fuel-efficient car); yet, with sufficiency strategies such as reducing or delaying consumption, this is not the case. Here, policy has to prioritize one goal over the other. Such conflicts both within the set of consumer policy goals (including low versus socially 'fair' prices) as well as with other policy objectives (for example, sufficient consumption versus increased consumption to stimulate economic growth) cannot be ignored but have to be decided on, preferably via democratic processes.

A consumer policy vision in which the maxim of individual consumer freedoms has its limits in *Leitbild* of responsible consumer behaviour is in sharp contrast to the existing market economy models, since it has a clearly ethical base. From an empirical perspective, it directs the behaviour of only a minority of consumers, and the number of consumers who vehemently oppose it – the so-called 'hedonistic consumers' – is significant. As opposed to consumers out to maximize self-benefits, the sustainability-conscious consumer weighs up not only the economic, but also ecological, social, cultural and ethical implications of his or her consumption choice. However high these demands, there is strong empirical support from experimental economics that the self-benefit rationale of individuals is indeed kept in check by equally relevant preferences for fairness, which, of course, have to be 'cultivated' and socially supported. An appeal to personal ethics, to the conscience, can spark change. But if it does not become anchored in the structures and institutions of a highly complex society, and if it does not take account of the multiple roles consumers play and the diverse demands they face outside the market place, it can easily lead to frustration and resignation. Hence, it is argued, that sustainable policy initiatives will only have an impact on the demand if a systemic or 'integrated' view of the consumer, as proposed below, is adopted.

9.4   AN INTEGRATED VIEW OF THE CONSUMER

A new perspective on the role and scope of consumer policy also demands a thorough rethinking and remodelling of its object – 'the consumer'. The question of the right model of 'the consumer' has been raised before (see for example Røpke in this volume; Reisch 2003b). It is sometimes answered by presenting and comparing discipline-specific definitions that have been developed in economics, sociology, psychology, anthropology and law on the basis of the discipline-specific explanatory demand. Consumer policy as a cross-cutting policy field is confronted with these different concepts of the consumers: consumers as consumer economics' neoclassical utility maximizers; consumers as contract partners in consumer law; consumers as psychologically and socially highly complex individuals making consumption choices on the basis of competing rationalities and multiple preferences (Kahneman and Tversky 2000); consumers as household members procuring their families and producing their final goods in a household production process influenced by communication, interaction and negotiation processes, and so forth.

Obviously, the term 'consumer' appears in different contexts and terminologies, and one can trace a struggle for ownership of the term between these different terminologies and spheres of action. However, consumer policy has to design and discuss policy options that have to be based on a certain common understanding of 'the consumer' – and hence of consumer interests, spheres of action, limitations and barriers to behavioural changes and so on. This is the backcloth against which the Scientific Advisory Board for Consumer, Food and Nutrition Policies to the German Federal Ministry of Consumer Protection, has proposed an *integrated model* of the consumer (Reisch 2004). The rationale to propose such a broadened approach is, at this stage, to provide politics with a more practically useful picture of the consumer, that is, to develop a heuristic with a modest methodological status but with high political impact. One aim is to avoid isolated policies that do not take into account where, how and why everyday consumption decisions really take place and are hence deemed to be ineffective. Another goal is to redirect attention away from market actions to the wide range of diverse consumption–production processes that take place outside a market environment. As proposed by household economics, consumption can also be viewed as household production, where market goods are only one of several inputs in the household production function (Becker 1965). Moreover, such a broader view should be able to take into account the many new forms of cooperative consumer–producer engagements in the form of, for example, prototyping strategies, cooperative product design, or co-producing. Where the lines between production and consumption are fading, the old conception of consumer as market actor does not hold any more.

Departing from the traditional approach of equating consumers with market actors, and extending the concept of the 'consumer-citizen' (for example, Micheletti 2003), the present model conceptualizes consumers as taking on three interrelated roles in three different spheres of action: consumers are market actors, consumer-citizens and participants in informal life and household production as community and family members.

Firstly, consumers are *market actors*, representing the corresponding opposite side of the fence to producers of goods and services in the market. Beyond the purchasing power of the discretionary income, market opportunities for consumers depend on several other factors such as national and international legal agreements, access of consumers to the courts, consumer competence (for example, media competence), state subsidies, the extent and quality of consumers' organizational structuring and power to fend for their interests, the symmetry or asymmetry of different market players' access to information. Due to asymmetric access to and costs of information (Nelson 1970), producers are typically better informed than their market counterpart. This is particularly the case in markets for goods and services with so-called 'credence characteristics' (Akerlof 1970; Darby and Karni 1973). Credence goods carry quality dimensions that cannot easily be evaluated by consumers via 'search' or 'experience', for instance, the contamination with pesticides in fruits or with the BSE pathogen in beef. Market developments in turn are significantly influenced by the timeframe market players choose for defining their own interests (short-term or long-term); by the dependence of consumer demands on available information (such as producer advertising and/or information sources focusing on consumer needs and interest and/or independent research); and by regard for or neglect of narrow market segments that are rather defined by financial clout than by consumer needs.

Secondly, as *citizens*, consumers are the sovereigns of our democracy. By their votes for specific parliamentary representatives they give orientation to the development of legal frameworks governing the market and their own role as consumers within that market. Also, in the role of consumers they can act 'politically': through their direct and personal purchasing decisions, by exercising 'exit and voice' (Hirschman 1970), they influence markets and living conditions, including the protection of human rights and the environment, in their own countries and elsewhere. Consumption does not only pacify consumers, it also empowers them (Micheletti 2003). Consumer-citizens 'vote' with their wallet and voice when they boycott (Friedman 1999) or 'buycott' (Friedman 1996) specific products or services and when they support or participate in pressure groups and non-governmental organizations. They organize themselves in collective action (Olson 1965) in order to deal with and promote consumer-related social affairs. Ideally, in a democracy, political will is generated by citizens through strategic discourse, inquiry and the creative balancing of conflicting interest. Hence, decisions on consumption made by consumer-citizens are not necessarily based on their own market-related interests only, but also on common welfare and social values.

Thirdly, consumers are *participants in informal life* and livelihoods that permeate both the private and the public sphere. Consumption decisions are strongly intertwined with the so-called 'informal' (that is, unpaid, voluntary, not counted for in the GNP) work consumers provide for their households and families, neighbourhoods and communities. As participants of the informal sector, consumers engage in information search and processing, coordination and control, transport, storage and waste disposal. These efforts compete with many cherished aspects of 'leisure time' use and voluntary work. Hence, buying decisions are often secondary decisions of the more general decisions on life time use. While informal life is influenced by culture, politics and the economy, it is predominantly seen as belonging to the so-called informal sector, which ranges from individual useful activities outside formal employment to family care, housework and mutual help between neighbours to subsistence farming that secures survival for many people throughout the world. The immaterial and material contributions generated for our societies in this way are not put on record adequately. Informal life remains a 'blind spot' between economics and politics. The market often externalizes its transaction costs into informal life – into housework and family care, and into consumers' so-called leisure time. This means, for example, that the reduction of the workforce in the formal sector often places an additional burden on the customers who spend more time in queues and do not get paid for that time.

Last but not least, it is important to recognize that consumers often do not act as individuals, but as members of private *households*, that is, a group of relatives or a personal network who join together in sharing income and consumption. The caring for the household members requires a multitude of different skills and competences in gaining transparency of markets, goods and services, reflecting needs and following sustainable patterns of consumption. While in formal education, household and caring work play a subordinate role, this type of so-called 'informal work' is of major importance for consumer policy. Consumer policy measures targeted at the whole product chain will only have an impact if they are supported by respective use strategies and consumption processes of the individual households. Apart from private households, there are institutional households in which people are either partially (for example, institutional feeding in schools and companies) or entirely (institutional households, for example, retirement homes and homes for the disabled or hospitals) cared for. As bulk consumers and key customers, such institutional households could play a key role in market development for sustainable product-service systems, for example, in public provision.

The realization that the term 'consumer' does not always mean the same thing leads to the urgent need to clarify the complex interactions between the three concepts and systems, to focus on their interrelationships and to strive for integration. Such a task is not well suited for mainstream economics which focuses solely on the consumer as market actor. It is much better suited for a more encompassing approach such as institutional economics (for example, to explain the negotiations within households), ecological economics (to explain the interrelatedness of the three systems of consumption), evolutionary economics (to explain the evolution of markets), economic psychology (to explain the so-called 'attitude-behaviour gap' in sustainable consumption), political economy (to discuss possibilities of public governance), to name some of the relevant dissenting economic approaches.

Each of the three systems is indispensable and must be dealt with in their own right at the highest level of quality possible if we are to acknowledge consumers' functions as market players, as consumer-citizens, and as participants in an informal life in which purchased goods and services are being translated into quality of life through home production, nurturing of friendships, voluntary work, political activities and unpaid services for neighbours. It is important to realize that decisions on consumption in the formal market are often the secondary results of decisions made on how to live one's life, allocate one's time, and relate to the other household members. The criteria and rationale behind these decisions can, therefore, not be completely understood and hence hardly be influenced, for example, to promote sustainable lifestyles, if consumers are seen as nothing but market players and citizens.

9.5   REFLECTIONS

The concept of 'sustainable consumer policy' is young and in a turbulent stage of development. As part of a politically desired sustainability strategy, it focuses not only on individual short-term interests involved in consumer protection, but also on collective long-term economic, social and cultural needs and a life-sustaining and health-promoting environment. Consumer policy, which has been primarily a policy for the consumer, that is, his or her short-term direct benefits and protection of rights, has witnessed an extension in scope in the form of a macro-policy for consumption, which aims at directing demand according to politically set goals – an extension in scope that does not happen without tensions. Such a policy has three major tasks. Firstly, to design *market conditions*, that is, institutions and infrastructure ranging from the taxation system to deposits on disposable drink containers, so that demand not only supports consumer interests but all those of the economy and society. Secondly, to advise, inform, and *motivate consumers* to enable them to make more sustainable consumption decisions as market actors, consumer-citizens, and participants of the informal sector. Thirdly, to pave the way for structural change in such a way as to *retain strategic consumption options* towards sufficiency-based behaviour.

Such a difficult intention demands both a solid theoretical foundation and decisive political implementation at many levels. Firstly, to provide that *theoretical foundation* could become a challenge for ecological economics, which could build on prior research on the meaning and implementation of sustainable consumption. One task could be to further test the idea of an integrated view of the consumer regarding its usefulness, and, eventually, to improve its methodological status of the concept from 'working hypotheses' to 'theoretically sound'. Another potential research field could be the interplay between micro- and macro-consumption issues and of governance questions in consumer policy.

Secondly, *political implementation* will largely depend on how sustainable consumer policy as cross-sectoral policy will be positioned in and backed up by the other policy fields and departments (that is, economics, research and development, education, environment, health and welfare, legislation and so on). Welcome activities in the area of sustainable consumption, such as research programmes on sustainable consumption and production funded by the Federal Ministry of Education and Research or the concept of the 'sustainable shopping basket' of the German Council for Sustainable Development will need a solid coordination in order to have political and scientific impact. Unfortunately, despite evidence of the many welcome and positive activities in the form of top-down state initiatives, bottom-up Agenda 21 processes, and businesses' initiatives, consumer policy is still lacking an ongoing forum and an institutionalized framework for sustainable consumption as agreed at EU level and more generally at the Johannesburg Summit in 2002. Unlike the years before, there is now a window of opportunity, which should be opened.

REFERENCES

Akerlof, G. (1970), 'The market for "lemons". Quality uncertainty and the market mechanism', *Quarterly Journal of Economics*, **84**, 488–500.
Becker, G. S. (1965) 'A theory of the allocation of time', *The Economic Journal*, **299**, 495–517.
Darby, M. R. and E. Karni (1973), 'Free competition and the optimal amount of fraud', *Journal of Law and Economics*, **16**, 67–88.
DTI (Department of Trade and Industry) (1999), *Modern Market: Confident Consumers*, Implementation plan for the Consumer White Paper, London: DTI.
DTI (Department of Trade and Industry) (2003), *Comparative Report on Consumer Policy Regimes*, British Department of Trade and Industry, October, London: DTI.
European Commission (2002), 'Consumer policy strategy 2002–2006' (COM (2002) 208 final), (2002/C), *Official Journal of the European Communities*, 8 June 2002, C 137/2-C137/23.
Friedman, M. (1996), 'A positive approach to organized consumer action: The "buycott" as an alternative to the boycott', *Journal of Consumer Policy*, **19**, 439–51.

Friedman, Monroe (1999), *Consumer Boycotts. Effecting Change Through the Marketplace and the Media*, New York: Routledge.

Government of the Federal Republic of Germany (2002), *Perspectives for Germany. Our Strategy for Sustainable Development*, Berlin: Federal Government.

Government of the Federal Republic of Germany (2003), *Action Plan for Consumer Protection*, Berlin: Federal Government, 323/03.

Hansen, U. and U. Schrader (1997), 'A modern model of consumption for a sustainable society', *Journal of Consumer Policy*, **20**, 443–68.

Hirschman, Albert O. (1970), *Exit, Voice, and Loyalty. Responses to Decline in Firms, Organizations, and States*, Cambridge, MA: Harvard University Press.

Kahneman, Daniel and Amos Tversky (eds) (2000), *Choices, Values, and Frames*, Cambridge, MA: Cambridge University Press.

Lampman, Robert J. (1988), 'JFK's four consumer rights: A retrospective view', in Scott Maynes (ed.), *The Frontier of Research in the Consumer Interest*, Columbia, Missouri: American Council on Consumer Interests, pp. 19–33.

Michaelis, Laurie and Sylvia Lorek (2004), *The Future for Sustainable Consumption in Europe*, Report for the Danish EPA (Draft),.

Micheletti, Michele (2003), *Political Virtue and Shopping: Individuals, Consumerism, and Collective Action*, New York: Palgrave Macmillan.

Micklitz, H.-W. and S. Weatherill (1993), 'Consumer policy in the European community. Before and after Maastricht', *Journal of Consumer Policy*, **16**, 285–321.

Nelson, P. (1970), 'Information and consumer behaviour', *Journal of Political Economy*, **78**, 311–29.

Olson, Mancur (1965), *The Logic of Collective Action. Public Goods and The Theory of Groups*, Cambridge, MA: Harvard University Press.

Reich, N. (1992), 'Diverse approaches to consumer protection philosophy', *Journal of Consumer Policy*, **14**, 257–92.

Reisch, L. A. (2003a), 'Potentials, pitfalls, and policy implication of electronic consumption', *Information and Communications Technology Law*, **12** (2), 93–109.

Reisch, Lucia A. (2003b), 'Consumption', in Edward A. Page and John Proops (eds), *Environmental Thought*, Edward Elgar Series, Current Issues in Ecological Economics, Cheltenham, UK and Northampton, MA, US: Edward Elgar, pp. 217–42.

Reisch, L. A. (2004), 'New consumer policy principles and visions', *Journal of Consumer Policy*, **27** (1), 1–42.

10. Lifestyle approaches as a sustainable consumption policy – a German example

Claudia Empacher and Konrad Götz

10.1 INTRODUCTION

Industrialised countries have experienced a considerable social change during the past three decades, a process that has often been referred to in terms such as erosion of traditional values, individualisation and pluralisation of social groups (see Beck 1986; Fitzgerald 2003; Giddens 1996). As to consumption, these developments have resulted in the pluralisation and individualisation of consumption patterns as well. But has this social change been adequately dealt with in the ongoing discussion on sustainable consumption?

In the decade following Agenda 21, numerous activities have taken place to enable and promote sustainable consumption policies, such as research projects, the initiation of an integrated product policy, and eco-labelling schemes, and so on. However, a clear shift towards more sustainable consumption patterns can still not be observed. Somehow, sustainable consumption policies simply do not seem to reach consumers or affect them enough to bring about a change in behaviour.

This is partially due to the fact that there are still no sustainable consumption policies that systematically and effectively aim at consumers; instead, policies aim predominantly at changing the basic conditions for consumption (for example, by achieving more transparency through more or better information on sustainable products, eco-labels), or at producers to reduce the environmental impact of their products (for example, by sustainable product design). By doing so, strategies neither take the living conditions of consumers into account nor their attitudes, orientations and wishes that influence actual consumer behaviour. Results of consumption research are not sufficiently heeded (see Wimmer 2001, p. 80) and use is hardly made of the experiences of market research and marketing (Götz

1999). Only recently, a growing discussion on the role of advertising and marketing for sustainable consumption has evolved (Longhurst 2003).

In the following, lifestyle approaches are presented as policies towards sustainable consumption that directly refer to consumers, to their living conditions, their attitudes and their wishes. The potentials of lifestyle-oriented approaches for the promotion of sustainable consumption patterns are illustrated on the basis of the results from a study on sustainable consumption patterns carried out in Germany.

First, a brief introduction into research on lifestyles and the connection of lifestyle research and the sustainability discourse is given before the social-ecological lifestyle approach is presented. The fourth section presents the results of the empirical study in Germany. Finally, conclusions for sustainable consumption policies are drawn.

10.2   RESEARCH ABOUT LIFESTYLES

Lifestyle concepts have been developed simultaneously in sociology and in market research.

10.2.1   Lifestyle Research in Sociology

The roots of lifestyle concepts can be found in the work of Max Weber. He was the first to use the terms *Lebensstile* and *Stilisierung des Lebens* in *The Protestant Ethic and the Spirit of Capitalism* ([1920] 1986). He analysed the group of Protestants and argued that this social group could be distinguished clearly from the societal mainstream, because their behaviour was driven by their religious normative orientations. Thus, he concluded that social groups act differently depending on their normative orientations.

In contrast to Weber, the mainstream of sociology emphasised the importance of objective criteria, such as professional position or income, for influencing behaviour. These models of social structure broke down the population, according to these objective criteria, into social classes or strata.

But at the beginning of the 1980s, due to the societal change that took place in Western European countries, these traditional models were no longer adequate. The erosion of traditional institutions along with the individualisation and pluralisation of society, implied that traditional sociological categories such as professional position or education, were not sufficient to analyse new social differences.

The segmentation of society into different lifestyles, as suggested by the newly emerging lifestyle research, represented a means to take these developments into account. On the one hand, lifestyle concepts emphasise the importance of socio-cultural criteria and attitudes for the classification of social segments (Schultz and Weller 1997). By subdividing societies not only *vertically* (that is, into upper, middle and lower classes), but also *horizontally,* according to socio-cultural criteria, a picture of different milieus in the social sphere is created. Each of the milieus can be distinguished by its own lifestyle. Elements of lifestyles characterise the self-identity of a group, but they also distinguish the group vis-à-vis other groups (Götz 2001).

Thus, lifestyle research is able to map the pluralisation of societies. But on the other hand, lifestyle concepts provided an explanation why societies were not bound to disintegrate by the growing tendency of individualisation. Lifestyles can be understood as a mode of social integration that gives individuals the opportunity to be socially integrated while living in disparate and particularised surroundings (Götz 2001).

The most important impulses for the development of the lifestyle concept in sociology came from Pierre Bourdieu (Bourdieu 1979). He was the first to present a multi-dimensional model of social space, with demographic variables (income, professional position, education, number of children and so on) in the vertical dimension, and preferences and tastes (on media, art, literature, products, leisure, politics and so on) on the horizontal dimension. However, he still called attention to the importance of the vertical dimensions for the development of differences in taste and he did not name concrete groups or lifestyles.

Today, sociological lifestyle concepts are considered to be an extension and fulfilment of social structure analysis (Müller 1992, p. 369).

10.2.2   Lifestyle Research in Market Research

Although market research does not focus on the analysis of society, the development of lifestyle concepts in market research was motivated by similar reasons as in sociology: due to societal change, demographic variables and other classical segmentation variables had become less useful for predicting and explaining consumer behaviour (Hustad and Pessemier 1972, p. 296). Moreover, in order to improve advertising and marketing, there was an increasing need to know the consumer better (Grunert et al. 1993).

Lazer had introduced the lifestyle concept to consumer research as early as 1963. Instead of focusing on objective segmentation criteria, Lazer emphasised the importance of subjective variables such as culture, values and symbols (Lazer 1964, p. 130).

In the following years, lifestyle analysis as a method of market segmentation for the identification of target groups received steadily growing attention, and numerous different approaches were developed. One of the best-known approaches in Germany, which has also gained international attention, is the social milieu model of the SINUS institute. On the vertical dimension, the SINUS milieus consist of criteria of social strata (income, education, socio-demographics, and so on). The horizontal dimension divides the social milieus according to their basic orientations and values into those with traditional orientations ('to preserve'), material orientations ('to have'), hedonist orientations ('to enjoy'), post-material orientations ('to be') and, finally, post-modern orientations ('to have, to be and to enjoy') (SINUS 2000).

Unlike in sociology, there have been considerable efforts to develop lifestyle concepts for cross-cultural analysis due to the internationalisation of markets (Grunert et al. 1993, p. 7; see for example, Ascheberg and Ueltzhöffer 2003 based on the SINUS milieus).

10.2.3 The Definition of Lifestyle

Up to now, there has been agreement neither in market research nor in sociology on the definition of lifestyles. A more recent definition from consumer research emphasises the variability of the concept: 'Lifestyle is a summary construct defined as patterns in which people live and spend time and money. Lifestyles reflect a person's activities, interests, and opinions ...' (Engel et al. 1995, p. 449). In contrast, one of the sociological definitions reads as follows: 'We understand lifestyles as socially distinctive variants of cultural practices ... with a corresponding social position that can not, as a rule, be changed arbitrarily. Lifestyles are not simply symbolical derivates of available resources and "objective" positions' (Berking and Neckel 1990, p. 482, author's translation).

In market research, a purely descriptive approach to lifestyles seems to dominate, while sociological approaches emphasise the symbolic meaning of lifestyle for the self-identity of the individual as well as their affiliation to a certain group. But in spite of conceptual differences, lifestyles seem to be commonly understood as a multi-dimensional concept in which the subjective dimension, such as values, orientations, attitudes and so on play a decisive role for actual behaviour. Therefore, in lifestyle concepts behaviour is not described by social position (upper-, middle- and lower-class behaviour), nor is it conceived as the behaviour of a homo oeconomicus; instead behaviour is understood as guided by motivation (Stieß and Götz 2002).

10.3 LIFESTYLES IN THE SUSTAINABILITY DISCOURSE

The multi-dimensionality of the lifestyle concept and the importance attributed to the subjective dimension have to be kept in mind when transferring the concept to other disciplines or other areas of use. However, within the sustainability discourse, one can observe that the term lifestyle is taken up quite unreflectedly and without a clear definition, thus creating considerable confusion with regard to its meaning.

In the beginning, the term lifestyle was mostly employed in the singular in the environmental discourse by demanding a considerable change of 'our Western lifestyle'. But commonly used polarities in the environmental debate like 'materialism' versus 'post-materialism' (see Inglehart 1977) or 'environmentally oriented', versus 'not environmentally oriented', had gradually proved not to represent adequate categories for promoting more sustainable behaviour. It became clear that it was not sufficient, either analytically or strategically, to rely on average data and to concentrate on mainstream trends (Stieß and Götz 2002). This has finally led to a widely shared understanding of the lifestyle concept: lifestyles allow for the differentiation between different groups of people, and hence, between different target groups.

But beyond this, the term is still used in quite different contexts. Some understand lifestyle as determined by purely socio-demographic factors, such as income, household type, social position, age and so on; others differentiate lifestyles merely by subjective variables.

However, it is the multi-dimensionality of the lifestyle concept that makes it promising for formulating a sustainable consumption policy. A group-specific analysis is useful if social segments are identified in such a way that group-specific information campaigns or product marketing can be developed. This is only possible by drawing a holistic picture of the respective target group.

In Germany, the advantages of lifestyle approaches for the sustainability discourse have been widely recognised. By analysing different lifestyles within their different dimensions, innovative approaches to different target groups can become visible, single groups can be understood in their specific rationality, and potentials for changing behaviour can be identified and activated (Stieß and Götz 2002).

Moreover, with lifestyle-based typologies it is possible to operationalise those influential factors that are generally considered 'incalculable': attitudes, orientations, emotions and motivational backgrounds. The influence of these soft factors can even be measured in terms of actual behaviour. Since these so-called 'soft factors' have proven to be, in fact, the truly 'hard factors' when it comes to changing behaviour, typologies of different target groups contain invaluable knowledge as a basis for changing consumption patterns.

10.4 THE SOCIAL-ECOLOGICAL LIFESTYLE APPROACH

General objectives of lifestyle research in sociology and market research have been to describe societal change and to sell products and services. In addition to that, lifestyle approaches for sustainable consumption should consider specific characteristics of this field that are not emphasised sufficiently within these other disciplines.

To optimise the lifestyle concept for utilisation in the sustainability debate, the Institute for Social-Ecological Research (ISOE) has developed a social-ecological approach to lifestyles. This approach analyses the three following dimensions and their relationships:

- social background of households (social situation and household context);
- orientations: lifestyle relevant – general values, orientations with regard to work, leisure, consumption, the environment, health, and so on; relevant area of need – attitudes, emotions, preferences, dislikes and so on;
- indicators of actual consumption behaviour as practised daily.

The social-ecological typology evolves from group-specific patterns of orientations, behaviour and social situation and can be used as a target group model. According to the specific research interest or the area of need in question, we call this typology consumption, mobility, leisure or nutrition styles and so on. The identified lifestyles can be analysed with regard to the three dimensions and can be used as target groups for the development of socially differentiated information, marketing and consumer advice offers (Empacher et al. 2002).

This model implies some important advantages for the use in the field of sustainability. Firstly, it takes into account the household context and thereby acknowledges the embeddedness of individuals in a concrete social context, a family or household. Conventional lifestyle research sees individuals as embedded only in a lifestyle group and abstracts from the immediate social surroundings of the individual. But these surroundings can have considerable influence on individual decisions, because compromises and bargaining among the different household members are implied, meaning that a change of behaviour towards a more sustainable behaviour pattern also depends on other household members.

Secondly, an important advantage of this approach is the inclusion of the behavioural dimension. This allows for the testing of hypotheses concerning the extent to which orientation and motivational factors influence actual behaviour.[1] Moreover, it enables a consideration of the material dimension of consumption and thus allows this approach to link up with natural scientific studies of metabolic processes.[2] Therefore, it is possible to analyse environmental impacts of different lifestyles and estimate reduction potentials within lifestyles. Finally, strategies can be targeted more effectively if environmental impacts of consumption habits and the extent to which the different target groups are equipped with goods are known.

10.5 'CONSUMPTION STYLES': A GERMAN EXAMPLE

In the following, the results of a German empirical study of sustainable consumption based on this social-ecological lifestyle approach are presented.

The study entitled 'Household Exploration of the Conditions, Opportunities and Limitations Pertaining to Sustainable Consumption Behaviour'[3] had set out to identify a typology of consumption that could be used as a target group model for the promotion of sustainable consumption.[4]

10.5.1 Proceedings of the Study

The study was based on a qualitative empirical survey of 100 German households. The households were carefully pre-selected from a demographic, geographical and lifestyle-related standpoint to establish typical *consumption styles* within German households.[5] Lifestyle and orientations of respondents were ascertained using open interviews. In addition, a standardised questionnaire was used to record the key variables with regard to the extent to which respondents were equipped with consumer goods, together with indicators of their consumer behaviour relating to key areas of household consumption.

On the basis of these interviews, different consumption orientations within the household were identified. These orientations were related in a particular way and thus displayed specific patterns. In a heuristic procedure, these orientation patterns were collated with specific social situations and concrete behaviours, thereby developing a typology of *consumption styles*.

10.5.2 Consumption Types and Target Groups

In the beginning, the consumption typology consisted of ten consumption types, each of them representing an 'ideal type' distilled from several interviews. In reality, a mixture of types will frequently be found:

Type 1: fully-managed eco-families;
Type 2: childless professionals;
Type 3: self-interested youngsters;
Type 4: everyday life artists;
Type 5: people fed up with consumption;
Type 6: rural traditionalists;
Type 7: underprivileged who can't cope;
Type 8: run-of-the-mill families;
Type 9: active seniors;
Type 10: status-oriented privileged families.

The typology demonstrates typical patterns of consumer behaviour within German households, while at the same time the variability of user profiles becomes apparent.

In order to ensure operability when developing target-group-specific strategies, the ten consumption types were afterwards combined according to similarity of key consumption patterns to form four key target groups:

- environmentally oriented group (Type 1 and 4)
- group of people who can't cope (underprivileged) (Type 3, 5 and 7)
- group of ambivalent traditionalists (Type 6, 8 and 9)
- privileged group (type 2 and 10).

For each of these groups, strategies for sustainable consumption were developed and finally tested in group discussions with members of the respective target group.

10.5.3 Some Exemplary Consumption Styles

In the following, exemplary consumption types from each of the four target groups are presented more closely in order to provide an insight in the potential of lifestyle-specific approaches. Type-specific enabling and hindering factors for sustainable consumption are pointed out, as well as some possible target-group-specific strategies for promoting sustainable consumption.

10.5.3.1 Environmentally oriented group: The fully-managed eco-families

Social context

The fully-managed eco-families have one or more children and are in general well educated, often academics. Both parents practise a profession, which is the basis for the good financial situation of the household. However, it also results in an acute lack of time and a strong need to coordinate and optimise the processes of the everyday life of all family members.

Orientations

The model of partnership practised in these families aims at equal rights for men and women, and at the same time puts emphasis on including the children in family decisions and processes, which results in a democratic family model based on equal participation of all family members. On the other hand, the acute lack of time leads to a strong orientation towards time-economising so-called 'convenience' offers. At the same time these families show a clear orientation towards environmental matters, which nevertheless has to take second place when putting it into practice is too time-consuming. Furthermore, these families are distinguished by their openness towards anything new, an orientation towards social and ethical aspects, as well as a strong health and quality orientation.

Consumption equipment and behaviour

The degree to which thay are equipped with consumer goods does not differ considerably from most of the other consumption types. The fully-managed eco-families do not possess any luxurious appliances or leisure equipment. Regarding nutrition, they sometimes buy organic products and seldom use ready-prepared meals, but they own a deep freezer and often use frozen foods. The families go on vacation to other European countries once a year. They own a family car, which is rarely used, they cover most of their daily distances by bike and public transport. Nevertheless, the family car is seen as indispensable for the maintenance of the family organisation. Their energy consumption is comparably high, although they use energy-saving light bulbs.

Possible strategies

This consumption type is clearly open towards sustainable consumption strategies, such as the use of recyclable and easily repairable products or high-quality products with long durability. The families can even be convinced to consume less, as they do not attach great value to material goods. Hindering factors are, above all, a lack of time, although they are able to compensate this lack via financial resources. Therefore, more eco-efficient services that are not too time-consuming should be developed for this type.

This type becomes particularly sensitive to environmental aspects when children are born, and this event can be a door-opener for health-related sustainable strategies such as the purchase of organic food, untreated furniture, or solvent-free paint, and so on. During that phase, strategic consumption decisions (Bodenstein et al. 1997) are often made, for example, purchase of a new or bigger car, renting of a bigger flat, and can be influenced towards a more sustainable decision (car sharing, collective use of products, and so on). On the other hand, energy saving is difficult with smaller children in the household, although these families in general tend to save energy, not for financial, but for environmental reasons.

10.5.3.2   Underprivileged group: The underprivileged who can't cope

This consumption type represents a contrast to the fully-managed eco-families in many ways.

Social context

The underprivileged who can't cope lack financial as well as time resources, and often lack a social net that can support them. There is neither time nor space left over for environmental or other social or ethical issues. A lack of competence to master everyday life, and a lack of knowledge about how to get information, is often visible. A traditional gender-specific division of labour often results in a particularly acute overburdening of the women. Within this type many jobless individuals, poor elderly people or single parents can be found.

Orientations

Because of their financial problems the most important orientation is that towards low prices. Material goods are, nevertheless, of great importance for this type, as he/she still wants to comply with societal expectations. Therefore, an orientation towards cheap (and short-lived) products can be observed. On the other hand, convenience plays an important role. The underprivileged reject environmental matters strongly. They already feel overburdened by everyday duties and perceive environmental matters as a luxury issue for the ones that can afford it.

Consumption equipment and behaviour

The underprivileged who can't cope live in small flats. Sometimes, they have large quantities of children's toys. They are not buyers of organic products, and regularly use ready-prepared meals and frozen food. They generally have a small car, but do not go on vacation. Considering the size of their flat, energy consumption seems to be comparably high.

Possible strategies

A change towards more sustainable consumption patterns can hardly
be expected from this type as long as there is neither time nor financial
resources. Sustainable strategies that would meet their needs, such as
second-hand goods, are unthinkable for this type, because, in their eyes,
these symbolise social exclusion.

An overall strategy should be to strengthen this type's competence in
managing everyday life necessities in order to create a space in which he/
she can be aware of and reflect sustainability issues. The underprivileged
certainly are a target group for strategies that imply monetary savings, such
as energy and water saving, but the problem is now to impart corresponding
knowledge to them. They do not read print media, prefer to watch
entertainment broadcasts on television and are rather reluctant to accept
advice from the outside. The best way to approach them is through people
from their immediate surroundings.

10.5.3.3   Privileged group: The childless professionals

Social context

The childless professionals are professionally successful singles or 'dinks'
(double income no kids) with a relatively high income and lack of time,
and they predominantly live in bigger cities.

Orientations

Due to their strong orientation towards their profession and the resulting
lack of time, they are very much drawn to time-economising offers
(convenience) and tend to call on external household services (cleaners,
ironing service). The childless professionals are distinguished by a certain
status and enjoyment orientation. They think they deserve some luxury
as a reward for their hard work. In addition, quality and service are very
important for the childless professionals, and the women in particular are
strongly health-oriented. The childless professionals dissociate themselves
from those wholly committed to an, in their eyes, ideologically extreme
ecological lifestyle. An ecological lifestyle is associated with renunciation
and asceticism. However, ethical orientations are perceptible among the
childless professionals, especially among women.

Consumption equipment and behaviour

The childless professionals own big flats, possess numerous consumer goods
and electrical appliances, sometimes even luxury goods like whirlpools or

tanning beds. They own big cars and go on long-distance journeys several times a year. They are not consumers of organic products, and often use ready-prepared meals or eat out. Their energy consumption is very high, although they occasionally use energy-saving bulbs.

Possible strategies

The childless professionals, like the status-oriented privileged families, constitute the 'winner type' of Western societies. Due to their status and esteem in society, they serve as role models (and have leader functions). Therefore, it is especially important and worth the effort to reach these types and achieve a change in behaviour towards sustainable consumption. The biggest impediment is their rejection of anything associated with 'eco'. Nevertheless, they have certain health and ethical orientations that make them accessible to sustainable consumption. Childless professionals are not willing to reduce their consumption and asking them to do so will very likely result in even stronger rejection. The approach here should be to effectuate/ bring about a change in consumption habits and it seems advisable to avoid any ideological touch. More important is that sustainable products meet this type's demand for design/aesthetics and service on the one hand, and his/her orientation towards enjoyment/pleasure on the other. The advantages of sustainable consumption have to be emphasised: the enjoyment and pure flavour of organic food, the design and aura of a high-quality item with history, the relaxing value of a vacation in the region rather than the stress of flying abroad, and so on. Also conceivable are products that are highly visible and possibly symbolise status, such as solar energy installations.

10.5.3.4   The group of ambivalent traditionalists: The rural traditionalists

Social context

The rural traditionalists include elderly married couples or families who live in their own houses in rural surroundings or in small towns. They practise a traditional gender division of labour: women are responsible for house and garden; the men are employed.

Orientations

This type has a strong regional and social orientation and is embedded in his/her immediate social surroundings (neighbourhood, community). As for consumption, solid quality and the avoidance of any kind of waste or extravagance are important for this type. At the same time, he/she is keen to maintain his/her possessions and take particular care of them. Security and hygiene play an important role, as well.

Consumption equipment and behaviour

The rural traditionalists do not possess any luxurious consumption equipment, but they have a considerably high number of appliances for storing food (deep freezers and refrigerators). They occasionally purchase organic food from farmers they know, do not use ready-prepared meals, but prepare their own stored or frozen food. They have several cars, do not use public transport and go on vacation once a year, preferably in Germany or in German-speaking countries. Their energy consumption is comparably low.

Possible strategies

Generally speaking, this consumption type displays several enabling factors for more sustainable consumption behaviour. Their orientations towards traditional values, such as the maintenance of material and immaterial goods, social cohesion, as well as their rejection of any kind of waste, in principle, makes them a very sustainable type. Yet, one can make out a strong distrust of anything that is called 'ecological' or 'biological', because the rural traditionalists suspect the producers of eco-products of abusing the label to raise price, and hence rip them off. This is the root of this type's ambivalence.

However, this ambivalence can be used in favour of more sustainable consumption. Once again, as for the childless professionals, sustainable behavioural offers must avoid ecological ideology. However, for this type, it is important to overcome his or her distrust. This can be achieved by pointing out and explaining concrete ecological advantages. Another way would be to appeal to their sense of social responsibility rather than to ecological responsibility. Apart from organic food, suitable strategies for this type are the purchase of regional and fair trade products. In spite of their social orientation, strategies that are based on the collective use of products, such as pooling and sharing, contradict their wish to possess and to take care of their own material goods (Empacher et al. 2002, p. 81).

10.6   CONCLUSIONS: LIFESTYLE APPROACHES AS A SUSTAINABLE CONSUMPTION POLICY

The presentation of different consumption styles in the German study aimed at illustrating the potentials of lifestyle approaches for the promotion of sustainable consumption. The empirical insights into various spheres of consumption (that is, the social context, orientations and behaviour) provided by the social-ecological lifestyle approach produce knowledge on enabling and hindering factors for more sustainable consumption. The segmentation into different consumption types illustrates the diversity of consumers and at the same time presents a holistic and understandable picture of each type. Thus, the different rationalities of diverse societal groups become evident and potentials for target-group-specific strategies are revealed. Strategies can be developed that directly connect to target-group-specific orientations while taking into account their specific social context.

Moreover, the knowledge about actual consumption behaviour allows the prioritising of strategies to deal with those groups with the highest environmental relevance. Unfortunately, as the presented study was based on a qualitative approach, no statements can be made as to the size of the different target groups, which would make a further prioritisation of strategies possible. But the quantification of the target groups can be carried out in a second step via quantitative empirical surveys and clustering.

Lifestyle approaches as input for a sustainable consumption policy can be used by various societal players. In Germany, the consumption-style typology has been used to evaluate the range of advice offered by a consumer advice agency (the North Rhine-Westphalia Consumer Advice Service) with regard to its target group accuracy. This evaluation initiated a reflection process concerning the current target groups of the agency and has resulted in the optimisation of their advice policies and in the more effective use of their limited resources in the meantime.

However, in spite of the advantages of this policy, it is generally difficult for public organisations and politicians to work with this kind of segmentation, because it contradicts their understanding of target groups as purely socio-demographic groups. Moreover, their task of serving the public well discourages them from targeting specific groups. However, they tend to forget that every message, every act of communication, every idiomatic style and every message appeals only to a certain group of people, and puts off others. As such, its effect is always selective, even if this is not intended. Lifestyle concepts contribute to the reflection on this selectivity.

On the other hand, public players tend to think that marketing-like categories are politically incorrect or manipulative, thereby confusing target group segmentation with advertising. Finally, public players often have difficulties abstracting from their own political objectives. They are not accustomed to taking into account the perspectives of people with different lifestyles. However, lifestyle segmentation is particularly useful for understanding the wishes, values and demands of different groups of people, and thereby also for appreciating a perspective that differs from one's own.

Lifestyle-specific approaches are thus a promising policy for sustainable consumption. The value of lifestyle concepts for market research and social structure analysis has been widely shown, and in Germany, lifestyle approaches in the field of sustainable consumption are already widespread. However, the actual effects of such a sustainable consumption policy for the environment have still not been analysed in detail.

NOTES

1. In a study on mobility styles, we were able to demonstrate that within different mobility styles there is a close coherence of mobility orientations and mobility behaviour (see City: mobil 1999).
2. An environmental impact assessment of different consumption types was carried out for the first time in the field of leisure mobility (Götz et al. 2003).
3. The study was commissioned and published by the German Federal Environment Agency (see UBA 2002).
4. The term sustainable consumption used here refers to the definition of the Oslo Symposium in 1994 as '...the use of services and related products which respond to basic needs and bring a better quality of life while minimizing the use of natural resources, toxic materials and emission of waste and pollutants over the life cycle, so as not to jeopardize the needs of future generations'. This can be put into practice by consumers through (1) the purchase of products that cause less environmental and social impacts during production, use and disposal, such as organic food, energy-efficient washing machines, energy-saving light bulbs, fair trade products; (2) changes in what is consumed, such as vegetarian dishes instead of meat, local holiday instead of a long distance flight; and (3) changes in use behaviour, such as the lowering of room temperature when going out, the turning off the light or the standby modus.
5. The aim of qualitative research is not to determine the frequency of social action but to find a set of relevant and typical action patterns in a social situation (see Lamnek 1993).

REFERENCES

Ascheberg, Carsten and Jörg Ueltzhöffer (2003), 'Transnationales Zielgruppenmarketing. Die Methode der sozialen Milieus', ('Transnational target group marketing. The method of social milieus'), http://www.sigma-online.de/Forschungsschwerpunkte/Zielgruppenforschung/Transnationales_Zielgruppenmarketing/Transnationales_Zielgruppenmarketing.html.de.

Beck, Ulrich (1986), *Risikogesellschaft. Auf dem Weg in eine andere Moderne* (*Risk Society. On the Way to another Modernity*), Frankfurt/Main: Suhrkamp.

Berking, Helmuth and Sighard Neckel (1990), 'Die Politik der Lebensstile in einem Berliner Bezirk. Zu einigen Formen nachtraditionaler Vergemeinschaftung' ('The politics of lifestyle in a Berlin district. About some forms of post-traditional communitisation'), in Peter A. Berger und Stefan Hradil (eds), *Lebenslagen, Lebensläufe, Lebensstile*, Soziale Welt Vol. 7, Göttingen: Schwarz, pp. 481–500.

Bodenstein, Gerhard, Achim Spiller and Holger Elbers (1997), *Strategische Konsumentscheidungen: Langfristige Weichenstellungen für das Umwelthandeln – Ergebnisse einer empirischen Studie (Strategic Consumption Decisions – Longterm Setting of Switches for Environmental Action – Results from an Empirical Study)*, Diskussionsbeiträge No. 234. Duisburg: University of Duisburg.

Bourdieu, Pierre (1979), *La Distinction. Critique Social du Jugement (Distinction. Social Critique of Judgement)*, Paris: Les Editions de Minuit.

CITY:mobil (ed.) (1999), *Stadtverträgliche Mobilität. Handlungsstrategien für eine nachhaltige Verkehrsentwicklung in Stadtregionen*, Stadtökologie Vol 3, Berlin: Analytica.

Empacher, Claudia, Konrad Götz, Irmgard Schultz and Barbara Birzle-Harder (2002), 'Die Zielgruppenanalyse des Instituts für sozial-ökologische Forschung' ('The target group analysis of the Institute for Social-Ecological Research), in Umweltbundesamt (Federal Environment Agency) (ed.), *Nachhaltige Konsummuster: ein neues umweltpolitisches Handlungsfeld als Herausforderung für die Umweltkommunikation; mit einer Zielgruppenanalyse des Frankfurter Instituts für sozial-ökologische Forschung (Sustainable Consumption of Patterns: A New Field of Action for Environmental Policy as a Challenge for Environmental Communication, with a Target Group Analysis of the Institute for Social-Ecological Research*, Frankfurt), Berlin: Erich Schmidt, pp. 87–181.

Engel, James F., Roger D. Blackwell and Paul W. Miniard (1995), *Consumer Behaviour*, Eighth Edition, Fort Worth, TX: The Dryden Press.

Fitzgerald, Tony (2003), 'Globalization arrives', http://www.sociologyonline.co.uk.

Giddens, Anthony (1996), 'Leben in einer posttraditionalen Gesellschaft', ('Life in a post-traditional society'), in Ulrich Beck, Anthony Giddens and Scott Lash (eds), *Reflexive Modernisierung*, Frankfurt/Main: Suhrkamp, pp. 113–94.

Götz, Konrad (1999), 'Mobilitätsstile – Folgerungen für ein zielgruppenspezifisches Marketing' ('Mobility styles – conclusions for a target group specific marketing'), in Jürgen Friedrichs and Kirsten Hollaender (eds), *Stadtökologische Forschung. Theorie und Anwendungen* (Urban Ecological Research. Theory and Practice), Berlin: Analytica, pp. 299–326.

Götz, Konrad (2001), 'Sozial-ökologische Typologisierung zwischen Zielgruppensegmentation und Sozialstrukturanalyse' ('Social-ecological typologisation between target group segmentation and social structure analysis'), in Gerhard de Haan et al. (eds), *Typenbildung in der sozialwissenschaftlichen Umweltforschung* (Development of Types in Social Scientific Environmental Research), Opladen: Leske+Budrich, pp. 127–38.

Götz, Konrad, Willi Loose, Martin Schmied and Stephanie Schubert (2003), *Mobilitätsstile in der Freizeit. Minderungen der Umweltbelastungen des Freizeit- und Tourismusverkehrs (Mobility Styles in the Leisure Time. Decrease of Environmental Impacts of Leisure and Tourism Traffic)*, Nr. 02/03, Berlin: Erich Schmidt.

Grunert, Klaus G., Karen Brunso and Soren Bisp (1993), 'Food-related life style: Development of a cross-culturally valid instrument for market surveillance', MAPP working paper no. 12, Aarhus: The Aarhus School of Business, MAPP – Centre for Market Surveillance, Research and Strategy for the Food Sector.

Hustad, Thomas P. and Edgar A. Pessemier (1972), 'Industry's use of life style analysis: Segmenting consumer market with activity and attitude measures', in Fred C. Allvine (ed.), *Combined Proceedings*, Chicago: American Marketing Association, pp. 296–301.

Inglehart, Ronald (1977), *The Silent Revolution*, Princeton, NJ: Princeton University Press.

Lamnek, Siegfried (1993), *Qualitative Sozialforschung*, Weinheim: Beltz.

Lazer, William (1964), 'Life style concepts and marketing', in Stephen A. Greyser (ed.), *Towards Scientific Marketing*, Chicago, US: American Marketing Association, pp. 243–52.

Longhurst, Mike (2003), 'Advertising and sustainability: A new paradigm', in Admap, July/August 2003, http://www.uneptie.org/pc/sustain/reports/advertising/article_longhurst_admap.pdf.

Müller, Hans-Peter (1992), *Sozialstruktur und Lebensstile. Der neuere theoretische Diskurs über soziale Ungleichheit* (*Social Structure and Life Styles. The Newer Theoretical Discourse on Social Inequity*), Frankfurt/Main: Suhrkamp.

Schultz, Irmgard and Ines Weller (1997), *Nachhaltige Konsummuster und postmaterielle Lebensstile. Eine Vorstudie im Auftrag des Umweltbundesamtes*, (*Sustainable Consumption Patterns and Post-Material Life Styles. A Preliminary Study Commissioned by the German Federal Environment Agency*), UBA-Texte 30/97, Berlin: Umweltbundesamt.

SINUS (2000): *Kurzinformation zu den SINUS-Milieus*, Stand 05/2000, Heidelberg: SINUS.

Stieß, Immanuel and Konrad Götz (2002), 'Nachhaltigere Lebensstile durch zielgruppenbezogenes Marketing?' ('More sustainable lifestyle through target group oriented marketing?'), in Dieter Rink (ed.), *Lebensstile und Nachhaltigkeit. Konzepte, Befunde und Potentiale*, Opladen: Leske + Budrich, pp. 247–63.

UBA (Umweltbundesamt) (Federal Environmental Agency) (ed.) (2002), *Nachhaltige Konsummuster: Ein neues umweltpolitisches Handlungsfeld als Herausforderung für die Umweltkommunikation; mit einer Zielgruppenanalyse des Frankfurter Instituts für sozial-ökologische Forschung* (*Sustainable Consumption Pattern: A New Action Field of Environmental Policy as a Challenge for Environmental Communication; with a Target Group Analysis of the Institute for Social-Ecological Research in Frankfurt*), Berlin: Erich Schmidt.

Weber, Max (1920/1986), 'Die protestantische Ethik und der Geist des Kapitalismus' (*The Protestant Ethic and the Spirit of Capitalism*), in M. Weber, *Gesammelte Aufsätze zur Religious soziologie*, Vol. I, Tübingen: J.C.B. Mohr.

Wimmer, Frank (2001), 'Forschungsüberlegungen und empirische Ergebnisse zum nachhaltigen Konsum', ('Reflection on research and empirical findings about sustainable consumption'), in Ulf Schrader and Ursula Hansen (eds), *Nachhaltiger Konsum. Forschung und Praxis im Dialog*), Frankfurt/Main: Campus, pp. 77–102.

11. Community, reflexivity and sustainable consumption

Laurie Michaelis

11.1 INTRODUCTION

This chapter sets out to explore the role of communities, and in particular 'reflexive' or 'post-traditional' communities (Beck et al. 1994), in sustainable consumption. It starts in the next section by briefly sketching out the magnitude of the environmental and ethical challenge posed by current consumption trends. It notes in particular the recent calls for factor-of-four or more reductions in resource use associated with consumption in industrialised countries. But it also observes the strong ideological opposition to any initiative to reduce the level of material consumption.

In consumer societies, consumption is mostly understood as an individual behaviour. The following section reviews some of the ways in which consumption patterns are shaped by the collective, including well-known market mechanisms but also emphasising the role of culture and discourse.

The chapter then identifies potential sources of a culture of sustainable consumption, describing some of the diversity in current cultures of, and narratives about, consumption and also reviewing some perspectives on the ways in which new cultures may emerge. It focuses on the role of discourse in developing our personal and collective narratives, and hence our ethics of consumption.

It explores how some of these ideas apply in the cases of three existing networks of communities that are seeking to promote sustainable consumption cultures. Finally, it considers what can be learned from their experiences and what might be the implications for a widespread shift towards sustainable patterns of consumption.

11.2 THE SUSTAINABILITY CHALLENGE TO CONSUMPTION

Joachim Spangenberg, in this volume, sets out the environmental impacts of consumption. His work (Lorek and Spangenberg 2001), along with that

of others (for example, Brower and Leon 1999) points to the need for large
reductions in the resource use associated with the three most environmentally
significant areas of consumption: food, transport and shelter. On a lifecycle
or economy-wide basis, consumption in these three areas in industrialised
countries accounts for around 70–80 per cent of material flows, energy
use, land use and water consumption. As a consequence, food, transport
and housing are also responsible for the majority of greenhouse gas
emissions, local air and watercourse pollution, habitat disruption and loss
of biodiversity.

Calls for factor-of-four to -ten reductions in resource use in industrialised
countries have been justified mainly with reference to greenhouse gas
emissions (von Weizsäcker et al. 1997; OECD 1998), but estimates of
'ecological footprints' also point to the need for the citizens of these countries
to reduce their resource use by a factor of four or more (Wackernagel et
al. 2002). Much of this reduction will have to come from changes in the
patterns of production and consumption associated with food, transport
and housing.

Consumption patterns are strongly defended against government
intervention, especially in these three key areas. The defence comes mainly
from industry but also sometimes from special interest groups (such as
motoring organisations) and politicians. It is not just government that
has become reluctant to entertain the possibility of measures to change
lifestyles; mainstream environmental organisations have also shied away in
recent years from messages and campaigns on sustainable consumption.

A number of moral arguments are brought into play to deny the propriety
of any government or collective role in influencing consumer behaviour.
These arguments draw on concepts central to the ethics of modern consumer
societies, in particular those of 'needs' and 'rights' (Michaelis 2000). These
two concepts have been closely associated with the last four centuries'
developments in the understanding of human nature and the place of
people in society and the world. In particular, an understanding of the
self has emerged that emphasises both individual autonomy and the inner
complexity of the psyche (Taylor 1989).

The idea that we consume (whether emotionally or rationally driven) to
meet 'needs' has become pervasive, at least in the sustainable development
discourse. The central goal of sustainable development is to meet human
needs now and in the future (WCED 1987). This emphasis on a concept that
is closely associated with individualistic conceptions of the self is deeply
problematic, not least because sustainable development demands a shift of
our focus away from ourselves as separate individuals and towards other
people and the natural world (Michaelis 2000). Furthermore, attempts to
define human needs are apt to lapse into circularity (Douglas et al. 1998).

Clearly we 'need' something if we will die without it. Our survival depends on meeting certain needs, such as basic nutrition, warmth and healthcare. Max-Neef (1991) points out the distinction between needs (for example, for nutrition) and satisfiers (for example, bread). We often choose 'false satisfiers' and in any case, meeting our needs does not necessarily make us satisfied. Maslow (1954) suggested that this is partly because we have many different types of needs, and when we satisfy one, another takes its place. He suggested that in addition to basic physiological requirements, we have 'needs' for belongingness, esteem and self-actualisation.

Perhaps we can agree on some basic and universal human needs (Doyal and Gough 1991) but appropriate satisfiers depend on the social context. We can understand some needs in terms of the capabilities required to function satisfactorily in society and hence to flourish (Sen 1993). Satisfiers may include appropriate clothing, mobility, education and much else. Nussbaum interprets capabilities as freedoms, and hence as rights (Nussbaum 1998).

In the welfare state, which promises both justice and security, the presumption is that people's needs should be met. To be in need is to suffer. To neglect others' needs is to be heartless and immoral. But in casual use, the word 'need' is now used for anything that we lack or desire. Hence it has lost some of its earlier moral force. Yet it retains a currency in justifying the actions of businesses, which must produce more stuff to meet people's needs.

If needs or the appropriate means of satisfying them are shaped by our social context, perhaps we should be asking whether we can adapt our needs to fit with what is ecologically and socially sustainable. There is no reason why human needs should lead to ever-increasing resource use; why should our social norms not establish needs that entail behaving in ways that minimise our ecological impact?

Whereas needs are usually supposed to be inherent to people, rights are more clearly conferred by society – although the Enlightenment philosopher John Locke thought that he was able to discern pre-existing 'natural rights'. In modern society, rights are politically determined and declared, and established in law.

Certain modern concepts of rights have contributed to the emergence of the consumer economy and culture. In particular, the right to the pursuit of happiness – and to choose our own path to happiness – is central to a culture in which the pleasures of consumption are condoned as long as others are not harmed. This is contrary to the morality of medieval European Christianity, which viewed gluttony and avarice as deadly sins. The right to freedom of speech, which has been extended from individuals to apply to corporations, provides permission for the increasing presence of marketing in all communication media.

11.3 COLLECTIVE DETERMINATION OF CONSUMPTION NORMS

Even where the social contingency of consumption (and all human behaviour) is acknowledged (for example, Røpke 1999; OECD 2002; Jackson and Michaelis 2003), culture and social structure are understood primarily as influences on individual choice. While this focus on the individual is a useful and valid perspective, it is not the only one (Jaeger et al. 1998). As Shove explains in this volume, individual behaviour can also be understood as a phenomenon of the group. Practices may emerge in a community or society without any individual ever making a conscious choice. In any case, there is considerable evidence that our sense of individual agency is at best transitory, and in many circumstances illusory (Dennett 1993).

Consumption is perhaps one of the realms in which it is most obvious that norms are established socially, rather than being inherent to people. The collective determination of consumption norms takes place at many different levels, within households and organisations, in local communities and cities, in nations and internationally. In the following, three processes of collective determination will be considered:

- Aggregate consumption choices: the market, physical and economic infrastructure. These practical influences on consumption are quite widely acknowledged and fairly well understood by policy analysts.
- Social structure, cultural norms and symbols. These influences are widely acknowledged but their importance is disputed in discussions about strategies for sustainable consumption and production.
- Discourse and narrative. This area of influence is of particular interest in the discussion in the remainder of this chapter.

The three realms are interdependent and some analysts would consider aspects of some of them to be subsets of others. For example, discourse and narrative is a particular aspect of symbolic interaction.

11.3.1 Practical Influences of Aggregate Behaviour

Our behaviour is shaped in many practical ways by the actions of those around us: through the development of infrastructure, technology, products and services in response to demand; through prices in the market; and through the policies of democratically elected governments. As Shove argues, and as historians of technological change have long observed (Landes 1969; Freeman 1990; Rosenberg 1994), social, economic and technological change are closely interwoven. The complex interconnections create a system that can become 'locked-in' to particular technologies and the practices and social structures that surround them.

Sanne (2002) describes consumption patterns in general as 'locked-in'. We are captured by pressures to standardise our behaviour arising from the need to succeed in the job market, to behave in ways that are consistent with others' expectations. Those who do not own homes are subject to the condescension of local governments and communities; those without cars have a limited choice of work, home and services; and those who do not eat a 'normal' diet may be constrained in their ability to maintain a social life and to spend time away from home. These explicit pressures to conform go a long way to explaining the apparent increase in citizens' 'need' to consume (Segal 1998).

One of the most obvious examples of lock-in is the growing dependence of citizens in wealthy countries on the car. Transport technologies, infrastructure and practices show a tendency to lock-in because of the high costs of infrastructure and huge advantages of standardisation (if vehicles are to function throughout the infrastructure network). In most wealthy countries, the car has become the dominant form of transport because that is how everyone gets around. As a result of economies of scale and a century of development and mass production, the gasoline engine is remarkably cheap compared with alternative types of engine or motor. The main alternatives to car use – non-motorised and public transport – have become more difficult to use, more expensive, and in many ways more dangerous. Meanwhile, the barriers to market entry for alternative transport forms, and even for alternative car technologies, seem tremendous.

11.3.2 Social Structure and Culture

It is perhaps in the discussion of competition for status that it is most apparent that individuals may be motivated to increase their consumption levels without becoming any better off. The 19th century critique of the 'conspicuous consumption' of the lower middle classes by Veblen (1899) is taken up in less snobbish terms by Hirsch (1977), with his discussion of positional goods and the need to establish social limits to growth, and by Frank (1985) in his work on 'relative consumption'.

Surveys and focus group studies (for example, Dake and Thompson 1999; Hines and Ames 2000) find that status consumption is associated mostly with certain cultural subgroups. Dake and Thompson use the framework of cultural theory to link status competition with individualist culture.

Schor (1998) finds that consumption is driven as much by the desire to belong to a group as by the desire for status. Thus, a large car enables parents to participate in a group of people who drive each other's children to school. Participation in social groups may require particular standards of dress, and reciprocity in treating others to restaurant meals. When it is clear that the alternative to belongingness is to be socially excluded, this kind of consumption appears less a luxury and more a necessity.

Bourdieu (1984) provided an empirical demonstration of the social determination of taste for inhabitants of Paris suburbs. Warde (1997) finds that, despite an increasing perception and ideology of individualism, food tastes in Britain remained socially determined in the late 1990s, although the particular preferences, and the nature of the social divisions, had changed substantially since the 1960s. Schor (1998) finds in the United States that many consumption preferences are determined by the need to belong to a particular community or group, and that television plays an increasingly strong role as celebrities are emulated as if they were high-status members of viewers' own communities.

Baudrillard (1970) is scathing about the conformity of the majority in a system of mass consumption, promulgated through the mass media. Beck (1988) writes of 'individualisation' in modern society as the illusion of individual choice and freedom, which is actually conformity to a new set of social norms. We talk and think about ourselves as if we were free but are in fact trapped by a system that forces us to establish an identity – a story about ourselves – that will endure as we move through portfolio careers and ephemeral communities.

The role of consumption in identity formation and communication has been explored in a variety of contexts. Douglas and Isherwood (1979) show from ethnographic studies, for example, how consumption is used to establish suitability for marriage. Csikszentmihalyi and Rochberg-Halton (1981) show the importance of material possessions for personal identity and a psychological sense of meaning. However, the nature of the symbolism and the implications for the environment vary considerably among different cultures (Ger et al. 1998).

The advertising industry has made particular use of the symbolic function of consumption, and indeed has augmented it tremendously. For example, TV advertising in particular uses sophisticated artistic and dramatic techniques to create associations between particular brands and deeply held values in the collective consciousness. A make of car might represent reliability. A brand of coffee might symbolise sophistication. Or a clothing label might be associated with celebrity and status. The associations are also made with idealised lifestyles and identities – happy families use the right kind of ultrasoft toilet paper. Independent and confident young people use a certain underarm deodorant, and so on.

11.3.3 Discourse and Narrative

Despite the importance of the social forces and mechanisms mentioned above, it is perhaps discourse and narrative that is of most interest in the context of sustainable consumption. Narrative is fundamental to our sense of self (Dennett, 1993) and our worldview – our understanding of human nature, of our relationship with society and of the natural world around us (Campbell 1959). It also lies at the heart of our sense of meaning, whether we describe it in terms of divine purpose, biological evolution, pleasure or survival. Hence, narrative helps to shape the identities, worldviews, values and symbols that are associated with lifestyles and consumption patterns (Jackson and Michaelis 2003).

It is through discourse that we develop and change our narratives, and even when our discourse is internal, it originates in communication with others. It is through discourse that we question and affirm the values, goals and priorities that shape our system of production and consumption. Our conscious choices about how to live and consume are largely mediated by discourse. And it is partly through discourse that we learn from parents, teachers and others to associate particular practices with values, status and belongingness, and with meeting our own needs. Dickinson (1998) describes how people draw on narrative from many types of media programming to construct their own discourses about food and food choices.

Current mainstream discourse, emerging over centuries of debate by philosophers, theologians, scientists, economists and politicians, encourages material consumption by emphasising:

- an understanding of human beings as autonomous, rational individuals whose highest potential is to be achieved through their work and demonstrated in increasing levels of material wealth and consumption;
- an understanding of society as nothing more than a collection of individuals, whose collective purpose is to enable individual members to meet their needs;
- an understanding of the natural world as a resource base for meeting human needs.

A central challenge for sustainable consumption is to question this narrative (Michaelis 2000) and to find storylines that will support a different set of priorities.

11.4 SOURCES OF SUSTAINABLE CONSUMPTION CULTURE

This section explores two possible sources of cultural approaches or storylines to support sustainable consumption. The first is in existing cultural groups. The second is in the evolution of culture, whether through developments in mainstream discourse or through the emergence of groups supporting alternative discourses. My starting point is a brief look at the range of existing cultures of consumption, but my emphasis will be on emerging cultures, awareness and forms of consciousness that support sustainability.

11.4.1 Diversity

Ethnographic studies of consumption behaviour and the associated values and attitudes show that only a minority of consumers fully accept the mainstream worldview outlined above. Dake and Thompson (1999), for example, identify five distinct cultures of consumption which can be summarised, as follows:

- *Traditional* consumers place emphasis on values such as duty and order. They eat a conventional diet and have homes that contain old or antique furniture reflecting continuity with the past. Their consumption patterns demonstrate their established place in the community.
- *Cosmopolitan* consumers emphasise values such as liberty and innovation. They are individualists who keep up with fashions in food, home furnishing and personal transport. These are the conspicuous and competitive consumers.
- *Natural* consumers are politically engaged, concerned with environmental and social values. In their consumption they tend to avoid anything artificial and distinguish 'real' needs, which can be met by nature, from 'false' needs that we cannot meet except by depriving future generations. Their consumption choices are a moral statement.
- *Marginal* or *fatalist* consumers do not make active choices, but muddle through, perhaps being constrained by budget or unable to take control of their consumption patterns for other reasons.
- *Hermits* are not socially isolated (as fatalists are) but make a positive choice to be independent of social expectations. They live simply without making a political or moral point of it.

Each of these cultural types or 'solidarities' (as Dake and Thompson call them) has the potential to be concerned about, and take action for, environmental and social issues. A study of British consumers by the polling survey company MORI (Hines and Ames 2000) also found five clusters, based on attitudes and approaches to ethical consumption. The clusters do not correspond exactly to Dake and Thompson's categories but there are some interesting overlaps, with the largest groups corresponding roughly to 'traditional', 'cosmopolitan' and 'fatalist' consumers, and a small group (5 per cent of the sample), which Hines and Ames called 'Global Watchdogs', corresponding roughly to Dake and Thompson's 'natural' consumers. All of the groups except for the one that appears closest to the 'fatalist' solidarity shared a concern about environmental and social issues, but they had different ways of acting, or not acting, on their concern. Only the Global Watchdogs were prepared to make significant lifestyle choices based on ethical concerns.

One option for any government or other organisation wishing to promote sustainable consumption is to work with these cultural segments, developing strategies that address the different attitudes and values of the groups. Natural consumers may respond to information and advice on reducing the environmental and social impact of their consumption. Traditional consumers might respond better to arguments about conservation of our heritage; they might also be attracted by more traditional, low impact patterns of consumption and production. Cosmopolitans are more likely to respond to innovative, eco-efficient products and services that provide them with new ways of being up-to-date and fashionable. Hermits may be particularly attracted by technologies and lifestyle options that enable them to combine self-sufficiency with environmental sustainability. Fatalists may be influenced only through regulations and standards that force manufacturers to offer more environmentally friendly products, and through tax changes that make it expensive to consume environmentally damaging products.

However, these approaches all assume a benevolent external person or institution seeking to shape the behaviour of the various groups. Behaviour changes that occur because of coercion or persuasion are very easily reversed. In any case, in democratic societies, coercion is rarely feasible or acceptable. Popular support is required from an electoral majority if governments are to introduce policies that make a real contribution to sustainable consumption. What would it take to develop cultures that are intrinsically supportive of sustainable lifestyles?

11.4.2 Reflexivity and Learning

According to Beck (1988), increasing consciousness of environmental and other risks is encouraging society to become more reflexive. Giddens (1994) writes of an emerging post-traditional society, where values, goals and practices are developed through deliberate discourse rather than received as tradition.

Living in a post-traditional society exposes us to tensions between fundamental principles, setting freedom against equality, individual against community, our rights against others' needs and humanity against nature (Michaelis 2000). The relaxation of traditional expectations about roles and behaviour may also increase the difficulty in choosing how to act given our own desires, our perception of others' expectations of us, and the guidance of our values, beliefs and ideals. These tensions are often reflected in our consumption and lifestyle choices. Life has become more complicated, partly because we have no simple, shared narrative about our goals and ethics as a society.

The issues surrounding sustainable consumption are as complex as any, and the result is often that we take the path of least resistance – we do what is easiest rather than what we think is right. Even people who believe that a change in lifestyle is needed for environmental reasons have a wide range of reasons for delaying action (Kasemir et al. 2000; Stoll-Kleeman et al. 2001). They are well aware of the wide range of competing discourses on environmental action and generally construct their own narratives to support their current choices (Hobson 2002). To take a common example, many car drivers say that, because of their environmental values, they would like to drive less. But they need their car to live up to their social values, for example, by giving people lifts or by having time to make their contribution to family and community (Michaelis 2003). They also believe that they need to make a trade-off between their own well-being and that of the environment.

Part of the difficulty here is that each of our many different value systems are supported by different narratives that seem incommensurate. We hear conflicting voices supporting personal material well-being, community involvement, tradition and conventional practice, social change and environmental sustainability. It never seems possible to weave them together into a coherent framework of values and principles for action, or ethics. MacIntyre (1985) laments the state of ethics in modern society, in particular the interminable debates over ethical principles and priorities. He argues that ethics cannot work as universal principles, but only if they emerge as practical rules for living within a specific functioning cultural tradition. Such a tradition includes a set of cultural practices, a narrative framework and an ideal of the good life. Gare (1995) believes that the creation of practical traditions for sustainable living depends on re-establishing local communities and reducing the power of nation states. This may seem a lost cause in the face of the globalisation of markets, media and human relationships, and it might be more helpful to look for the development of such traditions at a variety of different scales, in a large number of overlapping and intersecting communities.

Groups have found different ways of overcoming the tensions inherent in developing a living, reflexive system of values and ethics. Perhaps one of the first tensions communities have to come to terms with is that over their own existence. Bauman (2001) describes the tension between individual and community – between freedom and security – as interminable. Society currently puts great emphasis on individual freedom, or at least an illusion of freedom, and communities have deteriorated as a result. But we would not want to go too far in the opposite direction, giving up liberty for the security of the community. Another major question for communities relates to the source of their values. Some communities are established by an individual or organisation asserting leadership and imposing a set of values. Other communities adopt values based on an existing tradition, perhaps expressed in religious scriptures and elucidated by established experts or exegetes. Still others allow their values to emerge out of a process of discourse, negotiation or voting within the community.

Responding to complex challenges such as sustainability, with rapidly changing circumstances and information, demands a continuous learning process. Simple theories of government or business management become defunct very rapidly. Creativity is needed to expand the options available. Some of the best thinking and practice on learning processes to deal with complex contexts has come from business and management schools. One of the most interesting threads stems from the systems thinking of Bateson (1972) and in particular his concept of 'deutero-learning', now more widely termed 'double-loop' learning (Argyris and Schon 1996; Senge 1990; Griffin 2002). Single-loop learning occurs when we respond to new experience or information without changing our worldview, priorities, values or culture. For example, we might insulate our home once we realise that it will save us money and make us more comfortable. This action fits within mainstream cultural assumptions that comfort and cost-saving are important goals. Double-loop learning occurs when we respond to experience by changing the rules we live by. For example, following a visit to an African shanty town, we might be shocked on our return to Europe by the luxury and waste in our society, and radically revise our lifestyle expectations and values, adopting values such as simplicity and equality as our guiding principles. Argyris and Schon emphasise the lengths to which individuals and groups will go to avoid double-loop learning. Yet it is precisely this kind of cultural change – a shift in values and consciousness – that seems to be needed to approach sustainable consumption.

11.4.3 Emerging Consciousness

Part of the difficulty in double-loop learning is that our narratives and worldviews are structures that we use to feel safe in a complex environment. New perspectives bring new risks, challenge our existing choices and may require us to give up habits and comforts to which we have become attached. They may even require us to give up our sense of who we are, and of who others think we are.

Table 11.1 illustrates one framework for thinking about personal and cultural change, learning and emerging consciousness. It is based on the idea of 'modes' of consciousness and civilisation (Neumann 1954; Graves 1982; Beck and Cowan 1996). Each mode combines a view of human nature, a worldview, a sense of the purpose of life and a set of core values. It may be expressed in personal and communal narratives, in social structures and in individual and collective behaviour.

The modes emerge in succession, alternating between individualist differentiation and collective integration, liberty and belongingness. The development of consciousness is a dialectic process leading to increasing complexity, in which each phase reacts against and builds on the mental structures of the previous stage. In healthy development, each stage incorporates the functions of the earlier phases in a new synthesis. A similar approach is adopted in various theories of personality type (for example, Myers and Myers 1993; Riso and Hudson 1996), which view healthy development as the incorporation of additional attributes and functions. As we develop, we gain greater flexibility, maintaining the capabilities, conceptual frameworks and emotional patterns of earlier phases, although we also sometimes become trapped in reversions to the needs or limitations of those phases. Hence Beck and Cowan's phrase, 'spiral development', to emphasise that developmental progress is not simple and linear nor firmly bound to particular ages or sequences. At each step a particular mode or complex of worldviews, attitudes, values and goals is expressed (Beck and Cowan use their own language for these complexes but here they are referred to simply as 'modes'; I have also adopted my own labels for the modes, which Beck and Cowan refer to by colours; see Table 11.1).

Beck and Cowan's modes correspond roughly, but not exactly, to stages of development identified by others (for example, Torbert et al. 2001; Wilber 1981, 1996). There is also some association with Maslow's hierarchy of needs and with Piaget's and Kohlberg's stages of cognitive and moral development.

Perhaps more significantly in the context of the discussion of consumption, the hierarchic, strategic and pluralist modes appear to correspond to cultural theory's hierarchists, individualists and egalitarians. These are the three modes that are most prominent in the cultures of industrialised countries (Beck and Cowan 1996).

Within this framework, individuals, organisations and communities can be characterised as expressing particular modes. In Western society the heroic power, hierarchic and strategic modes tend to dominate. For much of the last 300 years, political debate has taken the form of a dialogue among these modes.

11.4.4 Awakening to Sustainability?

Many economic historians (for example, Schumpeter 1928; Rostow 1990) have followed Marx in looking forward to a time when a more communitarian, egalitarian worldview would dominate. Such a worldview is, indeed, emerging in the form of growing pluralism. It can be seen in the values of post-modernism and the current academic rejection of hierarchies – including the idea of stages of development (Wilber 2000). A new emphasis on community was one focus of the politics of the 1990s (for example, in the US Clinton administration and in Tony Blair's 'Third Way'). But in its undiscriminating inclusiveness, Beck and Cowan observe that the pluralistic mode can be an ineffectual basis for governance. There have been political backlashes in Britain and the United States, with an unhealthy reversion to heroic power in the 'War on Terrorism'.

Responding to the sustainability challenge may be partly a matter of values and attitudes, but it is also a matter of capability. Society must develop the ability to adapt to its environment; to learn from experience. Torbert et al. (2001), focusing on corporate organisation and transformation, write about the need for managers to develop to a level where they are able to function with multiple worldviews, if they are to lead 'learning organisations'. Such managers are able to communicate with and respond to people within their own frames, providing them with motivations that they can understand. Similarly, society needs leadership that can integrate different perspectives and worldviews. In Beck and Cowan's framework, we need an evolution in culture so that the synthetic and holistic modes are expressed more in our society. They describe these as 'second tier' modes with the emerging ability to synthesise the goals, narratives and symbols of the first tier modes. Figure 11.1 interprets this process in terms of the synthesis of recent cultural movements into 'post-consumerism'.

11.5 THREE LEARNING NETWORKS

This section will focus on three organisations that are involved in working for a new awakening, or new awareness. They are looking for solutions to

Table 11.1 Psycho-social modes (based on Beck and Cowan 1996)

Mode	Setting where mode dominates	Human nature, needs, self-image	Worldview (and theology)	Effective sustainability policies and communication strategies
Survival	Survival groups Excluded/street culture in Western society	Impulsive; reactive; instinctive; physiological and survival needs	Concrete challenges to be overcome	Planning, standards
Kin-attachment	Tribes, clans, extended families Youth/street culture Team sports	Centred on kin; belongingness needs	Magical; animistic capricious (trickster myths)	Qualitative guidance on lifestyle and consumption
Heroic power	Feudal kingdoms Sporting/street culture	Heroic power Assertion of force Esteem needs	Superstitious Symbolic (warring gods)	Regulation and policing
Hierarchy	Bureaucratic states and industries Team sports	Emphasis on role in hierarchy Absolute truth and right Esteem needs	Strong principles and justice (dynastic gods)	Codes of practice Incite duty, moral obligation Seek to develop new social norms
Strategic	Stock markets	Strategic, rational individual calculating and pursuing personal advantage Actualisation needs	Impersonal Obeying comprehensible laws (deism, atheism)	Objective information, pricing, clear responsibilities backed up by contract law
Pluralistic	Stakeholder forums	Emotional, communitarian, focus on personal growth, equality	Permissive pluralism: all worldviews allowed (one God, many faces)	Education Stakeholder processes Ensure opportunities for green lifestyles, consumption

Synthetic	Permaculture action learning guilds; quakers	Compassionate: able to take multiple perspectives Motivated by learning, integration of complex systems	Discerning pluralism: Intimacy with many worldviews (different theologies address different aspects of spiritual life)	Comprehensive policy packages justified by multiple rationalities to address different subcultures and situations
Holistic	Present in rare individuals and groups – currently mostly a vision	Integrated Creative synthesis of perspectives	Holism: creative synthesis of worldviews (focus on spiritual connectivity)	Cultural awakening to develop true communities at multiple scales

1500	1600	1700	1800	1900	2000
Reformation	*Enlightenment*	*Romanticism*	*Modernism/ early consumerism*	*Post-modernism/ late consumerism*	*Post-consumerism*
Rejects feudal system, church hierarchy	Scientific discovery of truth	Rejects Enlightenment materialism	Combines earlier values. Enlightenment important in business; romanticism in consumption	Rejects modernist certainties: kaleidoscope of worldviews	Creative synthesis of worldviews
Religious revelation of truth	Rational self	Interior discovery of truth		Self becomes increasingly abstract, aloof	Relativity of truth and values
Soul as true self	Goals of progress, utility	Emotional, inward self	Self as multiple personas	Goal of enjoyment/ amusement	Relational self
Goal of worshipping God through everyday life	Human rights: freedom and equality before the law	Goal of aesthetic/ mystical experience	Goal of efficiency	Hypermarket truth (competing experts)	Goal of people, communities and planet flourishing
Liberty in practice of religion	Nature as resource base	Human needs	Expert truth	Anything goes	Truth tested in discourse
Equality before God		Nature as ideal	Liberty, equality extended to new groups	Multiple views of nature	Nature as community of life
Nature to be subdued or managed			Nature as amenity		

Figure 11.1   Emergence of new worldviews

the challenge of sustainable living and employing reflexive processes in one way or another. They are:

- Global Action Plan (GAP), an international organisation promoting lifestyle change by setting up 'EcoTeams': small groups of neighbours who meet together regularly over several months to learn about the environmental impacts of their lives and adopt targets for change.
- The Religious Society of Friends (Quakers), in particular the Living Witness Project, a network of Quaker meetings in Britain exploring approaches to 'sustainable living'.
- The Permaculture Association, an international network of individuals and local groups and communities, which adopt an 'action learning' approach to search for solutions to sustainable land management and communities.

11.5.1   Global Action Plan

Of the three organisations, GAP is perhaps the most mainstream. It works with people in their neighbourhoods, workplaces, churches and schools to change lifestyles in an evolutionary rather than revolutionary way. Originating in the United States, GAP now has programmes in several countries including Britain. This section will draw mainly on the UK experience.

GAP sets out to encourage a change in lifestyles through awareness raising and dialogue (Burgess 2003). When GAP began to work in Britain, it initially focused on providing households with information packs, enabling them to work out their own environmental impacts and identify priorities for changing their habits. Surveys and interviews show that participants valued the information but did not feel strongly motivated to change their behaviour (Hobson 2002). On the whole, reflecting on their choices helped them to become clearer about their reasons for maintaining their current lifestyles, rejecting the rational arguments for change offered in the packs. They were more concerned about issues of social justice linked to their consumption than about the environmental impacts.

More recently, GAP UK has begun to adopt the EcoTeam approach, which has been the main strategy in other countries, especially the Netherlands. GAP starts from the assumption that many people have attitudes consistent with moving towards environmentally sustainable behaviour, but that they do not have sufficient information to do so, nor do they believe that they alone can make a difference. Hence a collective, community-based approach is crucial.

The EcoTeam is a group of six to 10 people who might be neighbours, members of the same religious organisation, or members of some interest group or club. They meet once a month and discuss ideas, experiences and achievements related to the EcoTeam programme. The programme is based on a workbook provided by GAP, which addresses six areas in turn: waste, gas, electricity, water, transport and consumption. The workbook explains each theme, the goals of GAP, and a number of actions that can be taken by households to reach those goals. The programme takes a total of eight months. Each team is supported by a coach or by a reporting centre.

EcoTeam members work towards becoming 'global citizens' by changing aspects of household behaviour. The emphasis is on the household rather than the individual, so that EcoTeam members work with other household members to change behaviour in areas such as waste separation and recycling, water use, energy use and travel.

GAP has set up EcoTeams in several countries and has developed workbooks and support material for different countries. While GAP monitors the results of its programme, the most detailed evaluation of quantitative results has been carried out in the Netherlands (Staats and Harland 1995), where EcoTeams have typically achieved reductions in car use and consumption of energy and water of around 10 per cent, and reductions in waste of around 40 per cent (presumably partly as a result of composting and recycling). Similar results are achieved in British groups (personal communication, GAP UK 2003). Maiteny (2002) found that behaviour changes that respond to negative incentives (for example, price or regulation) or anxiety are not maintained when the incentives are removed. Participants in GAP's programmes were most likely to maintain behaviour changes if they were motivated by a strong and positive link to personal meaning and identity. For some, the deciding factor was a spiritual experience, changing their sense of their relationship with nature.

11.5.2 Quakers

Quakers offer an unusual, if not unique, example of a reflexive community in which values, practices and collective identity are continually open to reflection and discussion by all members. Whereas GAP seeks to meet people where they are, within the mainstream consumer culture, Quakers (or 'Friends') have a 350-year history of maintaining alternative values, based on equality, simplicity and opposition to violence and war. They emphasise an approach to religion that is based on personal experience, tested within the meeting, rather than on belief and scripture.

Friends make decisions in business meetings modelled on their normal spiritual practice of sitting in silence, waiting or listening. The issue under consideration is presented to the meeting, after which Friends may stand and speak, usually interspersed by periods of silence. Throughout, there is a central emphasis on silent listening, and on individuals letting go of their own interests. The meeting has a clerk whose main responsibilities are to facilitate the process and to prepare a minute capturing the 'sense of the meeting'. Friends may then comment, suggest changes, or suggest that the minute be accepted. When this process works properly, participants in the meeting are supposed to be seeking the 'will of God', the 'sense of the meeting' or the right path forward, rather than trying to persuade others of their view. The business meeting is looking for a kind of collective narrative, and individuals are seeking to identify with a collective or transcendent consciousness. Morley (1993) emphasises that this process is different from consensus – it is a search for a collective sense of direction, rather than an effort by individuals to agree.

The 'Quaker business method' is applied to all kinds of decisions. It is used by small committees in local Quaker meetings considering the colour of the meeting house curtains, and by annual gatherings (Yearly Meetings, which in Britain can include over 1000 Friends) considering fundamental questions about the values, ethics, rules and actions of the Society of Friends. Minutes of Quaker meetings may determine corporate policies, or encourage individual Friends to take particular moral stances – for instance, against war, inequality, or injustice.

Over the last ten years, a narrative about the environment has begun to emerge among British Friends. The process has started from individuals who have written or spoken from their own perspective (Dale 2000; Finch 2000; McIntosh 2001). It has also drawn on narrative sources throughout Quaker history with the compilation of anthologies of past Quaker writings on the environment and on simplicity (BYM 1995; Adams 1996). The annual gathering of British Quakers, Britain Yearly Meeting, has agreed advice to Friends to live simply, show a loving consideration for all creatures, and work to ensure that our power over nature is used responsibly (BYM 1995). However, the narrative still retains many diverse strands and tensions, and has not yet cohered to produce a practical ethic for sustainable living.

Some Quakers are exploring the next step in this process through the Living Witness Project (of which the author is the coordinator). The project involves a 'learning network' of 17 Quaker meetings around Britain (Michaelis 2003). They are exploring corporate approaches to sustainable living, experimenting and learning both within the individual meetings and in the network that links them. Outcomes range from environmental improvements in meeting houses to projects involving local communities. They include practical advice to Friends on 'greening' their lifestyles, and campaigning on environmental issues at local and national level. Eventually, many in the network hope that their experiences will feed back into the collective Quaker narrative to produce a more coherent response to the challenge of sustainable living.

The initial experiences of those involved in the network show that quite significant lifestyle changes are possible with the support of a community that shares and talks about environmental values. Several individuals report becoming vegetarian or vegan, joining organic box delivery schemes, giving up their car or deciding to avoid air travel. A few are searching for opportunities to move into shared housing or communities. However, it is too early to tell how these decisions will hold up in the long term, and what the influence will be on others.

11.5.3 Permaculture

The third organisation considered here is a loose, worldwide network of practitioners, following the philosophy of permaculture, which has been developed and promoted since the mid-1970s by the Australian ecologists, Bill Mollison and David Holmgren. Permaculture is presented by practitioners and by the UK Permaculture Association as a design philosophy. Its central principles bring together the goals of taking care of the Earth, taking care of people and ensuring a fair distribution of resources. It emphasises the use of ecological principles in the design of land use systems and communities. And it adopts a range of tools and processes to support strategic and reflexive approaches to design.

In its most public face, permaculture comes across mainly as a set of practical, concrete principles – or even an ideology – for ecosystem management. Permaculture principles are being applied by a growing range of communities and organisations, in the production of food, recovery of degraded land and in the design of settlements that maintain the functioning of surrounding ecosystems.

The principles are also applied to social systems, treating knowledge, values and culture as aspects of biodiversity to be nurtured in the search for more sustainable ways of living. There is a well-developed, and still developing, process of reflexivity and learning through which permaculture principles evolve. Permaculture teachers, who must be experienced permaculture designers, are trained through a diploma that involves 'action learning', centred on personal reflection within regular meetings of an 'action learning guild'[1] of about four people (Permaculture Association 2003). They are encouraged to continue with the process beyond their diploma, as an essential support for their practice.

'Action learning' is a collection of approaches that are being used in an increasing variety of settings, with an emerging academic literature (for example, Reason and Bradbury 2001). The approach recommended to permaculture practitioners involves identifying a small group of people who are trying to 'change the world' in some way – not necessarily through permaculture – and willing to commit to a sequence of about four action learning meetings. In each meeting, the participants take turns to talk about, or present, the issues they are currently facing in their work. Each person has a fixed period of time during which the others listen without interruption. Afterwards, there is a period for comment and feedback with a clear set of ground rules to ensure that the group supports the learning process of each individual.

In contrast to the Quaker reflexive process, which is fundamentally corporate, action learning as practised in the Permaculture Association is primarily an individual and mutual learning process supported by a group. However, permaculture practitioners are networked through tiers of local, regional and international 'reference persons'. Hence, individual learning feeds into the learning of the organisation as a whole. Practitioners are encouraged to develop action learning guilds that include people involved in all kinds of social and political action and campaigning, as long as they are working for a better world. Participants in guilds are also encouraged to find new groups of people to work with, with the aim that the approach spreads to develop a wider network of activists and practitioners.

Permaculture is having a growing influence, in particular among co-housing projects and intentional communities that seek to adopt its principles and establish a fully sustainable lifestyle. However, at the moment it clearly appeals primarily to those already committed to environmental values and its focus remains on land management.

11.5.4 Evaluation

The three organisations reviewed here provide contrasting models of reflexivity. In GAP, overall strategy, values and principles are developed by a central organisation. The function of local groups or EcoTeams is mainly to implement the strategy, following the EcoTeam Handbook. However, the organisation does certainly learn through the experiences of the local groups, revising its approach when setting up new EcoTeam projects. The GAP approach is designed to reach a mass audience and may be the most promising of the three in reaching the general public. In Beck and Cowan's terms (see Table 11.1) it seeks to engage people in the hierarchic, strategic and pluralistic modes.

Of the three organisations, Quakers probably have the best-developed system of collective reflexivity, with an established practice of reflection and decision-making used at all levels within the Society of Friends. At its best, the Quaker business method can entail a group functioning in the synthetic or holistic mode (Table 11.1) although Quaker meetings often operate in the hierarchic, strategic and pluralistic modes. While they can be very supportive of the creativity and learning of individuals and small groups, the process of waiting for 'the sense of the meeting' to emerge can make Quakers very slow to change their practices or reach decisions. Nevertheless, the Quaker approach does seem to offer unique opportunities for the development of collective approaches to sustainable living, with the resolution of some of the tensions and difficulties posed by the conflicts within consumer culture. Furthermore, the Society of Friends is the largest of the three organisations, with approximately 24 000 people attending Quaker meetings in Britain. Hence there is considerable potential for the ideas and practices developed within the Living Witness Project to spread within a community of shared values.

The permaculture approach offers the best support for creative experimentation by individual practitioners and small communities. It operates at the strategic and pluralistic modes of Table 11.1, with individuals functioning in the synthetic and holistic modes. The use of ecological principles in its social organisation seems to have enabled the permaculture movement to spread rapidly and achieve a wide influence. However, for the time being it appeals mainly to enthusiasts and it is not clear whether it can generate a sustainability ethic that will appeal more widely.

11.6 CONCLUSIONS

Consumption-oriented lifestyles in industrialised countries are environmentally unsustainable, with food, transport and housing accounting for the majority of greenhouse gas emissions, land use, water consumption and material flows. Moving towards a sustainable society, in which the 'needs' of all can be met now and in the future, may require that we redefine our needs. A first step may be to recognise that many of our needs, or at least our chosen material means of satisfying them, are shaped by our social context rather than by motivations inherent to people. The social contingency of consumption takes many forms, from the 'lock-in' effect of aggregate choice, to the construction of shared narratives about the good life, wealth, human nature and the natural world.

Consumer culture is often talked about as if it were a single, monolithic body of narratives, practices and symbolism supporting mass consumption. However, ethnographic studies have found diverse cultures of consumption, among groups with varying levels of concern about environmental and social issues, and with varying propensities to act on their concern. Furthermore, the culture of consumption is evolving, and some sociologists see an increase in reflexivity stimulated by a growing perception of environmental risk, and involving collective examination of goals, worldviews and ethics.

This chapter explores three examples of reflexive organisations that seek to promote more sustainable ways of living: the NGO, Global Action Plan; the Religious Society of Friends (Quakers); and the permaculture movement. Individuals within the Quaker and permaculture networks have demonstrated the potential to reduce their environmental impacts to levels that might be sustainable if their lifestyles were replicated globally. The reflexivity in these organisations takes widely differing forms appealing to people with different cultural backgrounds and interests. GAP probably has the best ability to engage the general public, while the permaculture approach may be the most promising for generating new solutions. Of the three, Quakers have the best-developed methods for arriving at new collective narratives supporting sustainable living. There is considerable potential for these organisations to learn from each other and to share ideas and practices.

NOTE

1. 'Guild' is the ecological term for a group of species occupying a similar niche in an ecosystem.

REFERENCES

Adams, Anne (ed.) (1996), *Creation Was Opened to Me: An Anthology of Friends' Writings on that of God in all Creation*, Cheshire, UK: Quaker Green Concern, Wilmslow.

Argyris, Chris and David A. Schon (1996), *Organizational Learning II: Theory, Method and Practice*, Reading, MA: Addison Wesley.

Bateson, Gregory (1972), *Steps to an Ecology of Mind*, Chicago: University of Chicago Press.

Baudrillard, Jean (1970), *The Consumer Society – Myths and Structures*, reprinted 1998, London: Sage Publications.

Bauman, Zygmunt (2001), *Community: Seeking Safety in an Insecure World*, Cambridge, UK: Polity Press.

Beck, Don and Christopher Cowan (1996), *Spiral Dynamics: Mastering Values, Leadership and Change*, Oxford, UK: Blackwell.

Beck, Ulrich (1988), *Risk Society: Towards a New Modernity*, English translation by Mark Ritter (1992), London: Sage.

Beck, U. A. Giddens and S. Lash (1994), *Reflexive Modernization*, Cambridge, UK: Polity Press.

Bourdieu, Pierre (1984), *Distinction – a Social Critique of the Judgement of Taste*, London: Routledge and Kegan Paul.

Brower, Michael and Warren Leon (1999), *The Consumer's Guide to Effective Environmental Choices*, New York, NY: Three Rivers Press.

Burgess, J. (2003), 'Sustainable consumption: Is it really achievable?', *Consumer Policy Review*, **11** (3), 78–84.

BYM (Britain Yearly Meeting) (1995), *Quaker Faith and Practice*, London: BYM.

Campbell, Joseph (1959), *The Masks of God: Primitive Mythology*, Volume 1, New York, NY: Arkana, Penguin Group.

Csikszentmihalyi, Mihaly and Eugene Rochberg-Halton (1981), *The Meaning of Things: Domestic Symbols and the Self*, Cambridge, UK: Cambridge University Press.

Dake, K. and M. Thompson (1999), 'Making ends meet, in the household and on the planet', *GeoScience*, **47**, 417–24.

Dale, Jonathan (2000), 'Quaker understanding of testimony', in Quaker Home Service, *Faith in Action: Quaker Social Testimony*, London: QHS, Friends House.

Dennett, Daniel Clemens (1993), *Consciousness Explained*, London: Penguin.

Dickinson, Roger (1998), 'Modernity, consumption and anxiety: Television audiences and food choice', in Roger Dickinson, Ramaswami Harindranath and Olga Linne (eds), *Approaches to Audiences: A Reader*, London: Arnold, pp. 257–71.

Douglas, Mary and Baron Isherwood (1979), *The World of Goods – Towards an Anthropology of Consumption*, London: Penguin Books.

Douglas, Mary, Des Gasper, Steven Ney and Michael Thompson (1998), 'Human needs and wants', in Steve Rayner and Elizabeth L. Malone (eds), *Human Choice and Climate Change*, Columbus, OH: Battelle Press, pp. 195–263.

Doyal, Len and Lan Gough (1991), *A Theory of Human Needs*, London: Macmillan.

Finch, Suzanne (2000), *A Quaker Testimony to the Earth?*, London: Quaker Bookshop, Friends House.

Frank, Robert (1985), *Choosing the Right Pond: Human Behavior and the Quest for Status*, New York, NY: Oxford University Press.

Freeman, Chris (1990), 'Schumpeter's business cycles revisited', in Arnold Heertje and Mark Perlman (eds), *Evolving Technology and Market Structure – Studies in Schumpeterian Economics*, Ann Arbor, MI: University of Michigan, pp. 17–38.

Gare, Arran E. (1995), *Postmodernism and the Environmental Crisis*, London: Routledge.

Ger, Güliz, Hal Wilhite, Bente Halkier, Jeppe Læssoe, Miriam Godskesen and Inge Røpke (1998), 'Symbolic meanings of high and low impact daily consumption practices in different cultures', Working paper prepared for Second European Science Foundation Workshop on 'Consumption, Everyday Life and Sustainability', Lancaster University, England. See http://www.lancs.ac.uk/users/scistud/esf/title.htm.

Giddens, Anthony (1994), 'Reflexive institutions', in Ulrich Beck, Anthony Giddens and Scott Lash, *Reflexive Modernisation*, Cambridge (UK): Polity Press, pp. 56–109.

Graves, C. (1982), Seminar handout, http://www.clarewgraves.com.

Griffin, Douglas (2002), *The Emergence of Leadership: Linking Self-Organization and Ethics*, London: Routledge.

Hines, C. and A. Ames (2000), *Ethical Consumerism*, research study conducted by MORI for the Co-operative Bank. Presentation, http://www.co-operativebank.co.uk/downloads/ethics/ethics_mori.pdf.

Hirsch, Fred (1977), *Social Limits to Growth*, Revised Edition (1995), London: Routledge.

Hobson, K. (2002), 'Competing discourses of sustainable consumption: Does the "rationalisation of lifestyles" make sense', *Environmental Politics*, **11** (2), 95–120.

Jackson, T. and L. Michaelis (2003), *Policies for Sustainable Consumption*, UK Sustainable Development Commission, http://www.sd-commission.gov.uk/pubs/suscon/.

Jaeger, Carlo C., Ortwin Renn, Eugene A. Rosa and Tom Webler (1998), 'Decision analysis and rational action', in Steve Rayner and Elizabeth L. Malone (eds), *Human Choice and Climate Change*, Columbus, OH: Battelle Press, pp. 141–215.

Kasemir, B., U. Dahinden, Å. Gerger Swartling, R. Schüle, D. Tabara and C. Jaeger (2000), 'Citizens' perspectives on climate change and energy use', *Global Environmental Change*, **10**, 169–84.

Landes, David S. (1969), *The Unbound Prometheus: Technological Change and Industrial Development in Western Europe from 1750 to the Present*, Cambridge, UK: Cambridge University Press.

Lorek, S. and J. H. Spangenberg (2001), 'Indicators for environmentally sustainable household consumption', *International Journal of Sustainable Development*, **4** (1), 101–20.

MacIntyre, Alastair (1985), *After Virtue*, Second Edition, London: Duckworth.

Maiteny, P. (2002), 'Mind the gap: Summary of research exploring "inner" influences on pro-sustainability learning and behaviour', *Environmental Education Research*, **8** (3), 299–306.

Maslow, Abraham H. (1954), *Motivation and Personality*, Third Edition (1987), revised by R. Frager, J. Fadiman, C. McReynolds, R. Cox, New York: Longman.

Max-Neef, Manfred (1991), *Human-scale Development – Conception, Application and Further Reflection*, London: Apex Press.

McIntosh, Alastair (2001), *Soil and Soul*, London: Aurum Press.

Michaelis, Laurie (2000), *The Ethics of Consumption*, Oxford, UK: Oxford Centre for the Environment, Ethics and Society, Mansfield College.

Michaelis, Laurie (2003), *Friends Witness to Sustainable Living*, Oxford, UK: Living Witness Project.

Morley, Barry (1993), *Beyond Consensus: Salvaging the Sense of the Meeting*, Pendle Hill Pamphlet 307, Wallingford, PA: Pendle Hill Publications.

Myers, Isabel Briggs and Peter B. Myers (1993), *Gifts Differing*, Oxford, UK: Oxford Psychologists Press.

Neumann, Erich (1954), *The Origins and History of Consciousness*, Princeton, NJ: Princeton University Press.

Nussbaum, Martha (1998), 'The good as discipline, the good as freedom', in David A. Crocker and Toby Linden (eds), *Ethics of Consumption: The Good Life, Justice and Global Stewardship*, Lanham, MD and Oxford, UK: Rowman and Littlefield, pp. 312–41.

OECD (Organisation for Economic Co-operation and Development) (1998), *Eco-Efficiency*, Paris: OECD.

OECD (2002), *Towards Sustainable Household Consumption? Trends and Policies in OECD Countries*, Paris: OECD.

Permaculture Association (2003), 'Action Learning, the Diploma in Applied Permaculture Design and the Diploma WorkNet', http://www.permaculture. org.uk.

Reason, Peter and Hilary Bradbury (eds) (2001), *Handbook of Action Research*, London: Sage.

Riso, Don Richard and Russ Hudson (1996), *Personality Types*, Boston, MA and New York, NY: Houghton Mifflin.

Røpke, I. (1999), 'The dynamics of willingness to consume', *Ecological Economics*, **28** (3), 399–420.

Rosenberg, Nathan (1994), *Exploring the Black Box: Technology, Economics and History*, Cambridge, UK: Cambridge University Press.

Rostow, Walt Whitman (1990), *The Stages of Economic Growth*, Third Edition, Cambridge, UK: Cambridge University Press.

Sanne, C. (2002), 'Willing consumers – or locked-in? Policies for a sustainable consumption', *Ecological Economics*, **42**, 273–87.

Schor, Juliet (1998), *The Overspent American – Upscaling, Downshifting and the New Consumer*, New York, NY: BasicBooks.

Schumpeter, J. (1928), 'The instability of capitalism', *Economic Journal*, **XXXVIII** (151), 361–86.

Segal, Jerome (1998), 'Consumer expenditures and the growth of needs-related income', in David A. Crocker and Toby Linden (eds), *Ethics of Consumption: The Good Life, Justice and Global Stewardship*, Lanham, MD and Oxford, UK: Rowman and Littlefield, pp. 176–97.

Sen, Amartya (1993), 'Capability and well-being', in Martha C. Nussbaum and Amartya Sen (eds), *The Quality of Life*, Oxford, UK: Oxford University Press, pp. 30–53.

Senge, Peter M. (1990), *The Fifth Discipline: The Art and Practice of the Learning Organisation*, London: Random House.

Staats, Henk J. and Paul Harland (1995), 'The Ecoteam Program in the Netherlands, Study 4: a longitudinal study on the effects of the EcoTeam Program on Environmental Behaviour and its psychological backgrounds, Summary Report', E&M/R-95/57, Leiden: Centre for Energy and Environmental Research, Faculty of Social and Behavioural Sciences, Leiden University, the Netherlands.

Stoll-Kleemann, S., T. O'Riordan and C. Jaeger (2001), 'The psychology of denial concerning climate mitigation measures: Evidence from Swiss focus groups', *Global Environmental Change*, **11**, 107–17.

Taylor, Charles (1989), *Sources of the Self: The Making of the Modern Identity*, Cambridge, UK: Cambridge University Press.

Torbert, William R., Dalmar Fisher and David Rooke (2001), *Personal and Organisational Transformations Through Action Research*, Boston, MA: Edge/Work Press.

Veblen, Thorstein (1899), *The Theory of the Leisure Class*, 1993 Edition, Mineola, NY: Dover.

von Weizsäcker, Ernst-Ulrich, Amory B. Lovins and L. Hunter Lovins (1997), *Factor Four*, London: Earthscan.

Wackernagel, Mathias, Chad Monfreda and Diana Deumling (2002), *Ecological Footprint of Nations, November 2002 Update*, Sustainability Issue Brief, November 2002, Oakland, CA: Redefining Progress.

Warde, A. (1997), *Consumption, Food and Taste*, London: Sage Publications.

WCED (1987), *Our Common Future*, The Brundtland Report, Oxford, UK: Oxford University Press.

Wilber, Ken (1981), *Up From Eden*, 1991 Edition, Wheaton, IL: Quest Books.

Wilber, Ken (1996), *The Atman Project*, Second Edition, Wheaton, IL: Quest Books.

Wilber, Ken (2000), *Integral Psychology*, Boston, MA: Shambala.

12. Macroeconomic stability: Sustainable development and full employment

Jesper Jespersen

12.1 INTRODUCTION – QUESTIONS TO BE DISCUSSED

Today, the paradoxical situation is that goods are produced not because they are needed – agriculture and the car industry are the outstanding examples – but to prevent unemployment from going up any further. The Western societies seem to have given up the ambition of creating a sustainable development in an attempt to rescue the labour market from rising unemployment.

Anyhow, this vicious cycle could be broken if governments started to implement the zero growth strategy as presented below. Then people would get more leisure time organized according to individual preferences. They would be able to keep their present standard of living. This would make it possible to employ the productivity gains in such a way that the Western societies could embark on a production path leading to sustainable development.

What are the macroeconomic consequences of such a rigorous implementation of *sustainable development* with special regard to the negative impact on employment/unemployment? What can economic theory tell us, in general, about the interrelationship between the traditional macroeconomic variables and increased environmental considerations?

Does an economic system based on capitalist principles require an ever-increasing output to keep itself 'on track'? Is the market system like a bicycle – does it have to keep on going at a certain speed not to be wrecked? Or does the economic system start to 'spin' when the growth process is slowed down – like the bicycle that starts to wobble when the speed is lowered? Is it likely that the market economy has these bicycle-like properties?

Sustainable development has to be analysed within a macroeconomic framework. In Section 3 I argue that one can get inspiration for a realistic macroeconomic theory from post-Keynesian economics. That theory places effective demand and economic policy as the pivotal elements for sustainable development with full employment. In the final section I present a concrete example of how unemployment can be avoided.

12.2   THE GROWTH-ADDICTED DEVELOPED COUNTRIES

Environmental degradation is a contemporary global phenomenon. Furthermore, as we know, the global economy is becoming more and more interrelated and interdependent. Bearing these facts in mind, I will begin this chapter by considering the likely impact of a change towards a more sustainable economic growth on the industrialized countries with a yearly per capita income of more than $ 20 000. This focus is chosen for two reasons. First, it is the material consumption and the continued economic growth of these rich (post-)industrialized countries that indisputably have the largest impact on the *global* environment (exhaustion of limited resources and accumulation of pollution). Second, a zero growth rate in these countries would not make any people starve, if work and consumption were distributed fairly.

The performance of these rich, post-industrialized economies in the post-war period was characterized until the early 1970s by high growth rates, full employment, exponentially growing energy consumption and a fast-deteriorating environment. From the 1970s economic growth rates started to slow down (from 4 per cent per annum to 2–3 per cent per annum). This, after all, minor slowdown in the pace of economic growth, which emerged simultaneously with the first energy price hike, made unemployment an inherent part of the Western economies. Until the early 1970s, the registered rate of unemployment in Europe had not exceeded 2–3 per cent, but suddenly it jumped and reached double digits in the 1980s and 1990s.

Superficially viewed, it is tempting to see a direct causality from higher energy prices and increased environmental concern in general to slower economic growth and further on to increased unemployment. Why this is only a part, in fact only a minor part, of the explanation of the macroeconomic development will be explained in the following section on macroeconomic theory. Anyhow, from a market economic point of view one should rather have expected that higher energy prices would have increased the demand for labour at a given growth rate. This rising number of unemployed people tells us that productivity of labour together with changes in the strength of the growth process seems to dominate the substitution effect caused by changes in relative (factor) prices.

Before examining the macroeconomic arguments of how energy prices, economic growth and employment are related in greater details, it is also important to investigate developments in energy consumption. The picture is, of course, blurred. Energy is a strategic and highly politicized commodity. Nonetheless, a general pattern can be discerned in which a doubling or tripling of energy prices have caused a fall, but only a relative fall in the energy consumption compared to GDP (increased energy productivity). Although this substitution effect has been sluggish, energy efficiency has, at least in Europe, increased ever since the first oil price hike took place. This trend has continued even in periods when world market prices have fallen, because domestic and world energy prices have been separated due to energy taxes. In fact, it would be a better measure to use the domestic price level when the price elasticity of energy consumption by households is calculated. There has been, except for the US, an upward trend in energy taxes since the oil price collapse in the middle of the 1980s.

12.3   MACROECONOMIC CONSIDERATIONS

Unfortunately, macroeconomic analysis is not straightforward. There are many, and competing, schools of macroeconomic theory, each of which provides a somewhat different picture of the main driving forces behind the growth process. Phelps (1993) and Snowdon, Vane and Wynarczyk (1994) count seven schools of macroeconomics. At the end of the day the number of different schools can be boiled down. Depending on the purpose of one's analyses, it is not necessary to discuss all seven schools. I have, drawing my inspiration from Keynes, reduced the number of schools to two major ones (Jespersen 2000):

1. supply school, where 'the long-run general equilibrium' is determined by supply factors and relative prices (neoclassical economics);
2. demand and 'uncertainty' school' (Keynes-inspired economics).

> On the one side are those who believe that the existing economic system is, in the long run, a self-adjusting system, though with creaks and groans and jerks and interrupted by time lags, outside interference and mistakes.... On the other side of the gulf are those that reject the idea that the existing economic system is, in any significant sense, self-adjusting. The strength of the self-adjusting school depends on it having behind it almost the whole body of organised economic thinking of the last hundred years. (Keynes, 1934, pp. 286–7)

The above quote expresses Keynes's sceptical attitude towards the use of a general equilibrium model as a relevant analytical tool. It was primarily the deterministic and reductionist methodological approach underpinning macroeconomic theory of his time (neoclassical economics represented by A.C. Pigou, *The Theory of Unemployment*) that he revolted against.

According to Keynes, macroeconomic theory has to be grounded in 'realism'. What can we *know* about the *economy as a whole* today and in the future? Macroeconomic analysis is concerned with the performance of the entire economic system. Within that macro framework there is room for many different hypotheses about microeconomic behaviour. Keynes's main emphasis was to stress that individual actors have to act even though they only have a limited and uncertain knowledge about the future. Keynes did not quarrel about the postulated profit or utility maximizing behaviour – or any other reasonable behavioural assumption at the micro-level. His concern was how to establish a *relevant theory of the driving forces of the entire productive system*. For that reason he called his macroeconomics a monetary theory of production. It was the interplay of real and monetary factors in an economic system characterized by fundamental uncertainty that really made the analytical difference between him and his predecessors.

Uncertainty – caused by lack of knowledge about individual behaviour, structural organization and future events – cannot from an epistemological point of view be reduced to statistical uncertainty and, therefore, cannot be analysed within a general *equilibrium* model! When that is understood (and accepted) the neoclassical growth theory loses analytical force.

Post-Keynesian macroeconomics is grounded in realism. Having said that, it becomes more obvious why what any relevant macroeconomic theory can tell about economic performance in a long-run perspective is rather limited. Even the short run should only be predicted with a high degree of caution.

Anyhow, having the above-mentioned limits in mind, one can point to three analytical stepping-stones that might be useful for the detection of the development of the *economy as a whole* from a *sustainable development* perspective:

1. The *actual growth path* is dependent on history, the composition of effective demand, supply factors, innovations and mere chance.
2. *Effective demand* is the main macroeconomic factor determining the growth *rate* of any well-functioning market economy.
3. Supply factors: (1) productivity, (2) limited natural resources, contamination caused by outlet of waste and pollution and (3) microeconomic incentives:
   - supply factor (1): persistent *improvements of total factor productivity*;

- supply factor (2): absolute scarcity and relative factor prices – substitutability; and/or complementarity in the production process;
- supply factor (3): microeconomic incentives of any kind.

Ex. 1. The Western market economies have been growing for the last 200 years or more. The growth potential increases for a number of reasons: more capital equipment, specialization, technical innovations, a better-educated and trained labour force and the continuous depletion of natural capital. The point is that any specific growth process is influenced by a number of past and present factors that make the process *path-dependent* in the sense that history matters and can only very slowly, if at all, be reversed. For instance, when a country has based its power stations mainly on nuclear energy, the decision is binding for years to come.

Any radical transformation of Western societies in the direction of greater sustainability has to be a smooth process if historical experiences are to be of any relevance. Of course, I do not speak about a traditional neoclassical growth model analysis based on perfect factor substitutability, perfect foresight (rational expectations) and perfect competition. The approach I have in mind is what Joan Robinson (1974) later on, with inspiration from Keynes, coined the *methodology of History (in contrast to Equilibrium)*.[1]

> The object of our analysis is, not to provide a machine, or method of blind manipulation, which will furnish an infallible answer, but to provide ourselves with an organised and orderly method of thinking out particular problems; and, after we have reached a provisional conclusion by isolating the complicating factors one by one, we then go back on ourselves and allow, as well as we can, for the probable interactions of the factors among themselves. This is the nature of economic thinking. (Keynes 1936, p. 297)

Ex. 2. Keynes defined *effective demand* as the proceeds that firms *expect* to receive from the production they plan to undertake in the future. Hence, the level of macroeconomic activity is guided by effective demand, which in fact is derived from expectations held by firms about future sales proceeds counterweighted by information about the costs of production. Firms do not necessarily maximize profits, but they have to expect that the proceeds one way or the other will cover costs – if not every day of production, then at least within the planning horizon.

The formation of expectations by business is crucial for effective demand. Firms are assumed to form rational beliefs about the future. They try to make as good use as possible of available information; but they can, of course, never get full information about the future or about the functioning of the entire macroeconomic system.[2] There will always be a certain element of the unknown, but firms have to decide what to produce and how much to produce. Hence, effective demand can never be fully described in mathematical language.

The economic growth process is in poor countries perpetuated by an increased population, although often too slow and too little to feed the increasing number of people (Malthus). In richer and more developed countries, where people have sufficient income to cover their basic needs, the growth process is primarily directed by *effective demand* (Keynes). Hence, supply capacity is running ahead of people's desire to consume material goods. When societies grow richer people's preferences are directed towards a reduced working load and good public care.

Ex. 3. Below I will set up a simple scheme of 'economic thinking' about a sustainable growth process from a post-Keynesian tradition.[3] Sustainable development is defined in political/physical terms, not in economic terms.[4] Factors of production at a global level consist of: labour, man-made capital, land, natural resources and the quality of the biological sphere (environment).

The degree of substitutability/complementarity within the economic system (of effective demand, production and use of factors of production) is of interest when the impact on the environment of different growth strategies is to be analysed.

'Stylized Thinking about Sustainability' as a Macroeconomic (Demand-driven) Process

(1) Effective demand $*(1 + g)^t = >$ economic growth $= >$

(2) [demand for factors of production, energy and outlet of pollution] $/$
$(1+ (e - g))^t$
where, e = average growth in total factor productivity; g = average growth in effective demand.

The starting point of the analysis is a specific historical context at $t = 0$. Using the national accounts, one can calculate the actual figures for demand, production and the use of factors of production (working hours, capacity utilization, depletion of resources and pollution).

One characteristic feature of modern societies is that labour *productivity* is increased year by year. The utilization of an unchanged amount of factors of production forces production to grow, or, said slightly differently, an unchanged level of production requires fewer and fewer factor inputs. This is the 'magic' of the market economy.

History also tells us that specific productivity gains are correlated with changes in relative factor prices. When land became scarce in Europe in the 19th century crops were improved and fertilizers applied, but not quickly enough to prevent starvation and an exodus to overseas countries. Then labour became scarce when manufacturing took the lead. Trade unions were formed and labour got, for a while, a rising share of the value-added. That changed the innovation processes in the direction of labour-saving machines and import of goods from Third World labour-abundant countries. Of course, it is not solely changes in relative factor prices that have caused the substitution and productivity gains. In addition a number of administrative regulations have supported labour protection and labour-saving inventions – for the benefit of business and of labour, but, unfortunately, not of the environment.

Now the time has come when exhaustible resources and unspoiled environments have become increasingly scarce. Those environmental factors, which are protected by private property rights, have experienced rising prices – the outstanding example is, of course, fossil energy. However, the market mechanism is only of limited use, because on the one hand the scarcity of exhaustible resources is a long-term *stock* phenomenon clouded by uncertainty (uncertain knowledge) and on the other hand, market prices are guided by short-sighted *flow* considerations. Market prices react to flow imbalances, but do not have the capacity to correct future imbalances in stock variables. The observation applies also to financial markets, where stock/debt can build up for years before the creditors suddenly lose confidence and the much-delayed devaluation of the currency occurs. The collapse of ecological systems might follow the same pattern – *we simply don't know* (to speak the language of Keynes).

But still, within the historical context, it is important to emphasize that it is the size and the composition of *effective demand* that primarily drives the growth process forward. Furthermore, the specific direction it takes with regard to the use of different factors of production depends on the production structures, innovations and relative factor prices.

12.4 MACROECONOMIC POLICIES, EFFECTIVE DEMAND AND ECONOMIC GROWTH

According to post-Keynesian macroeconomic theory economic policy is one of the main determinants of effective demand and by that of the size and the composition of economic growth. The use of factors of production is determined by the growth process, factor productivity and relative factor prices. The unfortunate thing is, that our knowledge of the productivity-enhancing factors is rather limited.

Just to give a feeling of the magnitude of productivity gains I have presented one rather simple, but presumably not atypical empirical study of the Danish economy in the post-war period in Table 12.1.

Table 12.1 Contribution by factors of production to economic growth, Denmark 1960–99

| Private sectors | (1) Economic growth % p.a. | Contribution by: | Growth rates[a] | | | Energy productivity[b] % p.a. |
			(2) Increased real capital % p.a.	(3) Working hours % p.a.	(4) Labour productivity % p.a.	
Manufacturing	3.0	=	0.9	-0.9	3.0	2.0
Private service	3.0	=	0.8	0.0	2.2	0.8
Agriculture	2.1	=	1.3	-4.4	5.2	2.1

Notes: [a] columns (2), (3) and (4) add up to (1). [b] Energy productivity is supplementary information (1966–90).

Source: Pedersen (2000), pp. 77–89 and Jespersen (1998), Table 10.3, p.151.

Table 12.1 shows that labour productivity has outpaced economic growth to such an extent – except for private service – that the number of working hours undertaken in the private sector has fallen throughout the entire period. This process of continuously increasing labour productivity seems to be a common feature of a well-functioning capitalist market economy. Unfortunately, we have only vague ideas about the extent to which increased productivity is an endogenous or an exogenous component of the growth process. There are arguments in favour of labour productivity being determined by (1) better education, (2) specialization, (3) on the job training, and (4) labour-saving innovations. One could say that (1) and (2) are ongoing processes largely independent of the underlying growth performance. Whereas 'on the job training' requires that jobs are available – fewer or more insecure jobs mean less training. The final argument (4) is probably the most important one, because labour-saving innovations are based on business expectation that labour will become relatively more expensive in the future.[5]

Furthermore, the government can twist the composition of effective demand between different kinds of demand for goods and services. In the Danish context there is one major dividing line with regard to use of energy and labour. This is on the one hand the demand for private goods and service and on the other hand the provision of public services. Production of traditional public services (care, education, administration and to some extent health) has a higher labour content and a much smaller (negative) impact on the environment (energy consumption) than private goods and services (in general). If we look at Table 12.2 we see that demand for goods and private services (transport, entertainment, charter travel, finance, communication and so on) have a surprisingly similar pattern with regard to employment and energy when we calculate the total factor input using an input–output table of the Danish economy. Looked upon from this holistic point of view, private services (as opposed to public services, at least in the Danish case which I have closely investigated) turn out, in the input–output table, to be even less labour-demanding than manufactured goods and to absorb approximately the same quantity of energy per million Dkr value-added, see Jespersen (1998).

This analytical result does not leave much room for obtaining beneficial effects by twisting private demand from goods to private services. It is by boosting the demand for soft services (healthcare, education, local activities) that some environmental alleviation could be expected.

Furthermore, it has been calculated that real capital and energy consumption are complementary factors of production. This means that if capital equipment is installed as a substitute for labour it will automatically increase the use of energy – given the historical record.

Table 12.2   Labour and energy per million DKR value-added in different production sectors, Denmark 1990

	Share of GDP %	Employment (persons)/ million DKR	Energy (TJ)/ million DKR
Manufacturing	18.3	2.65	1.12
Private sector services	46.4	2.35	0.92
Public sector services	22.5	4.18	0.41

Source: Jespersen (1998), p. 150.

As we have seen, increased traditional economic growth is good for employment, but a strain on the environment. In fact, the Danish government took that aspect into consideration when the economic growth process was speeded up during the 1990s. The expansive fiscal policy was combined with a 'green tax reform'. This policy measure detached, to some extent, the increased growth rate of private consumption from energy and water consumption and CO_2 emissions. In many ways it was rather exceptional that economic growth could be increased substantially, while the current pressure on the crucial environmental flows was kept unchanged.

On the other hand, one should not exaggerate this result, because the overall development was still far from being sustainable. Unchanged consumption and unchanged flows of pollution mean that the exhaustion of stocks of natural resources and the accumulation of CO_2 continued at the same (unsustainable) pace as previously.

If we take a longer time perspective on the relation between energy consumption and economic activity in the Danish case, then we see that the correlation between economic activity and the energy consumption has been rather weak for the last 30 years (Hansen 2000). Although the economy as a whole has grown by 2.5 per cent per annum, energy consumption has remained quite stable since the 1970s. This means that energy productivity with regard to GDP has gone up by approximately 2.5 per cent p.a.[6] If we go behind the aggregate figures for energy consumption, we find that there is a striking difference between consumption by households (electricity, heating and private transport) and by firms (process and transport). Apparently, it is the household sector that really has made the significant contribution to the detachment from economic growth by reducing its energy consumption by 20 per cent since 1973, whereas the production sectors have increased their energy consumption by another 20 per cent. These different developments demonstrate that the green tax policy does matter. Energy taxes imposed on households have made energy goods relatively expensive compared to disposable income ever since the first energy crisis hit in 1973. Firms, on the other hand, have been taxed much lighter for the sake of avoiding a unilateral deterioration of the international competitiveness. In fact, there has been a fall in the (real) world price of energy since the early 1980s, which has been passed through to the business sector and slowed down improvements in energy productivity.

Furthermore, it is an unsettled question as to what share of the reduced demand by households that is a direct reaction to increased energy prices and to what extent the reduction of the energy consumption can be referred to structural changes: improved supply of heating (from power stations) and a combination of forced and subsidized improvements of the insulation of private homes. The same question applies to the business sector that has also had access to a number of subsidized energy-saving schemes.

12.5 HOW TO REDUCE MATERIAL CONSUMPTION WITHOUT CREATING UNEMPLOYMENT

From a macroeconomic point of view there are quite a number of similarities between the balance of payments constraint and an environmental constraint. In the first case, the 'consumption' of foreign exchange has to be reduced, in the second case it is the consumption of non-renewable resources and emission of dangerous waste/pollution that has to be diminished. In both cases it is an important side condition that a negative impact on employment should be avoided.

This parallel has given me the inspiration to have a short look at how the balance of payments constraint can be lifted, see Thirlwall (2002). The standard textbook answer is to improve the international competitive position of domestic goods through wage policies and/or a devaluation of the national currency. This is the traditional export-led growth strategy with no consideration of its impact on the environment. A more environmentally friendly strategy would be to reduce the domestic demand for foreign goods by a reduction of the purchasing power through increased taxation. That would surely cause unemployment to rise, unless it is combined with a comprehensive scheme of work sharing. If one goes ten years back in time, the debate on how to share the limited workload was very present because at that time the unemployment rate was above 12 per cent (in Denmark and many other Western countries).

At that period, it was common to talk about 'jobless growth', because the annual growth rate was below the current increases in labour productivity. The idea of these work-sharing schemes was to distribute the reduced number of working hours obtained through the productivity gains in a fair way among the labour force. Forced unemployment is a scourge – whereas a collective and equal reduction in average working time either through a shorter working week, longer holidays, parental or educational leave, or early retirement is often considered as a welfare gain.

It is much easier to get political acceptance of the beneficial effects of work-sharing when unemployment has gone up. It is much more difficult to get the same hearing from the politicians when the concern is about the environment. But in real life people are worried about the deterioration of the environment, which they feel is a direct threat to their health, contrary to the abstract concept of 'balance of payments deficit'. In fact, even in periods of relatively low unemployment, workers have been ready to accept a shorter working week without income compensation as the outcome of the yearly collective wage negotiations. The ever-increasing productivity gives labour a real choice between shorter working hours and increased real wage (or any combination of the two choices).

We can employ this idea more explicitly when environmental protection is on the political agenda. Foreign exchange could be saved through higher import prices and/or reduced private consumption. The environment can be saved through higher 'green prices' enforced by 'green taxes' or reduced private consumption of goods and service (Table 12.1). The parallel is striking.

There are two kinds of popular resistance to 'green taxes'. One comes from people with low incomes because they will carry a disproportionate share of these taxes, which they, for good reasons, consider as unfair. This objection could rather easily be overcome by a progressive tax scale on electricity, water, gas and oil for heating and a reduced tax for collective transport combined with a specific tariff on emissions from power stations. Furthermore, the tax revenue could be redirected towards tax relief on labour income and public goods mainly provided for low income groups. The other objection comes from exporting industries using exhaustible resources and causing pollution. These firms argue that if they are 'punished' by green taxes, production will move abroad. That might be the case, especially if the international society keeps on producing in an unsustainable way. In that case currency devaluation could be needed. Environmental protection has a price that society, as a whole, has to pay through a slowdown of the traditional economic growth compared to what otherwise would be the case. Of course, if all Western countries introduced green taxes or pollution permits at the same time the reduction of the economic growth in any specific country would be smaller.

12.6 A THOUGHT EXPERIMENT

What might happen to Western societies if it was decided by, for example, the OECD that the current level of consumption is enough, see Durning (1992). This is, of course, a utopian idea as far as production is unequally distributed among nations and citizens. A society (not to speak of a world) with a relatively equal income (and wealth) distribution is more willing to accept the proposition that 'enough is enough' when the basic needs are generously fulfilled and the social pressure of having certain material status symbols is limited.

Anyhow, let us assume that a zero growth rate in GDP is decided by parliament. What would happen when such a restrictive fiscal policy is implemented in a decentralized market economy? That is not difficult to predict, because when effective demand is reduced the number of unemployed people increases. To prevent that government has to combine the zero growth in effective demand with an initiative to share the reduced number of working hours in a fair way among the entire labour force. In this case the government could get some inspiration from the tradable permits of pollution. The government could initiate this new era of zero growth by distributing a voucher/work permit to all people in the labour force, which gives the holder the right to undertake a certain number of working hours free of charge. If they want to work more than this (free) number of hours they have to buy (or receive as a gift) extra hours at the market for 'work permits'. If you want to work less than the average you are free to sell the excess amount of work permits. People who leave the labour force (permanently or for a while) and get a public income transfer will not receive any (free) work permits.

One may wonder to what extent this ceiling on the number of hours worked can restrict the growth rate. The point is that firms and wages earners know in advance that each year the amount of work permits will be reduced proportional to the increase in labour productivity. In that case the macroeconomic outcome is a zero growth process, but at the individual level any worker is free to work more hours (or shorter hours) if one can get hold of more work permits. The historical record tells us that by and large the requested reduction in the total workload is 2 per cent each year. In fact, if this policy was implemented, people would also know that the volume of consumption would not go on growing. The 'buy and throw away' culture had to change. People might be more conscious about what is really a necessity to consume when one cannot expect to get more of everything. One could even expect people to demand more durable goods.

Zero growth will be beneficial for the environment. When GDP stops growing the increased energy productivity will reduce the current/flow consumption of energy. Within 35 years, a 2 per cent yearly productivity gain will halve the demand for energy. If at the same time the supply of renewable energy is expanded, then the day of a sustainable energy sector is within sight. In a number of areas, environmental protection does imply that labour productivity is increased more slowly than previously. The use of pesticides and fertilizers in agriculture has increased labour productivity (at least until the pollutants reach the ground water). The division of labour nationally and internationally has increased productivity through specialization and economies of scale, but at the cost of long-distance transportation. Renewable fuel means higher transportation costs and hence a slowdown in future labour market specialization. It is likely that increased environmental concern will reduce the growth of labour productivity.

Unfortunately, I see at least two macroeconomic snakes preventing this paradise from coming about without difficulty. When labour becomes more scarce, successful firms will try to substitute manpower with robots, thus raising the GDP growth rate (and energy consumption). It would be a great mistake to restrict the number of machine hours when they are installed. The substitution of machines for manpower is a minor problem because the increased labour productivity will reduce the number of work permits distributed the following year. To be honest, it would just be nice if machines would take over all the boring jobs.

A much more difficult problem to handle would be how to prevent cost push inflation in periods where labour is in short supply. One may recall the 1960s and early 1970s when there was a scarcity of labour and cost inflation went higher and higher in an attempt by labour to get a larger share of the value-added. This period lasted more than a decade and caused high unemployment in order to squeeze inflation out of the wage–price–wage formation. One solution is, of course, through demand management policies, to ensure that effective demand for goods and services is also restricted to a zero growth rate. That would probably mean that in periods with shortages of labour, tax rates would have to be increased to moderate the imbalance. Another and more constructive way forward would be the introduction of a profit-sharing scheme as the main distributive mechanism in the private sector. In the public sector, there is no profit to share. I have no straightforward suggestion other than to let the public sector tail the private, because the international competitive pressure is somewhat stronger in the private sector.

The individual wage earners will not be constrained by the number of work permits they receive; because these permits are intended to be made tradable and therefore more flexible than a given and unchangeable maximum. Those people who want to work extra hours are allowed to do that when they have bought extra permits in the market – expenses that labour might be able (partly) to pass over to the hiring firms. In that case wage costs will increase, because labour has become more scarce than otherwise. That is, anyhow, the price that society has to pay for any full employment policy. 'Full employment' requires social responsibility by trade unions and an institutional shift in the concern of wage negotiations where emphasis should shift from nominal wage increases to real wage or even better to profit-sharing. Such a shift could prevent a deterioration of the international competitive position.

Of course, any specific national policy is difficult to implement in an economic system that is becoming more and more globalized. The standard reaction to any proposal of this kind is that if it is not adopted by a majority of countries, it is too easy to bypass. We know that answer from the debate about the Tobin Tax on international capital flows. Anyway, this problem of transnational activities is not that big when the labour market is considered. Labour markets, even within the EU, are still a national entity.

12.7 CONCLUDING REMARKS

Historically, it was considered a political necessity to have a substantial growth in GDP to improve welfare and at the same time to prevent unemployment from rising. Now, the welfare goals have been fulfilled, but at a cost of an unsustainable development. Furthermore, the ever-growing labour productivity makes it necessary to let the GDP grow by 2–3 per cent each year just to keep the number of people employed unchanged. Whenever the growth rate of GDP falls below this 2–3 per cent, unemployment seems to rise inevitably.

That unstable situation begs the question, is it possible to slow down the growth of (material) consumption without causing unemployment? The short, simplistic answer to this question is a plain 'yes'. Because, if the average working hours per employed person are reduced by 2–3 per cent each year, then 'unemployment' could be shared equally by all workers in the form of more leisure time. The scourge of unemployment would be transformed to the gift of a shorter working time combined with an unchanged real income and even more important a first step toward sustainable development! This proposal of work-sharing could be implemented through a system of tradable *work permits* distributed equally among all people within the labour force – much the same way as tradable pollution permits are introduced as a remedy for reducing the emission of CO_2.

To ensure macroeconomic balance on the labour market it is important that the government puts the brake on the growth of effective demand for goods and services through an active *demand management policy*.

It is a myth that a *capitalist economy* cannot function at a constant GDP by making the entrepreneurial climate stagnate. That does not have to be the case, because underneath the surface of an unchanged overall production there will be a myriad of business activities. It is also a myth that firms have to grow to be successful within a capitalist market economy. Growth is not a necessary condition for profit maximization. On the contrary, it is quite easy to demonstrate that firms that maximize growth are forgoing some profit in their fascination for growth. As a consequence of this trial and error process some firms are successful and they will expand; others are less successful and they will contract. Furthermore, each year society becomes one year older, which means that some shop owners/farmers and wage earners will decide to retire. That creates opportunities for newcomers to set up a new production unit or to fill a vacant labour market position. At the micro-level, firms are indifferent as to whether the total volume of the economy expands or contracts, because they have, anyhow, only a small fraction of the entire trade. Their task is to be as efficient and competitive as possible given, not the size, but the structure of the market economy domestically and abroad.

NOTES

1. The specific methodological approach has more recently been identified with 'critical realism', see Lawson (1997).
2. Which are the assumptions behind the concept of 'rational expectations' used by many neoclassical theorists.
3. A more elaborated scheme of thought on economic growth constrained by the balance of payments, see Thirlwall (2002).
4. There are several definitions of 'sustainable development' – ranging from 'strong' to 'weak'. I will not go into that debate here, I just want to stress that the value of 'sustainability' cannot be calculated, only the *economic costs* of fulfilling different environmental objectives might be quantified *and* compared.
5. Unfortunately, there is not space within this chapter to analyse the causes of increased factor productivity. I take the development of total factor productivity as exogenous, but the division of this overall gain of productivity on the separate factors of production I assume is partly explained by relative factor prices.
6. This is a bit higher than the number in Table 12.1, which covers the period 1966–90.

REFERENCES

Durning, Alan T. (1992), *How Much is Enough?*, London: Earthscan.
Hansen, Anders Chr. (2000), *Bæredygtig opsparing*, PhD dissertation, Roskilde: Roskilde University.
Jespersen, Jesper (1998), *Miljøøkonomi*, Copenhagen: DJØFs Forlag.
Jespersen, Jesper (2000), *Introduktion til Makroøkonomisk teori*, Copenhagen: DJØFs Forlag.
Keynes, John Maynard (1930), 'The economic possibilities of our grandchildren', in Elizabeth Johnson and Donald Moggridge (eds), *Collected Writings of J.M. Keynes* (1973), Vol. IX, London: Macmillan for The Royal Economic Society.
Keynes, John Maynard (1934), 'Poverty in plenty: is the economic system self-adjusting?' in Elizabeth Johnson and Donald Moggridge (eds) *Collected Writings of J.M. Keynes* (1973), Vol. XIII, London: Macmillan for the Royal Economic Society.
Keynes, John Maynard (1936), *The General Theory of Employment, Interest and Money*, London: Macmillan.
Lawson, Tony (1997), *Economics & Reality*, London: Routledge.
Pedersen, Erik Haller (2000), 'Demografi og vækst i Danmark', in *Danmarks Nationalbank, Kvartalsoversigt, 1. kvartal*, Copenhagen: Danmarks Nationalbank.
Phelps, Edmund (1993), *Seven Schools of Macroeconomics*, Oxford: Oxford University Press.
Pigou, A.C. (1933), *The Theory of Unemployment*, London: Macmillan.
Robinson, Joan (1974), 'History versus equilibrium', *Thames Papers in Political Economy*.
Snowdon, Brian, Howard Vane and Peter Wynarczyk (1994), *A Modern Guide to Macroeconomics*, Aldershot, UK and Brookfield, US: Edward Elgar.
Thirlwall, Anthony (2002), *Growth*, Cheltenham, UK and Northampton, MA, US: Edward Elgar.

Index

Printed and bound by CPI Group (UK) Ltd, Croydon, CR0 4YY

23/04/2025

14660986-0003